School Design

Educators often overlook the positive impact of changing the environment of the school itself when considering how to improve the quality of education.

First published in 1994, *School Design* shows how to create more effective schools through a design process that involves teachers, students, parents, administrators, and architects. It reveals how to create school environments that develop the whole child, instil enthusiasm for learning, and encourage positive social relationships.

Readers discover how to integrate design research, design participation, and design development to optimize school settings. Using a number of case studies, detailed practical methods show how to:

- Link behavioural objectives to spatial needs
- Achieve spatial efficacy without compromising education
- Match children's developmental needs to facility requirements
- Promote greater variety in physical facilities to accommodate various teaching and learning styles
- Gain more valuable feedback from teachers, parents, students, and local citizens on building performance.

In response to tight school budgets, Henry Sanoff discusses how relatively minor design modifications can have a major positive effect on school performance. This path-breaking volume will provide architects, teachers, and school administrators with a wide array of insights into creating spaces that promote better learning.

School Design

Henry Sanoff

Routledge
Taylor & Francis Group
REVIVALS

First published in 1994
by Van Nostrand Reinhold

This edition first published in 2017 by Routledge
2 Park Square, Milton Park, Abingdon, Oxon, OX14 4RN
and by Routledge
711 Third Avenue, New York, NY 10017

Routledge is an imprint of the Taylor & Francis Group, an informa business

Publisher's Note
The publisher has gone to great lengths to ensure the quality of this reprint but points out that some imperfections in the original copies may be apparent.

Disclaimer
The publisher has made every effort to trace copyright holders and welcomes correspondence from those they have been unable to contact.

A Library of Congress record exists under LC control number: 93007904

ISBN 13: 978-1-138-06427-0 (hbk)
ISBN 13: 978-1-315-16041-2 (ebk)
ISBN 13: 978-1-138-06437-9 (pbk)

School Design

HENRY SANOFF

To Joan

Library of Congress Catalog Card Number 93-7904
ISBN 0-442-01096-6

I(T)P Van Nostrand Reinhold is an International Thomson Publishing company.
ITP logo is a trademark under license.

Printed in the United States of America.

Van Nostrand Reinhold
115 Fifth Avenue
New York, New York 10003

International Thomson Publishing
Berkshire House, 168–173
High Holborn, London WC1V7AA
England

Thomas Nelson Australia
102 Dodds Street
South Melbourne 3205
Victoria, Australia

Nelson Canada
1120 Birchmount Road
Scarborough, Ontario
M1K 5G4, Canada

International Thomson Publishing GmbH
Königswinterer Str. 418
53227 Bonn
Germany

International Thomson Publishing Asia
221 Henderson Building #05–10
Singapore 0315

International Thomson Publishing Japan
Kyowa Building, 3F
2–2–1 Hirakawacho
Chiyoda-ku, Tokyo 102
Japan

ARCKP 16 15 14 13 12 11 10 9 8 7 6 5 4 3 2 1

Library of Congress Cataloging-in-Publication Data

Sanoff, Henry.
School design / by Henry Sanoff.
p. cm.
Includes bibliographical references (p.) and index.
ISBN 0-442-01096-6
1. School buildings — United States — Design and construction.
2. School facilities — United States — Design and construction.
I. Title.
LB3218.A1S33 1992
371.6′2′0973 — dc20 93-7904
CIP

Contents

Preface

Shaping the learning environment to support educational objectives is one of the central themes of this collection of unusual school building projects. In many ways the projects exemplify the participatory design process, where it is recognized that the student, the teacher, the parent, the administrator, and the architect are all vital ingredients in the process of educational change. Equally important is user feedback related to the successful achievement of the educational objectives.

An attempt was made to include a wide range of school types, from children's centers to university settings, public and private, wherever formal learning occurs. A variety of sources was used to identify appropriate case studies, including a literature search and numerous telephone calls to informed educators. Many of the case studies in this collection were built or in construction, while others not built were included for their innovative techniques of user involvement.

Since there was little published material available about the design process for each building project, the development of the case studies for this book could not have been done without the cooperation and assistance of many people. The following architects and educators were kind enough to respond to my questions through a microcassette tape recorder where they described the design process: Graham Adams, Lella Gandini, Joe Murguido, Craig Rafferty, Jeff Riley, and Maryann Thompson and Charles Rose. Others contributed by writing their comments and recollections: Eileen Driscoll, Gaylaird Christopher, Donald McDonald, Earl Flansburg, and Alan Patterson. In addition, a note of appreciation is due to the many teachers, staff, and students who willingly responded to my evaluation survey. Thanks also to my graduate assistant, Robert Chase, who was supported by a grant from the School of Design, for his technical and editorial help.

Finally, appreciation is acknowledged for the dedication and commitment of my Community Development Group design team members — Graham Adams, Terry Alford, Greg Centeno, Tun Sing Chen, Andy Hensley, Rob Overly, Theresa Rosenberg, James Utley, and Cheryl Walker — who helped develop and test many participatory techniques during the past two decades.

Introduction

In recent years a consensus has emerged that many school buildings do not properly serve the functions for which they were designed. School buildings are said to be made for people, yet ironically those who actually occupy or otherwise use school buildings are seldom able to influence the way in which they are designed. In fact, nearly all the important decisions are based on factors that have very little to do with the way people use school buildings or the way school buildings affect their users. Those decisions are made by administrators, public officials, builders, architects, and others, who, in most instances, do not occupy the buildings ultimately constructed. This lack of user-participation has been cited as a major reason for dissatisfaction. Yet these same users can serve as valuable sources of information in the building development process.

There is an apparent need for greater variety in physical facilities to accommodate various teaching and learning styles. Many instructional programs can be enumerated, such as independent study, teacher centered study, and individualized self-paced study that require different physical settings. The technological and material changes occurring in education also require new approaches for achieving spatial efficacy without compromising educational purposes. The social and learning problems experienced in middle schools and high schools, combined with the variations in learning and teaching styles, provide overwhelming evidence for the need to alter present approaches to school building design.

It is no longer practical either to disassociate building plans from overall education plans or to use outmoded decision-making processes for modifying existing school sites or for building tomorrow's schools.

The business of schools is not to ensure academic performance alone. Given the considerable amount of time that students and teachers spend in classrooms, it is not unreasonable to expect these places to be hospitable. Even in the current "back-to-basics" atmosphere, teachers and school administrators still think in terms of developing the whole child, instilling in her enthusiasm for learning and encouraging positive social relationships.

Considerable research evidence supports the contention of many educators that these goals are more compatible with comfortable, attractive, and interesting school environments. On the other hand, there is also considerable evidence that the classroom environment can affect many attitudes and behaviors. High levels of density have resulted in dissatisfaction, decreased social interaction, and increased aggression. "Soft" classrooms have been associated with better attendance, greater participation, and more positive attitudes toward the class, the instructor, and classmates. Relatively minor design modifications introduced into existing classrooms have been shown to produce changes in students' spatial behavior, increased interaction with materials, decreased interruptions, and more substantive questioning. These findings are important because it is possible that more positive attitudes and behaviors may eventually result in improved achievement.

IMAGES OF SCHOOLS

Metaphors shape the way school problems are defined and are influential in shaping behavior — metaphorical images of schools figure significantly in the debate about the quality of schools and school reform. In an article about school images Philip Schlechty and Ann Joslin (1988) describe the most commonly held school images as:

- The school as a factory
- The school as a hospital
- The school as a log
- The school as a family
- The school as a war zone

The *school as a factory* is a deeply embedded image in educational theory and practice. The factory metaphor suggests mass production, assembly-line techniques, and quality control. It supports the argument that principals should be viewed as managers, teachers as workers, and students as products to be shaped and manipulated. The *school-as-a-hospital* metaphor views the need to distinguish management and professional decisions. Hospital models, such as diagnostic-prescriptive teaching, individualized instruction, and batteries of tests, approach the more clinical aspects of schooling. The *school as a log* refers to a classic form of education where the basics are emphasized, teachers are given high honor and status, and are carefully selected and supported with materials and resources. The *school as a family* recognizes that children should be treated as unique individuals; the whole child should be taught; and children should not be pushed to perform until they are ready. This model assumes that the relationship between the teacher and the child is the most important relationship in the school. *School as a war zone* conveys an image of conflict and hostility, and that aggressive action is an expected part of school and classroom life. Winning and losing become more important than cooperation and accommodation.

The notion of the school as a place of work is clearly the most widely held image, an image reinforced by talk of homework, classwork, and busywork. The contemporary workplace, however, has shifted from the factory to the knowledge-based industry, suggesting a synthesizing metaphor — the *school as a knowledge work organization*. Drucker's (1969) prediction of the dominant occupation of the future will be "knowledge work." Therefore, the student of the future will be the "knowledge worker."

Achieving more effective educational facilities relies upon an approach rooted in the recognition of the differences in needs, values, and preferences of the building's users. Generally speaking, there are many social benefits that can be gained from a user-oriented approach to school building design, resulting in greater accommodation of social needs, as well as an increasingly more effective utilization of resources at the disposal of a particular community.

Since the ideas associated with the participation model are new to the design field, there are detractors, skeptics, and a more general body of professionals who regard this as a passing fad. As a result, there are numerous arguments against participation, some of which are valid while others are simply false assumptions. The most persistent argument against participation is the proposition that teams cannot design; that design is an individual activity.

The camel is facetiously cited as a horse designed by a team or committee. The emphasis, however, on individual genius has been over-romanticized by designers who report the creative act in terms of inexplicable insight, neglecting the daily routine that has given the insight an underpinning. Decision making by consensus has been the subject of considerable research and the evidence strongly suggests that a consensus approach yields more creative decisions and more effective implementation than does individual decision making (Schein 1969).

Overemphasis on the group as an ultimate creative context can be equally detrimental whether the group is called a team, a task force, or a committee. Quite often, groups without a disciplined approach degenerate toward the level of the safest or the most obvious solution. The thinking underlying most naive group activity holds that the capabilities of the participants are additive; that three moderately creative individuals are equal to one highly creative individual. Another mistaken belief is that if one member does not think of a solution, another may. If no one arrives at a solution, then the blame is equally spread throughout the group.

Many of these problems can be resolved practically if every member of the group is personally committed to solving the problem in the best possible way so that participants can shift their emphasis from personal capabilities to collective capabilities. The key ingredient for group success is a willingness to openly recognize better solutions. Similarly, effective groups would need to shape the collective expertise of each of the members. Psychologist William J. J. Gordon, author of *Synectics* (1961), describes a process aimed at the development of creative capacity, and substantiates the idea that the individual process in the creative act mirrors a direct analogy in the group process.

Since groups attempt to expand the expertise of the individual, then it is necessary to consider the limitations of the experts, whether they represent the school-user population, the client, the government, or other designers.

Quite frequently complaints result from experiences with user groups or committees: people's wants are rooted in their experience; many groups' aspirations are commonplace and mundane; and the designer's responsibility is to expand the horizons of the group. Since these observations are certainly valid, it may be useful to clarify these issues.

Expertise consists of access to special knowledge of a subject, an access that supposedly raises the individual's awareness above that which is obvious. In reality, the expert is the least able to create a new idea, since the problem is often described in the technical terms of the expert's language, which makes it impossible to view the problem in a new way. Yet the knowledge of the expert is necessary to state the obvious or the commonplace in order to expand the narrowness of vision often found in highly trained people. Sometimes an attack on convention is viewed as an attack on the people themselves, resulting in experts who function not as individuals but as images of themselves. Communication is necessary at the personal as well as the professional level if there is any expectation for group activity to achieve more than the obvious.

Another issue frequently cited refers to the mobility of both staff and students. Since the time span for the renovation or construction of a new building through occupancy may take several years, opponents of participation have argued that the original participants may leave, or will soon leave, thus invalidating their involvement in the design process. For many years this recurring myth has plagued designers: the design tailored to the departing individual — whether student, teacher, or administrator — will have to be redone. A similar misconception about school projects suggests that since there are individual differences among people, the best way to cope with this situation is to ignore individual differences and design for no one in particular.

Quite often building programs do not include an accurate assessment of existing facilities in terms of both students' and teachers' uses, preferences, or complaints. Lacking such information, the program usually relies on an idealized stereotype of the building's occupants. Institutional clients rely on building committees to advocate the user's point of view. Such committees are often far removed from the needs of those who actively use the building. Since students and teachers have such different needs, attempts to create a single standardized "ideal" environment works to everyone's disadvantage. However, simply creating physical variety does not solve the problem. The school user should participate in the design process as an agent to assure variety.

Consequently, designers can create places that encourage individual choice in spite of situations that involve high-occupancy turnover. People's desire for personal territory, privacy, flexibility, and appropriateness are all design concerns that are often difficult to measure directly in relation to the institutional balance sheet, but unfortunately it is often the user and his or her community who pay the psychic and social consequences of ill-fitting environments.

A participatory process developed by Halprin and Burns and described in their book, *Taking Part: a Workshop Approach to Collective Creativity* (1974), was the focus of the design of a Catholic secondary school in Berkeley, California. Their process entails involving the people who will use the project in a series of participatory workshops at the very outset of conceptual planning. For ten years the students, faculty, parents, administrators, and neighbors of St. Mary's College High School have been working together to determine changes in the environment of the 12-acre campus. The results that have emerged include a brothers' residence, a student center, a central plaza, and site planning.

At the initial workshop in 1974, students, teachers, administrators, parents, and people in the community began their planning process by exploring the physical and nonphysical qualities of St. Mary's. First, they were asked to prepare "real-life" plans for the campus on scaled base maps. With the help of a professional team, people prepared their plans to demonstrate their recommendations for the campus. The plans were then presented for discussion and commented on, with the workshop conductors offering a summary of the agreements and differences that emerged. The workshop had taken one full Saturday and more than 80 people participated. When the campus plan was developed, workshop representatives reviewed it to insure that it reflected the agreements that were previously reached. Soon after, actual work began on several projects. The new brothers' residence was itself the subject of a smaller workshop for residents.

In 1981, Marquis Associates and Burns (1983) returned to St. Mary's to involve people in updating and changing the campus plan according to newly stated needs. The professional team re-involved people in the wide range of campus planning issues — changing previous decisions and making new decisions with the aid of a take-apart scale model of the campus. Commenting on user participation as an aid to professional programming, Marquis' associate partner, Jim Caldwell, states that "workshops quickly gave us information for which we otherwise would have worked for weeks, and some of it we would never never discovered, buried as it was in people's personal feelings" (1983).

Architects Lewis and Gindroz (1974) describe their participatory experiences in the design of a human resource center in Pontiac, Michigan, as one that deeply influenced their mode of subsequent practice (1974). In the course of a complex and open process involving a great many people, sometimes in bitter confrontation, sometimes in quiet working sessions, a building form emerged that included learning areas for children and adults, a health center, theaters and a library, a community field house, a food co-op, workshops and studios, food service for the elderly, and a public restaurant and lounge. What Lewis and Gindroz learned there, and have since seen repeated in a number of situations, is that when consumers and citizens are openly enfranchised early in the design process and invited to assume creative and responsible roles, planners and architects suddenly find available to them undreamed of resources of local perceptions and wisdom, and the reinforcement of the community. In the design of Willamette Hall, Buzz Yudell (1991) notes that "They (workshops) unleashed the enormous creativity of individuals who were enfranchised as creative participants in the making of their workplace and community, rather than relegated to the sidelines as observers or critics. They built a sense of participation that translated into energy and advocacy along the often difficult path to realizing a project."

1
Child Care Centers

Child Development

This section describes the way in which research findings can be integrated into design decision processes. There is the need for a new approach that can engage the architect and the client-user group in a process that links children's developmental needs to facility requirements. Strategies are described that engage parents, teachers, and administrators in collaboration with the architect during the initial stages of design. This process has produced teachers with new capabilities in playroom planning and organization, as well as with an understanding of the way in which architects make decisions. Integral to the process, is the concept of the nonpaying client. For programming purposes, people who use the building are the clients of the architect, whether or not they pay for services. Reference to the user as the nonpaying client, then, attaches greater significance to the importance of user contributions, and to a nontraditional relationship between the paying and nonpaying client.

It is widely accepted that a developmentally appropriate environment — one with well-trained and consistent staff in sufficient numbers, moderately sized groupings of children, and proper equipment and activities, will lead to good child care (Whitebrook, Howes, and Phillips 1989). In all types of environments, working conditions affect services provided. Measures of quality child care have been discussed in several ways. Researchers have attempted to examine the *structural* aspects of child care, such as group composition and staff qualifications, *dynamic* aspects of child care that pertain to children's daily experiences, and the *contextual* aspects of child care, which are concerned with the type of setting and staff stability. One approach for obtaining a quality assessment relies on a rating scale. The Early Childhood Environmental Rating Scale, referred to as ECERS, developed by Harms and Clifford (1980), examine seven dimensions of quality:

1. Personal care
2. Creative activities
3. Language/reasoning activities
4. Furnishings/display
5. Fine/gross motor activities
6. Social development
7. Adult facilities, opportunities

Adding the scores across the seven factors provides an overall quality rating. The results of such assessments have shown that children in higher quality centers showed more advanced communication skills and verbal intelligence, and more positive social behavior and task orientation (Phillips, Scarr, and McCartney 1989). It is apparent from the literature related to quality, that classroom quality, child-care setting, and contextual features are measures of social interaction and *not* measures of the physical features of the environment. Consequently, there is a general lack of understanding, in the early learning field, of the role of the physical environment in contributing to quality child care.

In recent years there has been a surge in the construction of child care facilities. Each project is approached in a unique way with very little programmatic knowledge transferred or recorded. From the limited research related to children's environments, it is becoming evident that new facilities are meeting health and safety standards, but not providing the

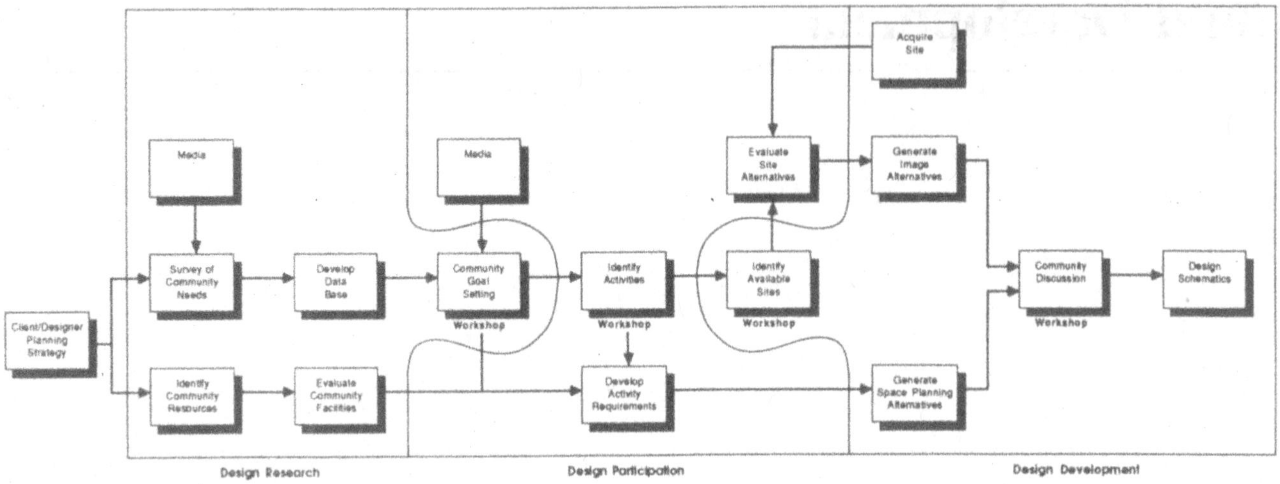

Major components of the collaborative design process.

physical conditions for the developmental needs of young children (Moore 1987).

This section represents a synthesis of numerous consulting efforts with a variety of client groups who are planning to construct a child care facility. The results of these experiences consist of a process and techniques that can be used by architects and teachers to facilitate a constructive dialogue concerning facility needs. The diagram shown above describes the integration of three major components of the collaborative design process: *design research, design participation, and design development*. These components precede production, construction, and evaluation. In this model programming represents the synthesis between design research and design participation. This collaborative design process is a departure from traditional programming approaches since the client, the nonpaying client, and the architect are directly involved in all decision-making stages. Furthermore, the stages described as design research and design participation subsume what is normally referred to as facility programming. This distinction enables the identification of discrete activities for each stage as well as clarifying the difference between information received from secondary sources, such as surveys and data bases, and information received from primary sources, such as direct, face-to-face involvement.

Research Findings

Since needs-assessment studies often yield conclusions far in excess of what is practical or feasible, the most important planning decision for the child care center is the number of children to be served. The research studies of Kritchevsky, Prescott, and Walling (1969) have shown that the developmental quality of child care services drops sharply with increases in the number of children served in one building. Prescott et al. (1975) found that center size was a reliable predictor of program quality. In centers serving over 60 children, major emphasis tended to be placed on rules and routine guidance. Conversely, teacher emphasis on these concerns was found to be significantly lower in smaller centers. Prescott et al. (1975) also found that large centers rarely offered children the experience of participating in wide age-range groups. These findings were also supported by Gump (1978). Mixing of ages in smaller centers offered opportunities for older children to serve as models and to enrich overall play possibilities (Moore et al. 1989).

The age groups generally served by most centers are infants (six weeks to 12 months), toddlers (12 months to two years), and preschoolers (three to five years). In order to achieve the needed critical number in each age group, a target number of 60 to 75 children is recommended (Moore et al. 1989) as a basic planning module. As the institutional needs increase, the number of children should then be increased in multiples of 60 to 75 administratively independent units, to keep the scale of the facility within the child's grasp.

In addition to the number of children in a center, an adequate amount of space for children's activities is necessary to insure a quality program that is developmentally oriented. In a commission study for the federal government, based on a review of cases of density and behavior in child care settings, Prescott and David (1976) recommended a minimum of 42 square feet of usable floor space per child. Cohen, Moore, and McGinty (1978), in conducting interviews as part of their national research, suggested that 42 square feet per child permits a much more flexible program, allowing simultaneous options in active and quiet pursuits without children disturbing each other, in contrast to the average minimum requirement of 35 square feet stipulated in most states. A study by Rohe and Nuffer (1977) showed that while increasing spatial density by reducing space tended to increase aggressive behavior, sheltering activity areas by inserting partitions increased cooperative behavior. Both density and partitioning affected children's activity choices (Rohe and Nuffer 1977). In a review of studies, Moore et al. (1989) concluded that the most desirable social environment occurs at a density of 42 to 50 square feet of usable activity space per child. These research findings provide the basis for facility size and classroom organization criteria.

During this stage of the process, background research findings are integrated into the activity analysis. Accompanying the area requirement for usable activity space for each child is the need for well-defined areas limited to one learning activity, with clear boundaries from circulation space and from other activity areas (Moore 1986). Well-defined activity areas or centers may be created with surrounding partitions, storage cabinets, changes in floor levels and surface materials, or other visual elements that suggest boundaries. Spatially well-defined areas support social interaction, cooperative behavior, and exploratory behavior (Moore 1986; Smith and Connolly 1980). Well-defined areas also prevent ongoing play from being disrupted by intruders (Field 1980).

A process by which the architect and teaching staff link behavioral objectives to spatial requirements corrects an inadequacy in the traditional practice of architecture in that it recognizes the behavioral requirements of the children in making design decisions. Decisions about classroom organization are usually delegated to the teachers, who attempt to create learning or activity centers, but who are often hampered by the lack of knowledge of how to shape the centers physically. Consequently, running and chasing activities are common in classrooms where boundaries are not well defined (Smith and Connolly 1980). Well-defined activity centers, conversely, separated by clear boundaries from circulation space and from other activity areas, and also with some visual or acoustic separation, decrease classroom interruptions and contribute to longer attention spans (Moore et al. 1989). This implies that activity centers within the classroom require a high degree of spatial definition. The design task, then, requires the development of a building program that can spatially respond to the developmental goals of the teachers of young children as well as to the literature on child development and behavior.

Jonesboro Child Development Center

Attitude Survey	
Charette Process	
Community Meetings	✓
Design-In	
Focused Interviews	
Fishbowl Planning	✓
Game Simulation	✓
Group Dynamics	
Public Forum	
Task Force	
Training	
Workshop	✓

SUMMARY

A collaborative approach to the design of a child care center helped to increase the client-user's awareness of how the physical environment could support their children's activities. This collaboration resulted in a design solution that was not only sensitive to the children's needs, but one in which the designer and client collaborated to achieve success. The process required a sharing of knowledge and expertise through the form of community workshops where participants discovered and valued the designer's contribution, and where designers learned from the expertise of the community members. Participants taking part in this process organized by a design team from North Carolina State University included sponsoring church officials, parents, and teachers of the Jonesboro Child Development Center, who were planning to move from their overcrowded facilities into a new building. Three workshops were developed during the course of this project. Beginning with the definition of the center's objectives, identification of appropriate children's activities, and finally the selection of a design solution acceptable to all participants. Each of the workshops was scheduled to allow sufficient time between sessions so that the result of each could be fed into successive sessions.

CLIENT

Jonesboro Child Development Center is currently located in the basement of the Jonesboro Methodist Church in Sanford, North Carolina. The center has been in operation for over ten years, serving an average of 36 children from two to five years of age. The Center accepts children from families of all incomes, using a sliding scale to accommodate children from poor families. The facilities used to accommodate the children's activities include three classrooms, a kitchen, a fellowship hall shared with the church, and additional office space. Due to the spatial limitations of the basement, the center has not been able to expand its program in order to satisfy the increasing requests for additional care. As a result, the church donated a portion of its land to allow for the construction of a new building.

PROJECT

The purpose of this project was to design a child care center that would directly involve the parents, the staff, and the church community members in the design decision-making process. This view was based on the client's belief that quality care can be achieved best through the involvement of all community members. In summarizing this process, the client stated that *"only when the staff is accountable to the parents and community members that it serves, only when the parents, the staff, and the members of the community are together, will the project be a meaningful experience — and only then will its effects be positive and far reaching."*

Community participation in the design of the children's center was divided into three Saturday sessions held at the fellowship hall of the Jonesboro Methodist Church. The first of the three workshops was aimed at informing the designers about the objectives of the Center and the Jonesboro community. A second workshop was held to discuss the way in which these objectives influenced the children's activities and the spatial arrangement of the Center. The third workshop integrated the results of previous sessions by providing alternative building design concepts for participants to discuss. To supplement the workshops' discussions, a program was developed through the use of staff and child care consultant interviews.

PROCESS

Faced with the need for expansion of their overcrowded conditions, the Jonesboro community explored several different options for providing child care to the residents of Sanford and Lee County. They initially explored child care from the private-for-profit corporations, but found they cater to families with predominantly higher incomes, and offer a standardized program. They also perceived that the profit centers do not usually respond to the unique characteristics of the community. Similarly, they discovered that the children's centers are often standardized buildings unrelated to the settings in which they are placed. Since the Jonesboro community had many residents that could not afford the fees of a private center, and since they were strong advocates of community involvement, they sought assistance from the Community Development Group (CDG) at North Carolina State University's School of Design to develop a design proposal suitable for fund raising by the Jonesboro community. CDG is a design group providing technical assistance to communities who do not have sufficient start-up funds.

The initial community meeting concentrated on the identification of the Center's objectives through a fantasy-oriented, goal-setting process using a "wish poem" as a catalyst. The purpose of the wish poem was to have participants express their aspirations about the Center by having them complete the phrase *I wish my center would . . .* in a free verse form. After completing the exercise, each participant read his or her poem to the group. This activity stimulated a lively discussion and set an optimistic stage for the next event. The statements listed in the wish poem were an important beginning to a series of exercises aimed at expanding the participants' awareness of many issues surrounding the development of a children's center. The setting of objectives, such as the wish poem, was used as a means of identifying the purposes of the Center. While the wish poem relied upon the spontaneity of the participants, the objective-setting process relied upon selections from a prepared list culled from educational literature. The intent of this stage in the process was to introduce research findings from the child development literature into the participants' discussions.

Teachers, parents, and church members divided into small working groups in which they made individual choices, defended their decisions, and yet reached a consensus to a mutually agreeable set of children's developmental objectives. The aggregated results from all groups were as follows (Figure 1-1):

- Develop motivation for learning through imagination, curiosity, and creativity

	PRIVATE AREA	HOUSEKEEPING AREA	DRESS-UP AREA	INFANT CARE	TODDLER AREA	CARPENTRY CENTER	INDOOR ACTIVE PLAY	LIBRARY	LAUNDRY	KITCHEN	TOILETS	CUBBIES	MANIPULATIVE PLAY AREA	READING AREA	PUZZLE AREA	MUSIC AREA	SCIENCE AREA	STORAGE AREA	LOUNGE	LUNCH AREA	NAP AREA	BLOCK AREA	OUTSIDE PLAY AREA	ADMINISTRATION	ENTRANCE	ADULT TOILET	OUTSIDE STORAGE
DEVELOP MOTIVATION FOR LEARNING THROUGH IMAGINATION, CURIOSITY, AND CREATIVITY.	■					■		■					■														
DEVELOP COMMUNICATION AND OTHER COGNITIVE SKILLS.																											
DEVELOP MOTOR SKILLS.					■	■	■						■														
DEVELOP SELF-ACTUALIZATION LEADING TO A POSITIVE SELF-IMAGE AND SELF-CONFIDENCE.	■							■		■		■															
ENCOURAGE GROUP INTERACTION							■																				
DEVELOP SOCIAL INTERACTION INVOLVING BOTH CHILDREN AND PARENTS SO THAT THEY MAY LEARN A TOLERANCE OF DIFFERENCES.																											

FIGURE 1-1. Goals-activity matrix.

- Develop communication and other cognitive skills
- Develop motor skills
- Develop self-actualization, leading to a positive self-image and self-confidence
- Encourage group interaction
- Develop social interaction involving both children and parents so that they all may develop a tolerance of differences

While the initial community meeting stressed the identification of objectives, the second session was designed to have participants match appropriate learning activities to those objectives. The final session was created to explore activity adjacencies as they might appear in a floor plan. The first step in the process was the objective-activity comparisons (see Figure 1-1), in which the objectives previously selected were matched with appropriate activities. The activity list was generated from a questionnaire distributed to the teachers prior to the workshop. Each participant completed the comparison chart by identifying two activities for each objective. This step provided an important link in the process of moving from objectives to achieving a desirable and responsive plan for the Center (Sanoff 1988).

The activity planning process (Figure 1-2) consisted

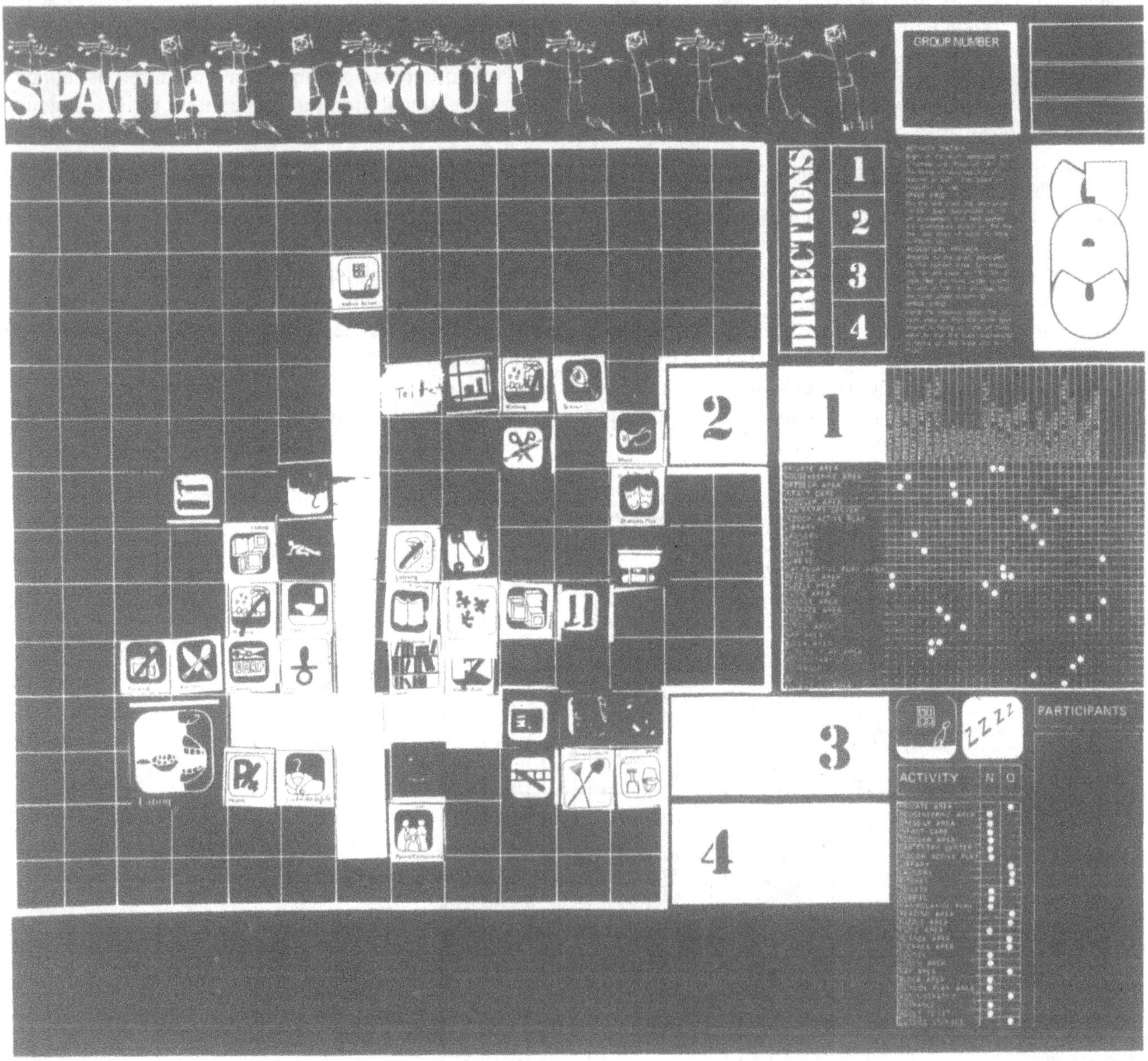

FIGURE 1-2. Parent-teacher workshop on spatial arrangement illustrating (1) the activity relationships matrix, (2) spatial layout grid, (3) activity symbols, and (4) noisy-quiet activity analysis.

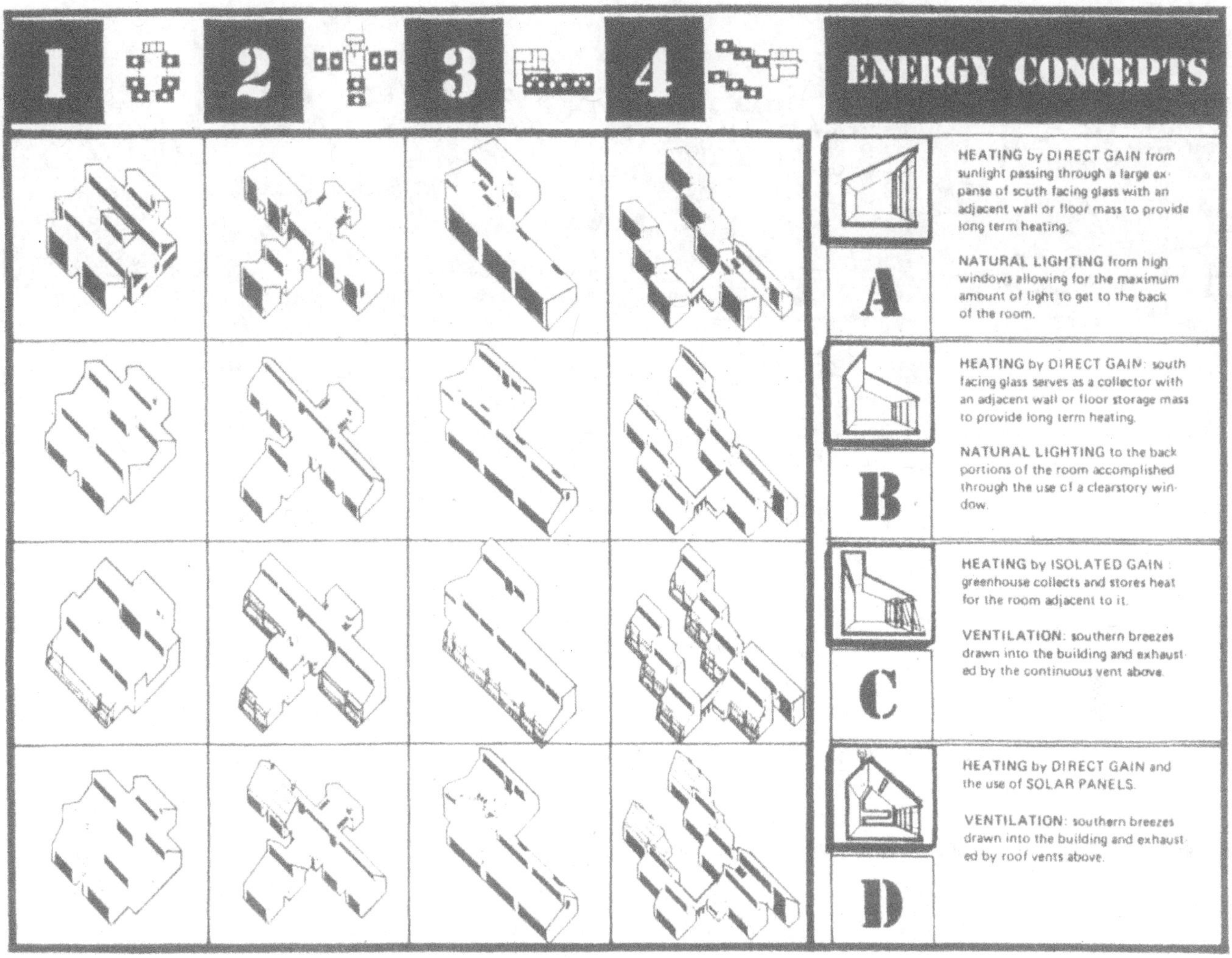

FIGURE 1-3. Spatial alternatives based on energy concepts.

of a large board with a printed grid. The sequence of steps began with the identification of activities with compatible adjacencies. Compatibility between activities was based on privacy requirements, traffic flow, and shared use of equipment or materials. Step one consisted of a matrix where each participant placed an "x" in the grid cell between compatible activities. Groups compared the results of the work and sought similarities in patterns of decisions. This information provided the basis for organizing the primary spatial relationships.

The second step in the Activity Planning Process was the Spatial Layout, in which participants were given symbols corresponding to each of the activities and strips of paper corresponding to corridors. The work groups then developed their plans based on considerations of noisy and quiet activities, and traffic flow between activities. Participants worked together, continuously modifying their ideas, until they reached agreement. When this phase was completed, participants fastened all symbols to the board for a general discussion and comparison between work groups. Several different ideas emerged from this exercise, including:

- Separation of administrative areas from the classroom
- Close proximity between the teachers' lounge and the infant playrooms
- Places for parents to observe their children without interfering with the children's activities

The final workshop was organized so that the design team used information from previous workshops to generate alternative design solutions. The design solutions were required to integrate programmatic requirements with appropriate daylight and passive heating, concerns that had surfaced earlier in the process (Figure 1-3). Participants discussed the merits of

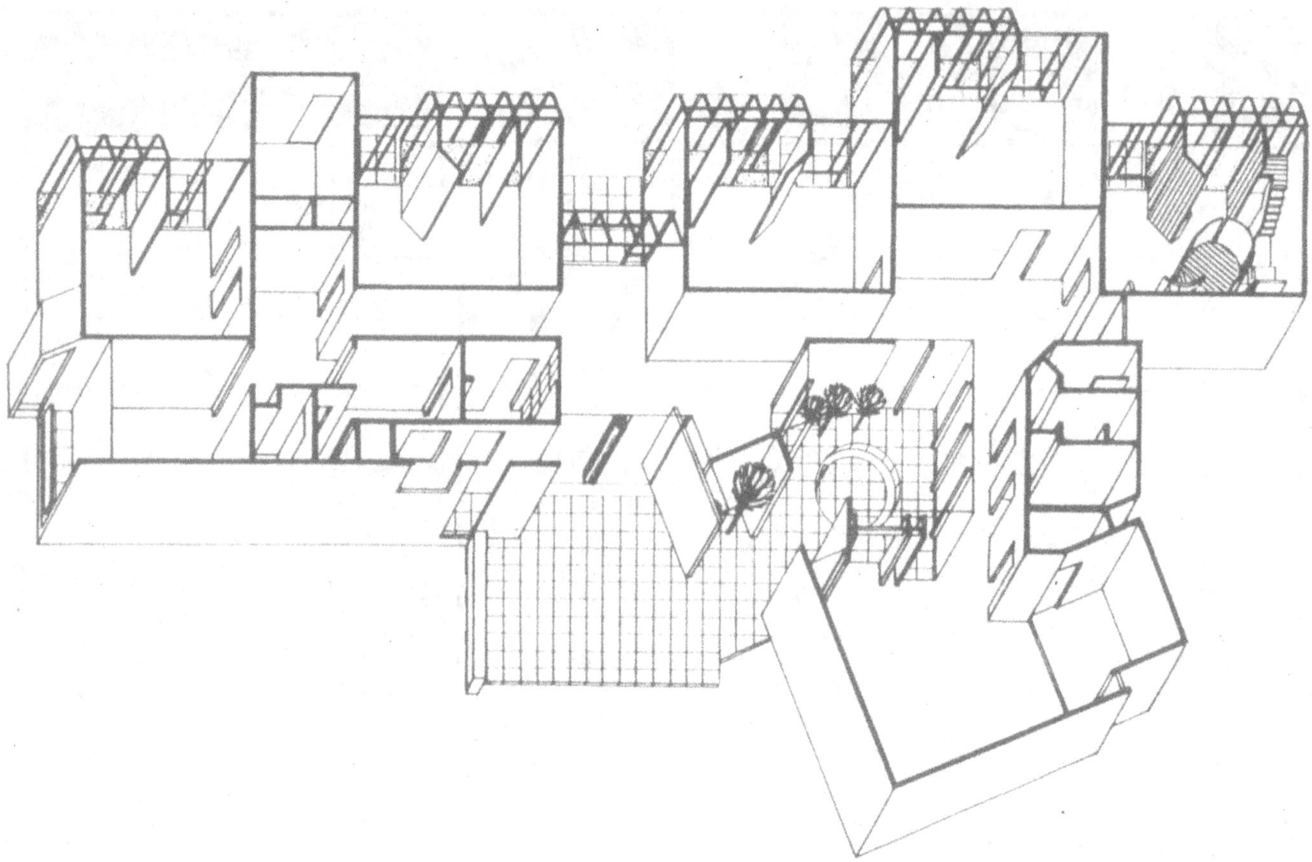

FIGURE 1-4. Proposed plan of children's center (Drawing: Tun Sing Chen).

each plan and recorded their comments on large sheets of newsprint paper. After comparing and contrasting, the design solution most preferred was 3C (Figure 1-4); however, work groups discussed the types of modifications that would improve the solution. The final step in this workshop was to locate the building on the site. In this exercise it was necessary to involve the church council and members of the church in the discussion of present and future uses that would accommodate church growth.

IMPLEMENTATION

The final program considered standards set forth by the Federal Interagency Day Care Requirements as well as North Carolina operating and licensing standards. The design team developed modifications to scheme 3C to include an infant and toddler area, and four playrooms for combinations of two-, three-, and four-year-old children. Each playroom provided clearly visible interest areas and allowed teachers to furnish these areas with appropriate materials and equipment. Adjacent to each playroom was a south-facing greenhouse to provide a continuous source of daylight as well as to act as a collector and storehouse of heat to warm each classroom.

This solution was unanimously approved by the Jonesboro child care community as well as by the church officials. The final approval, however, was clearly a formality, since the teachers, parents, and church officials were part of the design process from its inception. As a result, the design solution represented a partnership between the client-user and the design team, one in which the Jonesboro community had as much ownership in the solution as the design team.

ACKNOWLEDGMENT

The design team consisted of Tun Sing Chen and Rob Overly.

Reggio Emilia

Attitude Survey	
Charette Process	
Community Meetings	✓
Design-In	
Focused Interviews	✓
Fishbowl Planning	
Game Simulation	
Group Dynamics	
Public Forum	✓
Task Force	
Training	
Workshop	

SUMMARY

Reggio Emilia, a city in northern Italy, is widely recognized for its high quality schools for young children. Their infant centers serve children under three years of age, while the pre-primary schools are for children between three and six years. Combined, the schools serve almost one half of the young children in the city. Infant centers alone serve 37 percent of the city's children. Reggio educators see the development of young children as a part of a community responsibility, and require children's centers to be integrally located in the city to focus the interaction of all people connected with the school.

The particularly unique aspect of the school system is the belief that the quality of the children's interpersonal and physical environment supports their development and learning. The educator's goal is to transform a physical plant into a human environment, accomplished by personalizing rooms and hallways to reflect the lives of the children and adults who spend many active hours in that environment.

Named after a cinema located on the site, the Diana school serves children age three to six years, and, in 1970, was the first school to be built according to the Reggio Emilia philosophy. The Diana school's central location in the town reflects a mutual commitment to interaction between the local community and the school community. Its design was the result of collaboration among the architect G. Millo; furniture designer Ninio Sguarza; the founder of the program in Reggio Emilia, Loris Malaguzzi; and the teachers and parents of the schoolchildren.

CLIENT

The commune of Reggio Emilia, a town of 130,000 people, is located in the Po Valley of northern Italy. Reggio Emilia is widely recognized throughout Europe for its innovative and high quality public child care program. There, unlike the United States, day care is an integral part of the education program. In Reggio Emilia, there is a preschool program that was initiated by parents at the end of the Second World War. The town council established the first public preschools for all three- to six-year-old Italian children prior to the establishment of the national law in 1968. These schools are referred to as pre-primary schools. The city currently operates 22 schools for children between three and six years of age, and 13 centers, for infants to three-year-old children. In Reggio Emilia, all preschool-aged children attend some form of school, and almost half of infants and toddlers are in centers, the majority of whom are in the municipal centers.

This community of adults believes in a cooperative relationship of continuous dialogue between parents and teachers. They believe that no one group should decide what is best for children. Parent involvement includes decision making at the school and community levels. Each school has a Parent-Teacher Board or Advisory Council made up of elected representatives that include staff, parents, and citizens. The Board deals with problems related to the school. The Parent-Teacher Boards also have representation, along with the town council, and local Department of Education and influence local government policy.

The municipal pre-primary school and infant/toddler

center challenge notions of adverse effects of out-of-home care for young children and illuminate the potential for early childhood programs that are truly responsive to young children's interests and capabilities.

Citizens of Reggio Emilia do not see day care as an issue of maternal substitution, a view that is prevalent in the United States. Teachers acknowledge the critical role of parents, emphasizing that the child is also capable of developing other quality relationships. Teachers and parents also believe in the need for continuous collaboration in the development of the children. They achieve this end by grouping children and teachers together for a three-year period, so that children who begin as infants remain together until they are three years old, at which time they move to a preschool classroom where they will remain for another three years. This three-year grouping establishes a stable and secure environment for children, and, as a result of this continuity, enables more effective relationships between parents and teachers.

PROJECT

Each of the schools of Reggio Emilia has a unique history; in particular, the school called la Villetta, which dates back to 1970, where a group of women in a working-class neighborhood in a suburb of Reggio Emilia were driven to action. Since many of their requests to obtain a school for their children were ignored, they found an elegant but abandoned old house and forcefully occupied the building as a school for their children. In the days that followed, the women cleared away the overgrown garden, cleaned and repaired the dusty rooms, and looked for a teacher. Several years after the school was taken over by the parents, the city government assumed the operation and funding of the school, and began other neighborhood schools that were similar in character.

The philosophy underlying this preschool program has evolved through 25 years of collaboration, discussion, and work with children. Part of the growth has come from a partnership among teachers, parents, and educational advisors. This collaboration has generated many important ideas, one of which is the educational significance of the physical environment, and the impact of thoughtfully designed spaces. Loris Malaguzzi (1984), the founder of the education program for young children in Italy, describes the importance of the physical environment in this way: "We value space because of its power to organize, promote pleasant relationships between people of different ages, create a handsome environment, provide changes, promote choices and activity, and its potential for sparking all kinds of social, effective, and cognitive learning. All of this contributes to a sense of well-being and security in children. We also think that the space has to be a sort of aquarium which mirrors the ideas, values, attitudes, and cultures of the people who live within it." Lillian Katz (1990), Professor of Early Childhood Education and visitor to Reggio Emilia, indicates that the physical environment of a preschool center is considered a "teacher" in and of itself. The walls of the preprimary schools communicate the educational approach, and is the children's contribution to shaping the spaces within their school. Displays of children's work, descriptions of their work, teachers' remarks, and photographs that describe the educational process are exhibited throughout the school. In addition to contributing to the general character of the school, the displays communicate to teachers, parents, and visitors what goes on in the school.

Lella Gandini, liaison for the Reggio Emilia program, states in her chapter, Educational and Caring Spaces (Edwards, Gandini, and Forman 1992), "The environment is seen here as educating the child; in fact it is considered *the third educator* along with the team of two teachers."

In Reggio Emilia, because social development is linked to cognitive development, buildings are planned with spaces to facilitate interactions and social exchange among children, as well as among teachers, parents, and children. Malaguzzi believes that only through participation with parents and teachers can the architect understand the organization of people, space, and the school schedule. In the Diana school, which was planned in 1968, there is a central space similar to the "piazza," or city square, reflecting a key element in Italian cities and towns (Figure 1-5).

All other spaces open into the piazza. While many Italian schools have large open spaces, their use is

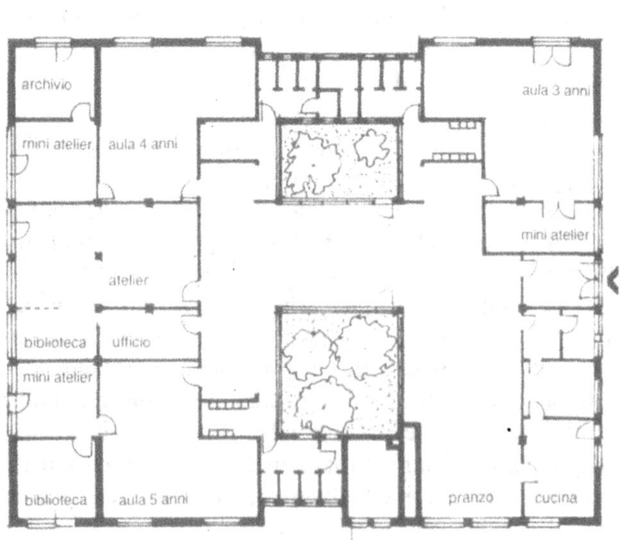

FIGURE 1-5. Plan of the Diana School (Drawing: Henry Sanoff).

limited by their intentions, which are often as a substitute place for inclement weather. Malaguzzi believes that for a large space to function, it must be planned to provide opportunities for social exchange. In Diana, the concept of a piazza is a place where social interaction and exchange of ideas occur. The piazza was conceived by the teachers as a place where children and adults may meet frequently.

Reggio educators are advocates of the concept of community, which is always evident in the philosophy of the school. The sense of community encourages children, teachers, and parents to work together and to build together. The location of the school, too, in a highly visible part of the city was an important issue for the founders, since the interaction between the school and the surrounding community is enhanced by the school's location.

A major feature of the Diana school is a large atelier, or studio, a key space where children explore ideas developed in the classrooms through the practice of visual arts. In an interview with Carlina Rinaldi, one of the pedagogical coordinators of Reggio, Gandini reports that the practical and sensitive use of space was an important element transmitted to the architect. Since, at the beginning, classroom space was inadequate, Malaguzzi conceived of a special space or atelier, where all children in the school could work on visual arts projects connected with activities planned in the classroom.

In the earliest meetings with the architect, Malaguzzi and the teachers also conveyed the importance of connections with the outdoors (Figure 1-6), and the need for daylight in the school building. This effect was achieved through the transparency of glass walls and bringing the outdoors inside through an atrium (Figure 1-7). The indoor garden in the central space becomes a gathering area for children and teachers for eating together, working in small or large groups, as well as for conducting casual interactions. Glass walls also separate work areas to create a communal feeling, though smaller more enclosed areas are available for intimate activities (Figure 1-8). In the outdoor play yard, there are many trees, with a tunnel for hiding and a tree house for the older children to climb (Figure 1-9).

In the mid-1970s, there were additions to the Diana school that came as a result of a fire, yet reflected the growth of new technological tools such as the computer and the video camera, and the need for more differentiated spaces. In preparation for the reconstruction of the building, research was conducted where parents and teachers analyzed their time and space use in several Reggio schools. They made observations on space use, and on quantity and quality of movement, in order to determine which locations had a special identity and which spaces needed to be modified. The results of this evaluative research led to the addition of a decentralized studio or mini-atelier, which provided each age group with a special workplace adjacent to their classroom. Also, parents and teachers agreed that there was a need for satellite spaces added to the central space to provide more opportunities for interaction, as well as for differentiated activity areas. In retrospect, these additions were perceived by the teachers as a major philosophical development in the evolution of the school. As a result of their past experiences, the teachers readily accept change and modification to welcome new ideas and different people (Gandini interview with Vea Vecchi 1992).

FIGURE 1-6. Glass walls bring outdoors inside (Photo: Lella Gandini).

Malaguzzi believes that the Reggio schools "show the attempt that has been made to integrate the educational project with the plan for the organization of work, and the architectural and functional setting, so as to allow for maximum movement, interdependence, and interaction" (Gandini interview 1992).

FIGURE 1-7. Interior view (Photo: Teachers of the Diana School).

FIGURE 1-8. Glass walls separate works areas (Photo: Lella Gandini).

FIGURE 1-9. Tree house (Photo: Lella Gandini).

ACKNOWLEDGMENT

The material for this section was generously provided by Dr. Lella Gandini, who also conducted and translated interviews with teachers of the Diana school in April 1992, and authored many articles about this innovative approach to education. Comments by Loris Malaguzzi, Carlina Rinaldi, and Vea Vecchi also helped to clarify the philosophical intentions of the Diana school.

The Stanford Arboretum Children's Center

Attitude Survey	
Charette Process	
Community Meetings	✓
Design-In	
Focused Interviews	
Fishbowl Planning	
Game Simulation	✓
Group Dynamics	
Public Forum	
Task Force	
Training	
Workshop	✓

SUMMARY

This children's center was designed to provide a home-like setting for 106 infants, toddlers, preschoolers, and mildly ill/recuperating children. Located near the arboretum on the Stanford University campus, the center was built in 1988 for the offspring of faculty, staff, and students in response to the growing need for child care, particularly for families with special needs. A programming committee worked closely with the architect to develop an environment that would satisfy the needs of very young children.

CLIENT

Stanford University provides a variety of child care programs through parent cooperatives, half-day, and daytime-only programs. With the increasing need for additional child care spaces as well as options for families who could not adjust their schedules to current programs, the Arboretum Children's Center offered a new approach. A "get-well" component is included in the center providing interim health care. The center also operates 18 hours a day to accommodate diverse family schedules.

PROJECT

Donald MacDonald Architects designed the Arboretum Children's Center to incorporate the natural environment and provide a home-like setting for the children. They conceived the building as a spiral of small modules with pitched roofs which offered the best access to sunlight because the building form followed the rotation of the sun. The interior of the site is dominated by a courtyard around which the building and its playgrounds emanate. A 12-person committee developed the basic program requirements for the child care center, basically following the California licensing requirements.

PROCESS

During the programming and schematic design phases, the Stanford University administration established a programming committee. The committee participated in four meetings in order to reach an agreeable solution for the program and building design. The committee included the architectural team, university facilities personnel, hospital personnel, child care consultants, student representatives, registered nurses, the dean of student affairs, and representatives of other campus child care centers. At the initial meeting this group expressed its aim: to develop an environment that would be conducive to the happiness, psychological growth, and physical well-being of the children. The committee also recognized the need to accommodate families who could not adjust their schedules to the current programs. Another urgent need that emerged from the discussions was for interim care for children who had an illness requiring them to stay home, but who were not recovered enough to join their groups. A special "get-well" facility was included in the center for recuperating children of parents who could not take the extra days from work or study to care for them.

At the second meeting, the architects prepared sev-

FIGURE 1-10. Model of preferred spatial arrangement (Photo: Magnus Stark).

eral block models to demonstrate the three-dimensional effects of different building configurations (Figure 1-10). The block models help to reduce potential client misunderstanding. Program requirements were also color coded to allow the client and architect easy manipulation of different building arrangements. Classroom blocks were cut in the form of square cubes to a realistic scale, thereby controlling construction costs resulting from the efficiency of the building form. The architects developed four schemes in response to the program. They included a radial form, a spiral form, a double-loaded corridor, and a fragmentary form. All schemes allowed for expansion and ample outdoor space. The group agreed, however, that the spiral form was the most versatile (Figure 1-11). Further meetings were devoted to detailed program information and to project scheduling.

The building design aimed to create a place that would be "home-like" in order to minimize the trauma of the child's transition from home to a social environment. Similarly, the building scale would complement the home-like atmosphere. To this end, the building is subdivided into small modules, making each playroom a recognizable, individual "house" with a pitched roof, giving it a residential character (Figure 1-12). The get-well facility is separated from the center by its own entry, kitchen, and laundry. This decision was the result of considerable discussion and concern for the spreading of viruses and bacteria.

The general layout of the center follows the spiral shape of a nautilus shell. Playrooms graduate in size from one end of the spiral to the other, where infants occupy the smallest playrooms located close to the entry and lobby, toddlers the larger ones, and preschoolers, the largest (Figure 1-13). As children grow older, they move up the spiral, symbolizing increased independence and growth. The spiral shape also follows the path of the sun, allowing all rooms to have sunlight during the daytime. This layout also permits expansion of the playrooms as well as enlarging the building by extending the spiral.

The director's office is located near the entrance with a view of the entire building. This location permits the director to monitor the activities of all parts of the building complex.

The building is located adjacent to the arboretum and incorporates the existing vegetation into the play yards to provide a varied environment with both sunny and shaded areas. The landscaped yards include sand pits, play structures, and tricycle paths.

Each playroom is designed to symbolically replicate the surrounding environment. The ceilings are painted light blue and clear skylights provide a direct view of the sky and trees outside. The green grass is extended into the building through the use of a soft green carpet, and by green doors and window frames. Each playroom also has an exterior covered play area providing shade on sunny days and cover on rainy days. The green of the roof blends in with the tree canopies and makes the building appear to be a part of the natural setting.

The building is heated with a radiant floor heating system and is partially carpeted, particularly conducive for children to use the floor for many activities.

AFTER-OCCUPANCY RESPONSES

Comments from the teachers using the building for several years supported many of the architect's intentions. The home-like, village scale of the project, with separate playroom modules, was one of the favored features (Figure 1-14). The color palette, too, seemed to reflect residential colors, which was a desirable feature of the building. The teachers reported the floor heating to be very successful, especially since many of the younger children spend most of their time on the floor.

Teachers' comments about disliked features of the building included the high noise levels. The compactness of the plan brings playrooms in close proximity to each other. The added advantage of cross ventilation and operable windows provides comfort, but also carries with it the noise generated by active children.

The location of the kitchens was also reported to be a problem since they did not allow for full supervision of children. Teachers involved in food preparation reduce the number of staff available for the surveillance of children. The only other reported

FIGURE 1-11. Floor plan showing spiral shape layout of the building. The courtyard faces north (Drawing: Thanh Do).

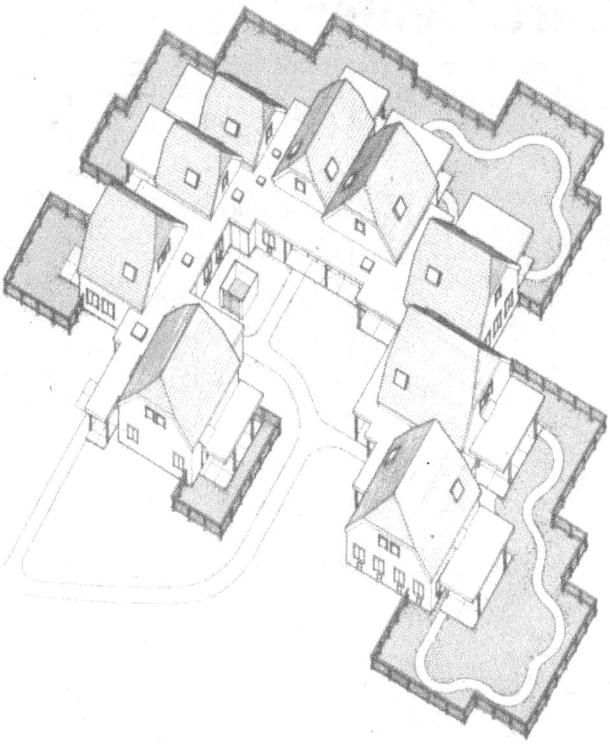

FIGURE 1-12. Aerial axonometric showing the modules linked by flat-roof circulation spaces (Drawing: Thanh Do).

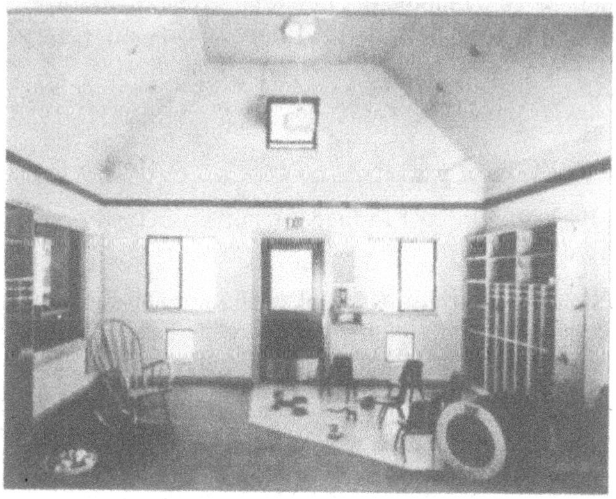

FIGURE 1-13. Interior of a typical playroom. Above are clear skylights offering a view of the sky (Photo: Christopher Irion).

FIGURE 1-14. Building exterior (Photo: Magnus Stark).

source of dissatisfaction was the excessive heat build-up from the skylights in certain portions of the building, although they are operable.

The initial goal of providing more individualized environments for children through the clustering of playrooms creates a residential setting sympathetic to the Palo Alto community.

ACKNOWLEDGMENT

For a detailed description of this project, refer to MacDonald, D. (1989) Deinstitutionalizing Architecture for Children: The Stanford Arboretum Center. *Children's Environments Quarterly,* 6.4:40–47.

SUNY Stony Brook Child Care Center

Attitude Survey	✓
Charette Process	
Community Meetings	✓
Design-In	
Focused Interviews	
Fishbowl Planning	
Game Simulation	✓
Group Dynamics	
Public Forum	
Task Force	
Training	
Workshop	✓

SUMMARY

A needs assessment of students, staff, and faculty conducted by the State University of New York at Stony Brook indicated that present care was inadequate to satisfy current demand. The present capacity of 90 children located in a residential setting in three small buildings would need to be relocated to accommodate a projected need of 200 children. A committee representing the university administration, parents, and students planned for the expansion of campus child care. A selection process involving several interviews retained a design consultant, allowing participation and collaboration of all groups to occur in the decisions regarding the design of the expanded facility. Several workshops considered site planning options as well as the design of playrooms for all age groups.

CLIENT

The choice of a collaborative strategy in the development of the children's center at the State University of New York at Stony Brook was prompted by a division between university administration, and parents and teaching staff who were part of a corporation that operated their present facility. The rift between the two groups was largely due to poor communication during a sequence of unfulfilled administrative promises and unclear expectations between parties. Since the organizational structure and goals of a university are different from those of a campus child care center, a dialogue between groups can foster administrative understanding. To prevent the university-community gulf from expanding, Henry Sanoff, a design consultant hired by a joint committee of representatives from adminstration, faculty, and parents, developed a process in which the responsibility for making decisions rested with those with competence and expertise in a particular area. As a result, the corporate board expanded to include a broad spectrum of parents and teachers who volunteered to work together to discuss, plan, and evaluate design options reflecting all facets of a child care center.

PROJECT

In 1987, the Provost formed a Child Care Task Force to:

- Review the space needs of child care and the allocations currently being made to child care
- Survey the extent and nature of the need for child care at Stony Brook
- Assess the current management model of child care at Stony Brook, study other management models of successful child care centers, and recommend a model best suited to maintain efficiency in providing child care
- Recommend a course of action for the expansion of child care

The needs assessment suggested expanded hours, part-time care, and underscored the need for expansion of child care facilities, for flexible infant care particularly, and low-cost child care. Once parent-run cooperatives, the centers at Stony Brook merged in 1985 and linked to the Empire State Child Care Services Inc., thus permitting Stony Brook to receive

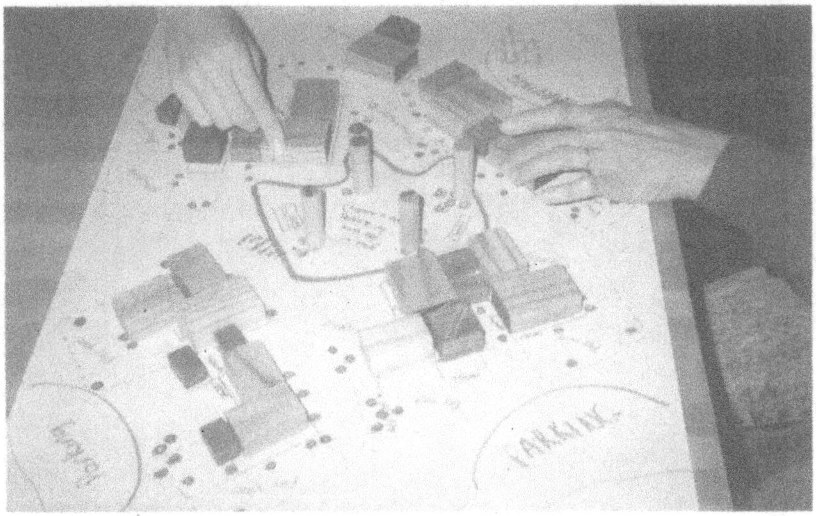

FIGURE 1-15. Parent-teacher work group (Photo: Henry Sanoff).

New York State and SUNY-wide child care funds. The task force further recommended a liaison between the university administration and the Stony Brook Child Care Center, Inc., in a separately constituted committee to plan for expansion of the delivery of child care services on campus. A further recommendation called for the new child care building to subsume the three existing buildings dedicated to child care under SBCC Inc., with the understanding that the three existing centers should be duplicated in the dedicated building.

The present facility, which had been in operation for over ten years, consisted of three adjacent houses located in a wooded site, accommodating 90 children. Staff and parents involved in this innovative program were adamant about retaining the intimacy, scale, and quality of their present facility, in spite of the university administration's endorsement of a needs assessment that would increase its capacity to 200 children. Since the existing site could not adequately accommodate the expansion, the campus planner offered an alternative site located strategically near parking and a major campus circulation corridor, referred to as South Campus. The site location and disposition of the existing self-contained centers plan were the most controversial aspects of the new facility since the teachers feared they would lose the intimacy of their present centers.

PROCESS

An initial workshop explored site planning options. The administration declined participation in this workshop, but agreed to abide by any decisions that would reflect consensus from the participants. Parents and teaching staff met with the design consultant at the children's center and worked together in groups of four with the aid of preassembled site planning kits. Scaled wood blocks were constructed to provide a three-dimensional quality that would be easily grasped. The wood blocks corresponded to all the room areas and classrooms. Work groups manipulated the pieces into various combinations of age-group classroom arrangements until they reached consensus about the appropriate solution (Figure 1-15). The groups devoted two hours to this exercise. They considered many issues that would influence the design of the facility, including solar orientation, circulation, age group clustering, and parking. Not surprisingly, each group arrived at similar solutions since they had numerous discussions about their new facility and had reached many areas of agreement. They divided the site into locations for four separate buildings to reflect the characteristics of their present facility (Figure 1-16). They admitted reservations about their solutions, and also remarked that the scale and complexity of the exercise were greater than they realized.

Involving the parents and teachers in a "hands-on" experience sensitized them to the myriad of decisions to be made and how those decisions could influence the outcome. They came away from the experience with an understanding of the need for a judicious balance of many critical factors, and an empathy for the responsibilities of the architect. In return, all work groups conveyed many ideas about site organization, though a few participants voiced frustration at not being able to achieve what they intended. Each group struggled to achieve the separation and autonomy contained in their present arrangement. All participants agreed that they had reached a point where the archi-

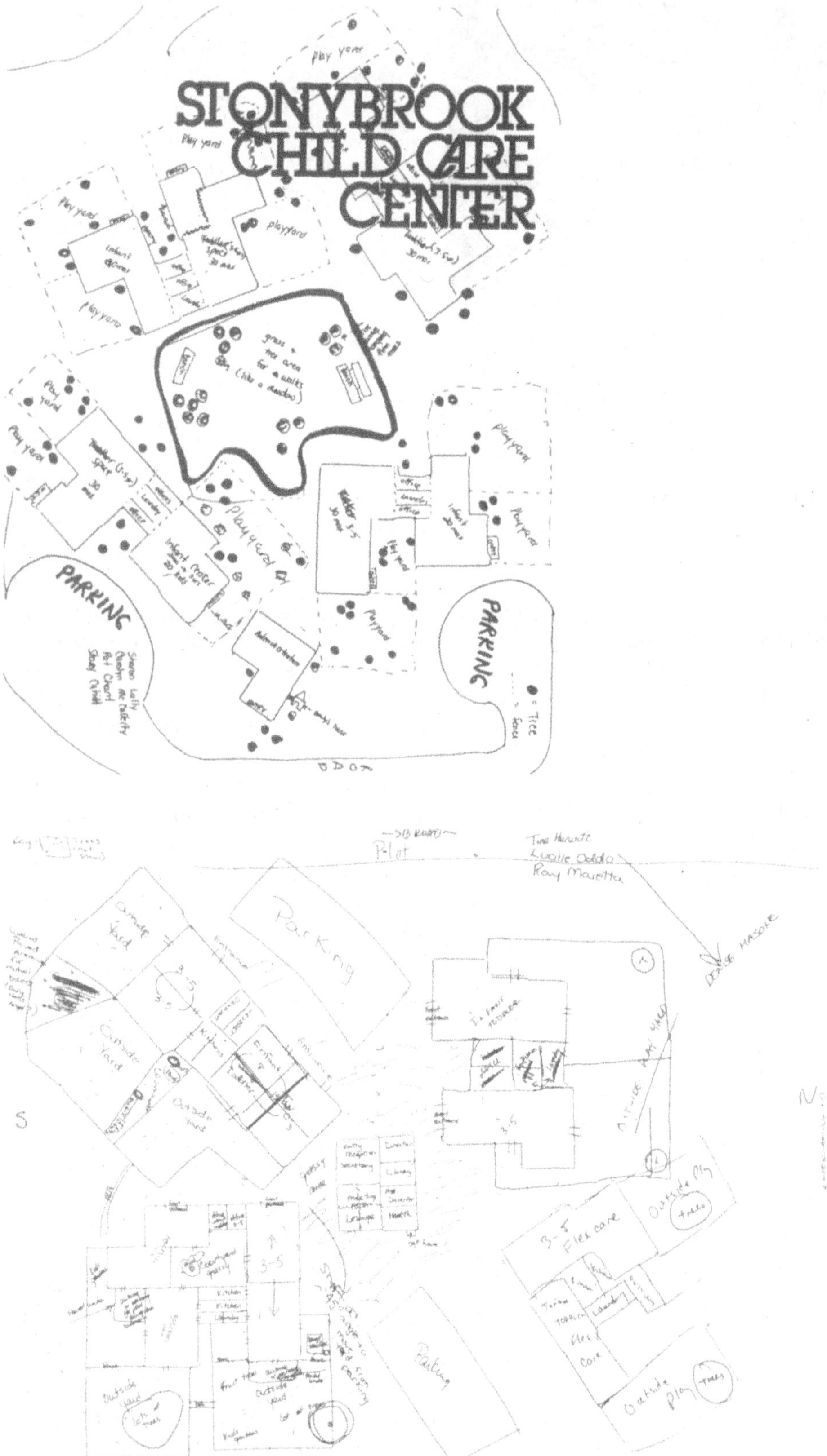

FIGURE 1-16. Site designs developed by parent-teacher work groups.

tect's expertise was necessary to evaluate their ideas as well as to solve problems beyond their capability.

Follow-up work sessions consisted of classroom organization concepts for different age groups and subsequent alternative building design solutions proposed by the architect. Sanoff asked teachers working in each of the three centers to organize the children's area for their respective age groups as a function of their prevailing philosophy, and the desired staff-child ratios in harmony with the New York State Day Care Licensing regulations. Teaching staff members developed activity diagrams and drawings of their ideas.

Three different conceptual schemes (or *parti*) were developed for group discussion by the design consultant, Henry Sanoff, all of which were based on the ideas generated at the first site planning workshop (Figure 1-17). Rather than the four isolated, single-focus buildings that appeared in the parent-teachers original solution, there was unanimous support for a building with separate entrances to achieve the desired autonomy and separation contained in their present facility. This solution also permitted easier food service during periods of inclement weather. Access for teachers and administrators would also be easier, since all movement would be under protective cover.

Many of the ideas related to infants, toddlers, and three- to five-year-olds were expressed by the teachers in the form of scenarios that describe children's daily routines. They currently employ multi-age groupings which they agree to be more natural and educationally beneficial than rigid age grouping. Multi-age grouping provides a classroom organization sufficiently flexible to accommodate children at different levels of maturity. Moreover, the younger children will have the experience of being the older children when the older group moves on and a younger group moves in.

CONCLUSION

From the university administration's viewpoint, the collaborative strategy improved relations between all groups, and provided a new channel of communication for parents and staff to share their child-related expertise. All voices were heard during the discussion sessions and, while there was not always total agreement with the decisions, there was general acceptance that the process was fair and open.

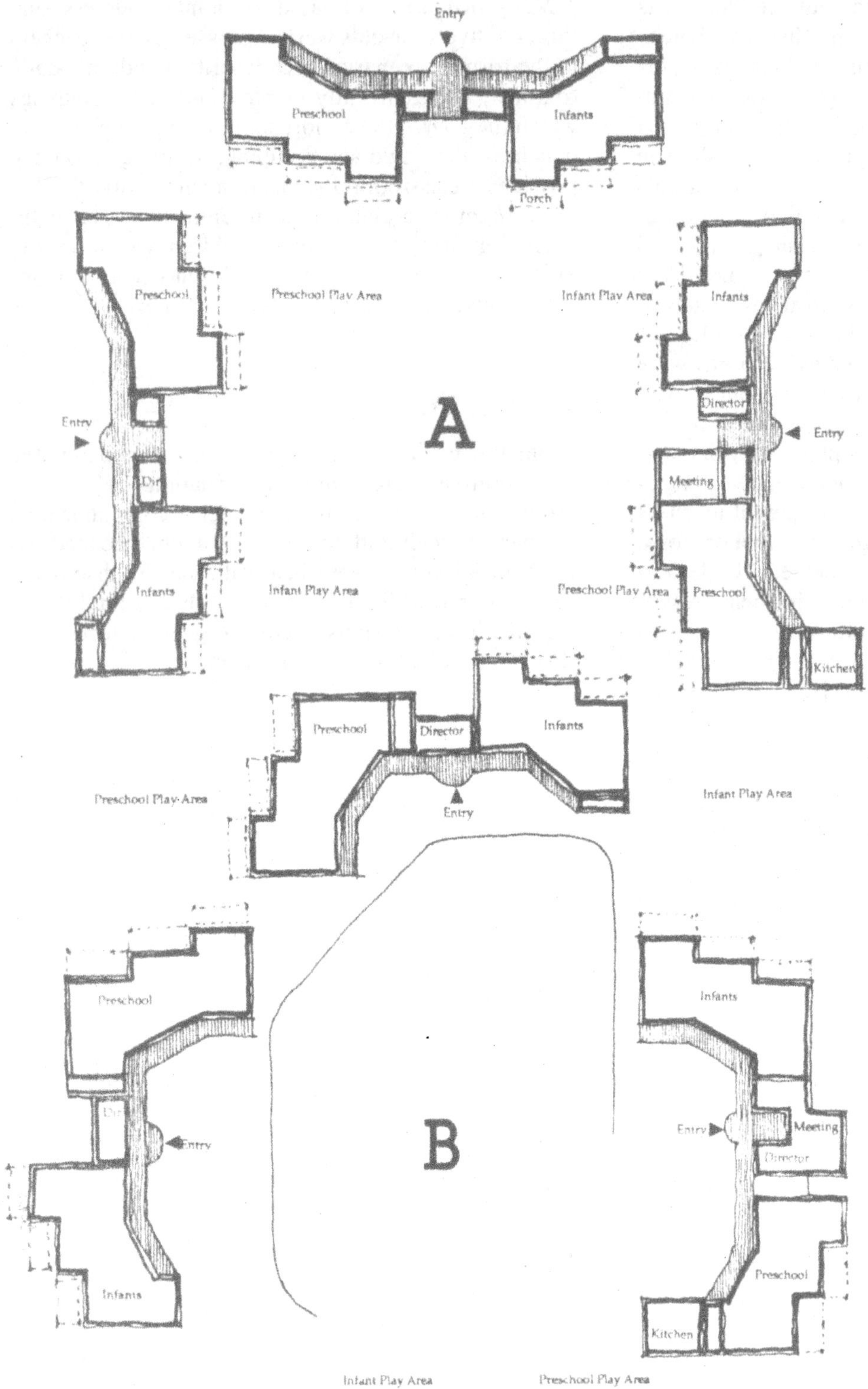

FIGURE 1-17. Sketches of three alternative design schemes based on results of work groups (Drawing: Henry Sanoff).

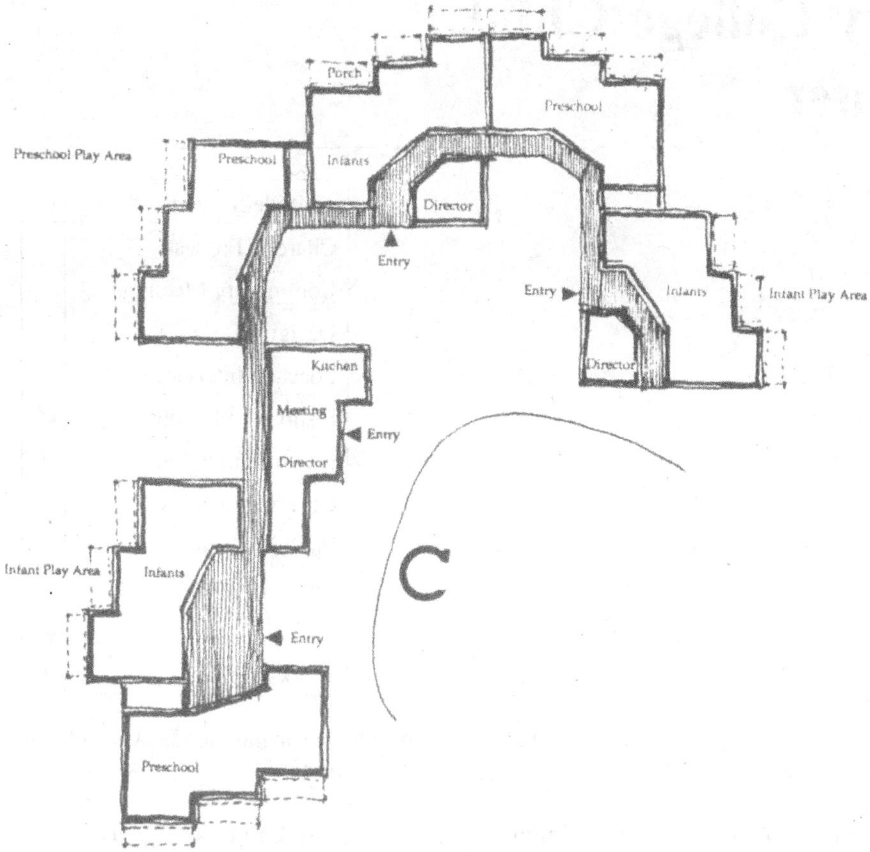

FIGURE 1-17. continued.

Wake Community College Child Development Center

Attitude Survey	✓
Charette Process	
Community Meetings	
Design-In	
Focused Interviews	
Fishbowl Planning	✓
Game Simulation	✓
Group Dynamics	
Public Forum	
Task Force	
Training	✓
Workshop	✓

SUMMARY

Programming and design consultation were requested by the planning group of a proposed 75 child facility and training center for Wake Community College's Child Development Program in North Carolina. They contacted the Community Development Group at North Carolina State University for design assistance to guide the planning group through design development (Sanoff 1989). Since this facility was intended as a demonstration site for the county, the department head and client representative, the teaching staff, and the educational consultants to the program were eager to follow a planning process in which research findings, their expertise, and educational philosophy would be linked to design decisions. This was particularly important since the architect was not identified at the inception of the project, and the planning team would need to be sufficiently informed about the design process to be effective advocates for their ideas.

CLIENT

The Child Development Program at Wake Community College currently occupies classrooms in a variety of campus and off-campus buildings. A component of the education program is a practicum where students are involved in observing and conducting exercises in children's centers throughout the County. For more effective student training, it was proposed to construct a new teaching facility with an integrated child development center.

Typically, institutional client groups planning the child care center initiate a formal needs assessment that includes the following steps:

1. Campus survey of student child care needs
2. Survey of campus child care centers
3. Site visits to child care facilities
4. Consultation with child-care experts
5. Departmental planning

The above steps constitute the *design research* phase of the collaborative design process. The *design research* phase included a needs assessment, visits to other child care centers, and the establishment of educational goals which included desired staff-child ratios and other factors inherent in a high quality center. Although typically initiated by the client, the architect can often provide guidelines for more systematic fact finding procedures.

Surveys and visits to existing facilities, if properly organized, can reveal valuable insights into their functions, since casual visits often reveal obvious results.

PROJECT

The purpose of this project was to create a demonstration child development center to serve as a learning laboratory for college students enrolled in an early childhood education program. It was also intended to create a building that demonstrated the use of space appropriate for different ages and levels of development. From infants to toddlers to preschoolers, playrooms were designed to accommodate a variety of activities into learning centers. The centers were spatially organized to provide for active areas, constructive exploration, and fantasy play, allowing for free and uninterrupted movement.

PROCESS

Early in the planning process, it is desirable for representatives of the user-client group to embark on a program of visits to other child care centers. The visiting team "walks-through" (Preiser, Rabinowitz, and White 1988) each facility and reports on their basic features. The walk-throughs consist of a briefing session, open-ended interviews with teachers, and observations of plan layout patterns of different facilities. Visitors should note positive and negative features of the facilities. Unless the visits are organized to include an interview schedule and specific features to be observed, the results can produce only obvious and superficial results. The visits help to familiarize client groups with the issues they will encounter during the facility development process. They also provide nonprofessional visitors with the direct experience of observing a child care center in action.

Since the playroom is the basic spatial unit of a children's center, prior familiarity with its constituent elements can enable teachers to enter into a productive dialogue with the architect. Modeling the playroom is an activity developed for a teachers' workshop, one that allows participants to manipulate fixed and movable playroom elements in order to achieve the desired developmental objectives. Working in teams of three, teachers are assigned a design task to create a playroom for a specific age group, such as infants, toddlers, or preschoolers. Found materials including cardboard, wood blocks, styrofoam, construction paper, and plastic are provided along with instructions to the teachers for measuring and cutting the materials needed to construct a three-dimensional model.

The model making is preceded by an exercise in which developmental objectives and corresponding activity areas for specific age groups are discussed and agreed upon by each team. Participants discuss model results, then join playrooms together to resemble a building for different age groups. At this juncture, participants discuss issues of playroom adjacencies, building flow, and location of services (Figure 1-18) in an exercise of four hours in duration. Walk-throughs and playroom modeling are effective methods for preparing the client group to participate actively and constructively in the planning stages of a child development center.

Planning began with focusing on the child as the basic unit of development. Next, the design participation phase involved the collection of behavioral data relating to each activity in which infants, toddlers, and

FIGURE 1-18. Teachers constructing a model of a classroom (Photo: Henry Sanoff).

preschoolers would be engaged. The conceptual framework used for the design of the facility was the activity center (Sanoff and Sanoff 1981). The teaching staff of the child development training program identified the developmental objectives for each activity by age group, and the "molecular" activities that would occur in the activity center.

The water play area, for example, the objectives of which would include sensory and perceptual acuity, concept formation, and eye-hand coordination (Sanoff 1982; Weinstein 1987), would involve such molecular activities as pouring, measuring, mixing, and floating objects, all of which are related to the primary activity. Activity data sheets recorded the relevant activity information which served as a program and resource for future decisions (Figure 1-19). The data sheets provided a format in which specific equipment needs could also be identified for future purchasing.

Since the planning of a child care facility also reflects a particular ideology about child development, a space planning exercise was developed to engage the teaching staff in decisions related to playroom layout. A planning guide of 50 square feet of usable space per child limited the number of activity centers that could be included in a playroom, and accordingly scenarios were written by teachers about a typical child's day. The constraints encouraged the teaching staff to use "trade-offs" effectively since they were required to decide which activity centers were most important for various age groups. Graphic symbols corresponding to each activity center (Figure 1-20) enabled the manipulation of children's movement patterns in the classroom. This element was the first step in providing environmental information to foster mental image development. Spatially organizing activity

Toddler

In this activity center the toddlers can learn about the properties of sand and water. The reaction of both to human manipulation and their flexible properties make them excellent tools for learning about natural forces. Manipulative toys need semi-private play environments so that the child can focus on the skill without major distraction. This hands-on type format for learning requires space that promotes this concept.

Manipulative
Sand
Water Play

100 square feet

Objectives

Sensory-motor; fine motor skills
Cognitive,math,visual motor
Socialization
Concept formation:math,science, cognition,self-help, language
Social skills
Building fine and gross motor
Relaxation

Notes

Outer rim on table for support and placement of toys
Child safe hooks for hanging toys
Water safe floor

Equipment	Storage Open	Storage Closed
12 transparent bins for objects	•	
Horizontal floor level work surface	•	
Wall display surface-interlocking toys	•	
Vertical display		
Storage for 24 extra bins		•
Pegboard storage.Puzzles		•
Floor height sand table with rim	•	
Storage for toys		•
Alternative materials storage		
Floor-level water table w/cover	•	
Storage for towels and toys		•
Smock hanging space	•	
Mop closet		•
Horizontal display for concept pictures	•	

Acoustical level- Moderate

FIGURE 1-19. Typical activity data sheet identifying the toddler age group and corresponding activity requirements.

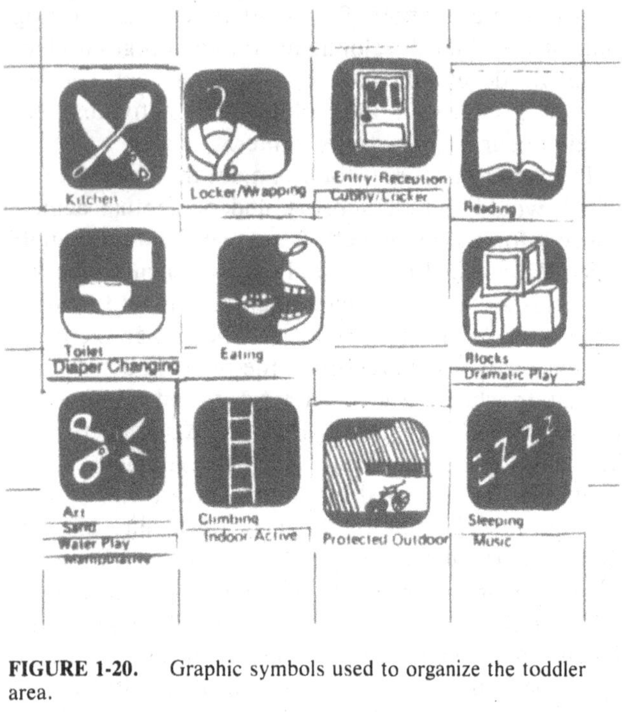

FIGURE 1-20. Graphic symbols used to organize the toddler area.

centers on a "game board" corresponding to a playroom permitted the determination of which centers were to remain fixed and which were to be flexible. The spatial layout process required teachers to consider planning concepts, adjacency requirements, circulation, and visual and acoustic privacy between activity centers. Most of all, the process reinforced the concept of activity centers.

The teachers worked through a playroom layout by manipulating activity symbols for each age group. They outlined the flow process from entering the facility, greeting the staff, removing their coats in the cubbie area, and moving to various activity centers. When planning the infant room, the teachers identified the diaper change as the focal point with surveillance to all other activity areas. To avoid the clustering of unsightly cribs, the teachers proposed decentralizing the sleeping activity into several crib alcoves. This process entailed small-group discussions that required consensus in all decisions. When agreement was reached, the symbols were fastened to the base to constitute a record of the group's decisions. The designer constructed cardboard scale models of each playroom using movable walls and furniture, corresponding with the flow patterns in the diagrams developed by the teachers (Figure 1-21). This stage of the process permitted the teaching staff to visualize the three-dimensional implications of their decisions. Simplified schematic models of the playrooms limited the amount of information presented at one time, conveying only the most significant issues in order to minimize information overload. Teachers could reconsider earlier decisions, particularly when they saw conflicts arise that were not easily predicted in the two-dimensional diagrams. Although circulation between activity centers was considered in the development of the activity symbol diagrams, the scale model conveyed the need to establish clear boundaries between centers to prevent distraction while permitting the teacher an unobstructed view of all children's play areas. The scale models included information not

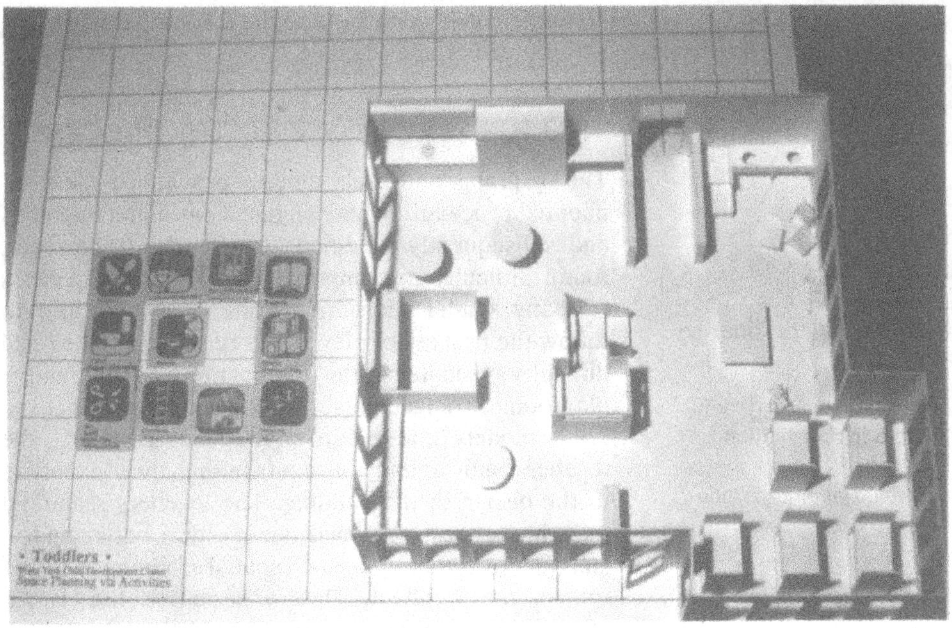

FIGURE 1-21. Model of classroom corresponding to form diagram (Model: James Utley).

shown on the activity diagrams, such as furniture and equipment, but the movable pieces were easily manipulated by the teachers as they referred to the activity data sheets.

When the teachers reached agreement about the best playroom arrangement, the designer developed form diagrams elaborating on their spatial decisions (Figure 1-22). These diagrams combined activity centers into playrooms for different age groups. Although abstract in nature, the diagrams allowed teachers to gain an understanding of "conceptual relationships." Teachers were better able to clarify their intentions regarding the way in which the educational program would be enhanced in the design of the classrooms. This exercise also provided the participants with the tools to evaluate plan alternatives and, most important, a procedure for further playroom modification after the building was in use.

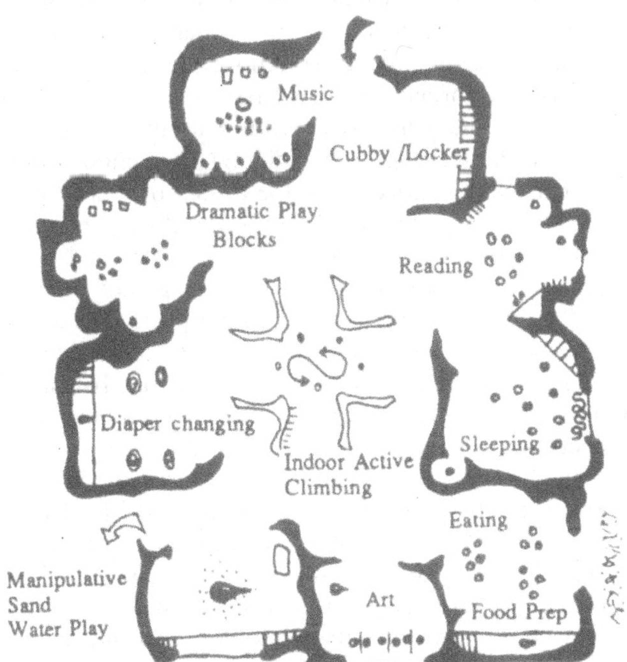

FIGURE 1-22. Form diagrams describing activity centers in the toddler area.

The results of the participatory exercises helped to generate design criteria, as well as to modify the requirements of the building program. Several statements described the fundamental environmental characteristics of an effective child development center. They were as follows:

The environment must be comfortable and inviting for children and adults. It should reflect an atmosphere conducive to children's growth. Materials and equipment should be easily accessible to children in order to encourage independence and self-esteem.

An effective means of organizing the environment is to develop interest centers where the playroom is divided into areas that focus on specific activities. It is advisable that quieter activity areas be placed in close proximity in order to promote a quiet atmosphere. Activity areas demand visual clarity and well-defined limits if children are expected to interpret cues on appropriate areas for certain types of play. A quality playroom would include the following activity areas:

- Creative expression/art
- Literature/language art

- Dramatic play/housekeeping
- Block building
- Self-image, personal hygiene
- Science and exploration
- Cooking
- Water play
- Carpentry
- Manipulative
- Music and movement
- Personal space

More specific guidelines that influenced the final solution included:

- Protected outdoor play area adjacent to each playroom
- South orientation for playroom and adjacent outdoor area
- Daylight to be provided by rooftop glazing and glazing orientation.

IMPLEMENTATION

The teaching staff was involved in organizing all the building components into a facility design using graphic symbols that corresponded to the major building parts, such as playrooms, kitchen, offices, corridors, and lobby area. Age-group adjacencies were considered with opportunities for different age groups to have visual contact with each other. This effect was ultimately achieved in many ways, including low windows in each playroom for children to be able to see into the adjacent room. The parents' "drop-off" was the initial step in the flow process that also examined connections between indoor and outdoor activities. The planning concept that emerged from the discussion was that of a "central spine" from which playrooms would be connected. The spine would be more than a corridor, yet similar to a street, where parents, teachers, and visitors could see into the playrooms, observing children's activities (Figures 1-23 and 1-24). To emphasize the street concept, it was necessary to fill the area with daylight through the use of overhead skylights (Figure 1-25). Each of the playrooms, too, would have a central spine leading to a covered outdoor play area. Spatially well-defined activity centers were located on either side of the playroom spine. These playrooms included fixed areas for art and water play, and centers that could change their focus at the discretion of the teacher. Spatially well-defined centers imply the need to be distinctly different from adjacent centers. This differentiation was characterized by physical features such as partially surrounding dividers or storage units, implied boundaries through the use of columns, changes in floor level or ceiling height, changes in floor covering, and changes in light levels (Figure 1-26). Learning materials, furniture, and equipment also contribute to the distinctiveness of the activity centers.

TEACHERS' RESPONSE TO THE PROCESS

The diagrams and scale models provided a clear sequential procedure where all decisions could be traced and subsequently modified. The teachers, however, found difficulty in comprehending the consequences of many spatial decisions. While they were able to follow the process of playroom organization, they had difficulty visualizing the implications of alternative playroom arrangements. A continual reference to scale models and perspective drawings aided the teachers substantially in contributing their expertise to the design of the building. The teachers remarked that this process provided them with a better understanding of the principles of spatial planning, and the role of the architect. They experienced the "ripple effect," in which minor changes in adjacency relationships manifest themselves into major revisions in the spatial layout of the playroom, or of the building. This diagnostic procedure of examining flow processes and linking objectives to activity centers enables teachers to develop a conceptual understanding of playroom and building layout principles.

CONCLUSION

The interaction between teachers and the designer described in this project is clearly a departure from the traditional approach to facility development. Conventional practice usually denies the expertise of the user (nonpaying client) and his or her involvement in design decision making. Traditional designers also focus on the formal and visual issues and give less attention to the behavioral factors that may equally influence the form of the building. This tradition could be carefully guarded since the design of a child care facility is normally developed at the floor plan level, defining relationships between classrooms and other areas, and disadvantaging the teaching staff because of their inability to comprehend floor plans. The teachers' expertise lies at the level of behavioral interactions within the playroom, but this is typically ignored by architects and left to the teachers to resolve after occupancy of the facility.

In the project discussed, a structured process enabled child development professionals to lend their expertise to the initial programming stages of the design process. Use of activity data sheets, activity symbols, and form diagrams permitted the designer to integrate knowledge about children's behavior and their requirements into a format that was conducive to making space planning decisions. Integrating the expertise of the staff in this guided process established

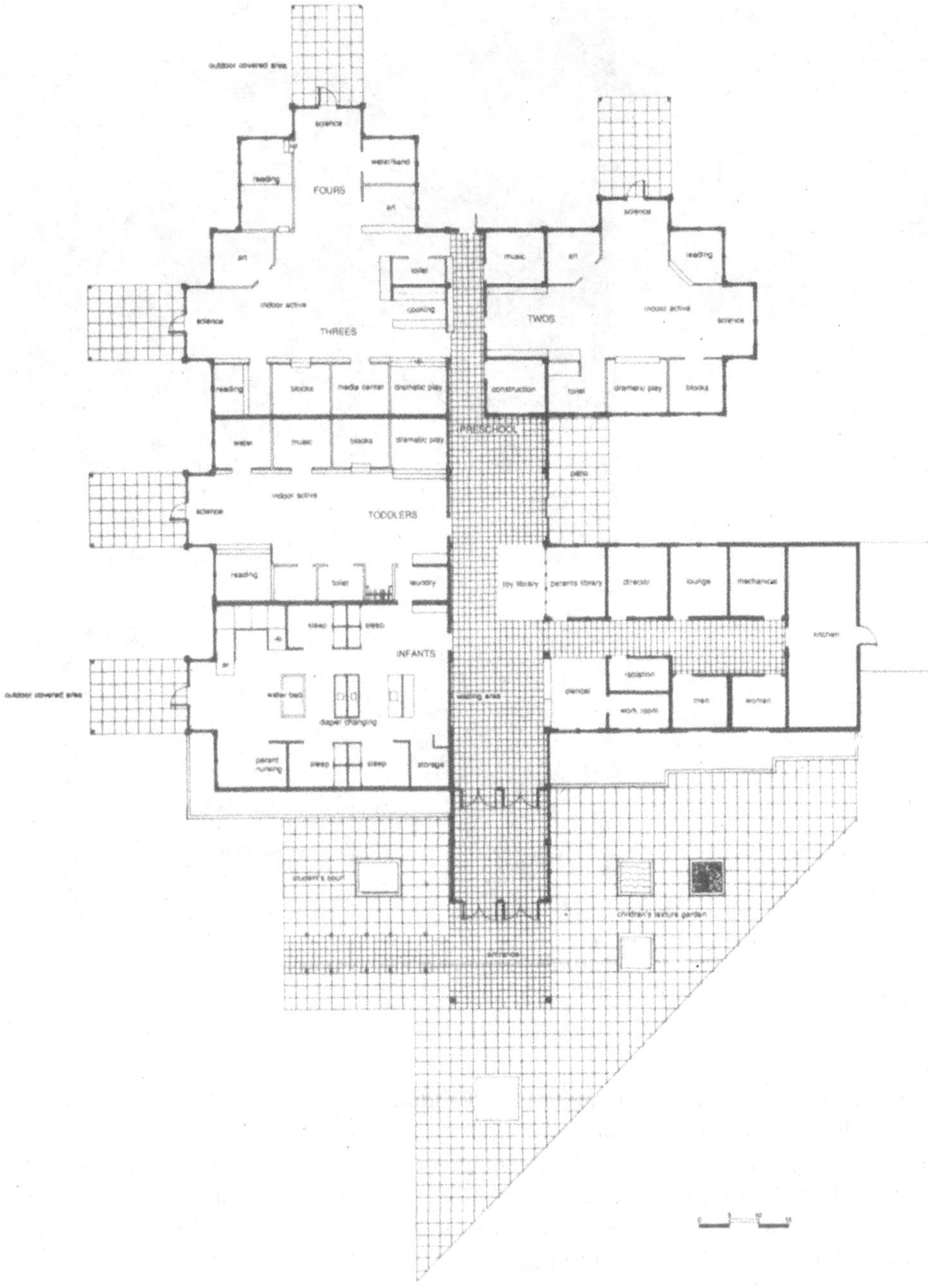

FIGURE 1-23. Floor plan of the children's center (Drawing: James Utley).

clear linkages between child development goals and the types of places where these goals could be fulfilled. The teaching staff's continual involvement in the building design process encouraged the exchange of ideas and concepts with the designer, which increased the staff's ability to act as effective design team members. The active part of the process usually terminated with the schematic design of the children's center, which is the result of the team's involvement.

These activities show that people who participate in design decisions have greater satisfaction with the product as a result of their involvement. It is evident from these experiences that the dynamics of a participatory process and product are different than the results of a more traditional design process. Not only is there a shared sense of ownership in the product, but participants are empowered by an understanding of the decisions that led to the physical form decisions. This approach has the further promise in enabling teaching staff to make spatial modifications after occupancy.

The effectiveness of a collaborative process is con-

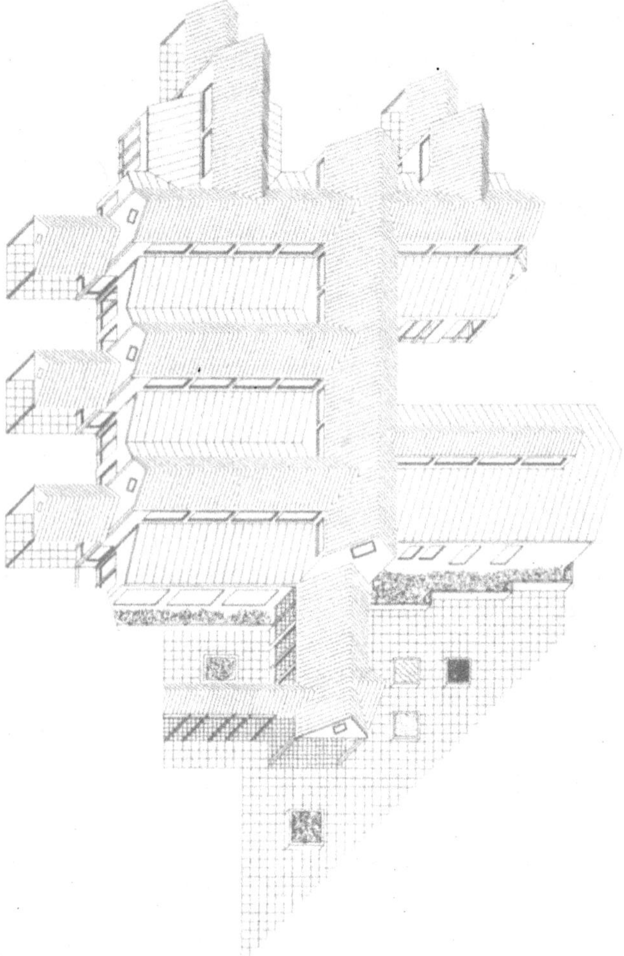

FIGURE 1-24. Roof axonometric (Drawing: James Utley).

FIGURE 1-25. Interior street of completed building (Photo: Henry Sanoff; Architect: Haskins Rice Savage & Pearce).

tingent upon the involvement of the architect from the inception of the project. When the architect is an integral part of the process, the building design proposals are clearly understood by the user-client group of teaching staff, parents, and administrators. On those occasions when the programming document was completed prior to the architect being commissioned for the project, significant communication problems can occur between the user group and the architect. In this instance, the architect of record was appointed by the college administration after the program and preliminary design had been completed by the consulting design team. Although considerable effort was made by the design team and teaching staff to explain the rationale for the programming and design decisions, the architect had great difficulty in grasping many of the nuances of the proposed design solution. Similarly, the architect's drawings were not understood by the teaching staff, since the drawings were prepared for construction purposes. This situation created difficulty in the working relations with the client because the architect often urged quick approval to expedite the production process. Construction of this facility was completed in 1991.

The language of the program should reflect the concepts developed by the teaching staff and conveyed in terms of educational goals and children's activities. The language of the architect — the floor plans and elevations — are the interpretation of verbal concepts, and are often unintelligible to the user group, especially if they are not developed simultaneously with the program. The implications of these experiences is that ownership in the design process, achieved through active involvement in design decisions, permits the user-nonpaying client to exercise free and informed choice. The separation of the programming and design stages not only limits participation of a wide range of experts but also jeopardizes the ability of the product to fulfill the expectations of the program.

ACKNOWLEDGMENT

The success of this project is largely due to Joan Sanoff, Department Head, Early Childhood Devel-

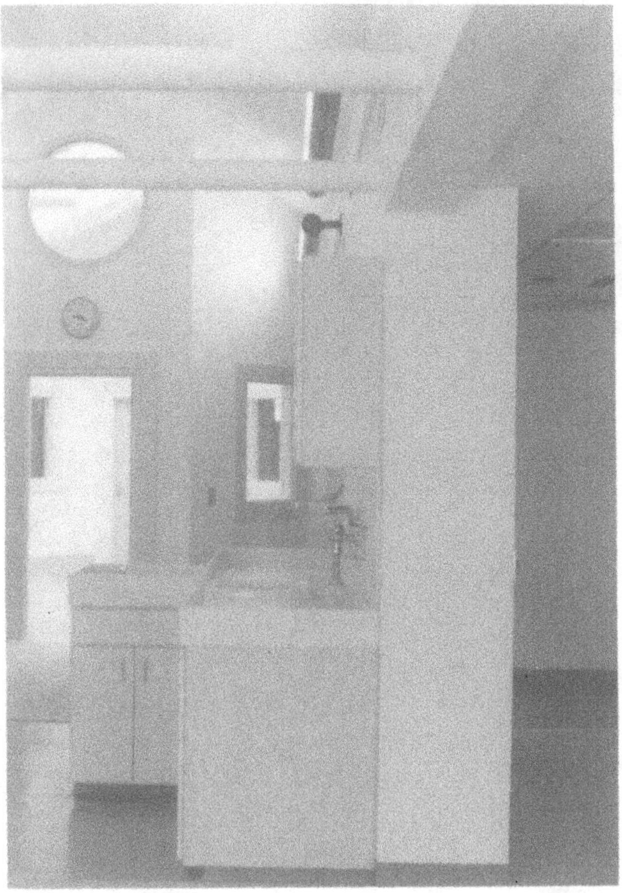

FIGURE 1-26. Interior view showing diaper change area separated from crib area (Photo: Henry Sanoff; Architect: Haskins Rice Savage & Pearce).

opment, Wake Technical Community College, who participated in the programming and design development, and urged the college administration and architect-of-record to produce a high quality building. A note of thanks is also due to James Utley, Community Development Group member, for his thoughtful design work.

An earlier version of this chapter appeared in *Children's Environments Quarterly,* Volume 6, No. 4, Winter 1989.

2
Responsive Elementary, Middle, and High Schools

Responsive School Environments

The amount of time young people spend in school, from preschool to twelfth grade, is so significant that it is important to recognize that much of this time is devoted to living as well as learning. The quality of this living, therefore, is an important matter (Gump 1987). Both the quality of student life and the quality of education are directly affected by the quality of the school environment.

School environments might refer to physical provisions as well as the patterns of a school's operations. Students' perception of their environment, whether supportive or hostile, interesting or boring, is also integral to an understanding of the school environment. Gump (1987) refers to this integrative conception as the ecological environment. Schools and classrooms can then be considered from the viewpoint of enclosure, size, and density, and the behavioral consequences of these characteristics.

Schools generally have been designed according to two basic patterns: open schools, or schools without walls and corridors, and traditional schools with enclosed classrooms along each side of a corridor, or "egg-carton schools.". While open-school environments were constructed largely in the 1970s, they represent a large proportion of the school building inventory. Open schools were envisioned as having a distinct economic advantage, since the space usually consumed by corridors became usable for learning. Open classrooms contained different activity areas and grouped students in a variety of sizes and abilities. While team teaching was shown to be more likely in an open school (Gump and Ross 1979), the lack of enclosure of basic activity areas created problems of noise and distraction. Studies have shown that noise and distraction were common complaints from children and teachers in open schools (Bennett et al. 1980). Studies at the elementary level have associated open-space classrooms with reduced task involvement. Decreased achievement in the open school was generally attributed to its more informal approach and to the design that failed to protect against distractions (Gump 1987). Data from achievement test results, comparing open-space schools with traditional schools, indicate that certain students may be unsuited to an open environment, and that this type of environment may encourage negative achievement effects.

The staff moving from a traditional school building to an open-space school also found the transition frustrating. It has therefore become common practice to partition activity areas to reduce the openness. Studies in the use of partitions to protect activity areas from community areas in secondary schools have shown that there were fewer interruptions where academic areas were distinct from nonacademic areas (Evans and Lovell 1979). Issues of spatial organization within elementary and high school classrooms, however, have not adequately been addressed in the research literature, except for the need for more small group space (Castaldi 1977).

Opportunities for privacy, which are never substantial in traditional school buildings, are less available in open areas. Privacy has been shown to contribute to a child's growth and development (Proshansky and Wolfe 1974) and consequently opportunities for increased privacy, such as secluded areas, have been recommended especially for reading (Ahrentzen 1982). Elementary students' desire for privacy niches (Mack 1976) has stimulated research into the "privacy booth"

— a classroom niche — in which a single student could work in relative seclusion. The booths often were secluded and did not permit a view to the outside. Students, however, often prefer a retreat, but not total exclusion (Curtis and Smith 1974). While the data on such experiments are not conclusive (Weinstein 1982), they do suggest that many physical arrangements can provide the opportunities sought in the privacy booth. Since students often seek seclusion, they might prefer spaces that are not visibly isolated or cut off from view. Students appreciate an environment that provides a variety of places to allow different learning experiences to occur.

There have been numerous studies on the effects of class size and learning; most studies, however, compare the effects of higher student population *without* an increase in the effects of the classroom environment and the amount of teacher resources (Gump 1987). With no expansion of space, social density will increase with the increase of students. Research on class size and learning has shown that smaller class sizes (lower densities) yield better achievement scores. Substantial differences occur when class sizes are reduced from 30 to 15 students (Glass et al. 1982). For teachers, on the other hand, a reduction from 30 to 20 students has a marked attitudinal improvement. Generally, research has shown that lower classroom densities improve learning as well as the attitudes of both student and teacher. This is partially explained by seating arrangements, student attitudes, and performance. Adams and Biddle (1970) found that an "action center" in the front and center positions of the seating area yielded as much as six times more student–teacher interaction than if the "action center" were in the more rear and peripheral areas. The results of greater participation in the front and center positions might be more effective learning and higher grades. Clearly, there are disadvantages to students on the periphery: less classroom participation and impaired learning ability. Consequently, with more students in the classroom, peripheries are more extended and remote. In classrooms that are heavily populated with students, the loss of open space to desks can imply fewer opportunities for small-group activities. Since students need some spatial separation, increased density could lead to negative student reactions to the classroom, and to their ability to learn within it.

The feasibility of smaller classes may not be economically possible for many school districts; however, arrangements can be made to reduce the instructional group size within the classroom. Small-group arrangements can be provided by the use of aides, parent volunteers, and student instructors. Many of these educational approaches are in operation now.

These findings related to the issue of class size are consistent with those in day-care research. The size of the student group can make a significant difference in the feelings of children and teachers, as well as in the conditions for learning.

THE TRUMP PLAN

Images of the Future by J. Lloyd Trump was a commissioned study aimed at improving the quality of secondary education for the school of the future. The study was commissioned by the National Association of Secondary-School Principals, who believed that America has met the challenge of quantity, in terms of students attending schools, but not that of quality. Written in 1959, the report suggests that "the secondary school of the future will not have standard classes of 25 to 35 students meeting five days a week on inflexible schedules." In terms of student-teacher relations, "the secondary school of the future will provide for closer relationships between students and teachers. The secondary school will make the teacher more a consultant than a taskmaster." Instructional time would combine small group and large group meetings, as well as time for individual study. Since students have different learning styles, they would pursue specialized studies and develop personal goals.

In the report a view of educational facilities was that "space within the building will be planned for what will be taught in it and how it will be taught." The school of tomorrow was one that consisted of flexibility of space in which large rooms will be divided into small seminar rooms for small-group discussions. Finally, the report suggested that architects, engineers, scientists, and educators will work together to design better structures to house these new requirements.

The Trump plan influenced the development of many schools during that period; one in particular was the Decatur-Lakeview High School in Illinois, a school of 1,000 students in six grade levels from 7–12. Former Principal, David W. Beggs III, describes the school planning process in his book, *A Practical Application of the Trump Plan* (1964). Based on a desire to find a better way to individualize instruction, the staff of the school, inspired by the Trump Report, began a series of meetings, identifying teacher strengths as well as different ways by which adolescents learn. After a number of conferences and meetings centered around theories of learning, the following beliefs about how adolescents learn were agreed on:

- Students learn when they see purpose to learning.
- Learning is an active process.
- Change in behavior is the central goal of instruction.
- Students learn at different rates and on various levels of comprehension in different content areas.

- Students learn best as a result of the appeal to the senses: seeing, hearing, touching, and smelling.
- The environment for learning, psychological and physical, is contributing to successful outcomes.
- Learning is affected by the students' concept of themselves and their attitude toward others.

The Decatur-Lakeview Plan was carefully structured to meet the needs of a particular staff at a particular time. This project was characterized by a vast amount of staff and community involvement. There was never a vote taken by staff; consensus determined acceptance. The Lakeview Lay Advisory Committee consisted of 54 members with an even distribution of parents from each of the six grade levels. Community participation was not on the level of professional decisions about how the Plan should be shaped, but it served as an arena for criticism. The focus of the activities of the lay group was on how the parents in the community felt about the new program, the building changes, and the implications for staff. Usually the committee would meet, hear a presentation, break into small discussion groups to consider the issues presented, and report back to the large group. In this school, the teachers were considered to be the source of ideas and policy recommendations. They were anxious to develop procedures to be understood and accepted by the majority. They were receptive to ideas evaluated by their worth, presented by individual teachers, administrators, or resource people.

Teaching teams were organized for each grade level, within single content areas. Lakeview teachers have a tradition of cooperative endeavors, though not necessarily working together in instruction. The results of this shift in mode of instruction was that teachers became more interested in their students' progress as teams developed. The Plan implied a reliance on team teaching to realize the fullest advantages of the small- and large-group program.

If teachers are to work together on instructional problems, an appropriate setting in which they confer, or do individual study, must be established. Beggs states, "The school's facilities partially determine what can be done and what cannot be a part of a school's program. Students are directly influenced by the physical features of the school they attend." He suggests that educators have given far too little attention to the facilities, buildings, furniture, and their arrangements. Space-planning is an important educational function.

Beggs concludes with a promise for the future when he states, "All of the changes and adjustments made in the schools will be to individualize instruction for students. The spotlight will be on the individual and how he can be assisted in reaching his full potential as a free man with limitless potential for self-realization." For Beggs and the Lakeview School it implied that students must be taught on a one-to-one basis, even when in groups.

RESPONSIVE ELEMENTARY AND MIDDLE-GRADE SCHOOLS

There is a gulf between what is known to be the needs of adolescents and their experiences in schools (Lipsitz 1977). Decisions about schooling are more often made on the basis of budgets and buses rather than on an understanding of the physical, intellectual, psychological, and social needs of adolescents. Schools that encourage the developmental needs of young people neither look the same nor do they have identical programs. Safety and academic achievement are necessary for all schools, but they are not sufficient in themselves to produce responsive schools for adolescents. The requirement for physical and emotional safety is an essential characteristic for the success of any school. Learning cannot occur in an environment where people fear for their personal security.

Researchers who have studied academically effective schools have found that student behavior and achievement is influenced by the overall school environment. Achievement, attendance, and behavior are better in schools where there are many opportunities for large numbers of students to assume responsibility and participate in the operation of the school (Rutter 1979). Achievement and attendance are higher in schools where students perceive the environment to be pleasant and comfortable.

Since young people vary in physical development, intellectual capability, and interests, the need for diversity would be an important characteristic of a responsive school. In such a setting, students and teachers would be engaged in different learning activities, in and out of the classroom, using a variety of print and nonprint materials, where a variety of teaching methods would be used. Small group work, lectures, individual projects, and experiential learning, combined with flexible scheduling, are features that would respond to the need for diversity.

Young people also need opportunities for meaningful participation in their schools, particularly those activities that will improve the school environment. This can include a voice in running their schools as well as in design and construction activities. Student involvement in establishing the school's structure, and in setting limits, leads to learning and responsibility.

In a responsive school, there are opportunities for young people to contribute to the school's structure, with increasing levels of independence and self-regulation as they grow and mature. There is an interdependency of needs that requires schools to understand the developmental stages of adolescents in order to design environments that encourage learning and healthy growth (Dorman 1981).

ASSESSING CLASSROOM ENVIRONMENTS

Physical space in the classroom is often characterized in simplistic terms such as "open" versus "closed," with very little insight into the qualities or attributes of the learning environment, except for the appearance of the shell of the building (David 1982). Although there have been efforts to assess the classroom environment, most studies have stressed physical features, such as lighting, temperature, acoustics, and floor-space-per-child, while School Boards use cost-per-square-foot as an objective measure. An important but missing factor in assessing classroom environments is how it is perceived and used by students and teachers or, as David (1982) suggests, the social functions of the classroom. The assessment strategy he proposes consists of a set of descriptive statements, printed on separate cards, which students sort into categories to describe the actual and ideal environment. The statements are further rated on a five-point scale whether they are "most like my classroom" to "most not like my classroom." The statements are based on student needs and performance, and are based on operational definitions of concepts such as privacy, personal space, personalization, social grouping, personal meaning, and participation. They are as follows:

I have enough space to work without others crowding me.
My room has places where you can be by yourself if you want to.
I have a place of my own where I can keep my things.
In my room it's easy to concentrate on what you're doing.
I get to choose where I sit.
I can see everything that goes on in our room from where I usually sit.
I spend most of the day at my desk.
The furniture in my room is arranged to help us work together easily.
I feel like I have a place here that belongs to me.
I can fix up my place the way I want it.
There are lots of good places to work in my room.
It's quiet enough for me in my room.
We often change the way my room is arranged.
My room is neatly arranged and clearly organized.
My room is just the right size for me — not too big and not too small.
My room is pleasant to look at.
My room is a special place for me.
There are a lot of comfortable places in my room.
I get to help decide how our room will be arranged.
There are lots of interesting things to do in my room.
I get to help add things to my room to make it even better.

Actual and ideal profiles were obtained from students in both open and traditional classroom elementary schools in California. Students from the traditional school described their ideal classroom as one that would provide them with "lots of comfortable places," and as a place where there were "lots of interesting things to do." In addition, they would prefer not to spend the entire day at their desk. Open-classroom students described their actual environment as one containing variety, with "lots of comfortable places." They also indicated that there are few places "where you can be by yourself," and it can be difficult "to concentrate on what you are doing."

This research aims at developing a language to assess the functional aspects of a classroom. David (1982) also points out that once a school has been built, the teachers become the "designers" of their classrooms. This assessment procedure can be an effective means used by teachers to gain systematic feedback about the performance of the classroom in response to their educational goals.

HIGH-SCHOOL ENVIRONMENTS

Environmental research at the high-school level is not as extensive as lower-level school situations. Studies related to the size of school based on student population were conducted by Barker and Gump (1964), who compared small and large schools according to curricular and extracurricular activities. Comparisons were made by the number of environmental units that make up a school. This unit, the *behavior setting,* is a particular place that has some type of physical enclosure, where habitual behaviors occur, such as the history class, the main office, rehearsals for plays, and so on. Since the social and psychological significance of extracurricular settings have been described as critical to adolescent peer relationships (Coleman 1961), school size can influence students' opportunities for participation. In extracurricular activities, students plan, evaluate, and execute their decisions, whereas in the classroom, teachers are the major decision-makers. Large schools present a different set of conditions than small schools. As the size of the school increases, the ratio of students to behavior settings increases, and the number of settings does not increase at the same rate as the student population. Small schools, then, have fewer students to carry out their extracurricular activities, requiring those students to work harder and assume more responsibility than students in larger schools. Consequently, students in small schools were more likely to occupy some positions of power and responsibility than were students in large schools. School-size studies also show that students' satisfaction was a result of being active and challenged, though large schools do not offer as many responsible positions per student as small schools. The larger school depends on more formal and impersonal controls, and tends to centralize administrative operations, becoming less responsive to the teachers and students (McPartland and McDill 1977), and is likely to find change more difficult.

To preserve some of the small-school advantages for a large school, the schools-within-a-school plan has been adopted (Plath 1965). This is a campus arrangement with clusters of buildings, where students' and teachers' experiences occur in smaller environments. As students move between classes, they cross one another's paths more frequently than they would in one large school building. The campus plan arrangement fosters closer peer and teacher relationships. Garbarino (1980) noted that when large numbers of students occupy an environmental unit, individuals become anonymous and are beyond the personal control of small groups, where deviance can be one result. Plath (1965) found that the campus plan substantially reduced serious student deviancy.

Another factor influencing school size relates to the environment around the school. In rural areas, the movement toward the consolidation of high schools requires that small communities may lose their existing small high school, often an important feature of the town's identity. Also, small local high schools often help to enrich the economy of a town.

In urban areas, attempts to build large high schools in urban neighborhoods often meet with community opposition because they usually require large-scale demolition, and threaten neighborhood stability. Gold (1975), a New York facilities planner, suggests that renovation of existing buildings for smaller schools is economically feasible and less of a wasted energy investment than large-scale demolition.

Clearly, small high schools involve a greater proportion of students in responsible positions than large ones. This involvement affects the likelihood of student satisfaction that comes as a result of being active and challenged in these positions. Although the large high school may be inevitable, it may be necessary to implement small-school effects.

Assessing Schools for Adolescents

Attitude Survey	
Charette Process	
Community Meetings	✓
Design-In	
Focused Interviews	✓
Fishbowl Planning	
Game Simulation	✓
Group Dynamics	
Public Forum	
Task Force	✓
Training	✓
Workshop	✓

SUMMARY

There has been an expressed need from citizens, educators, elected and appointed officials, and architects for guidance in assessing middle-grade schools. This need has been, in part, an outgrowth of reports of increased violence, dropouts, and youth unemployment. Quite often, decisions need to be made about the closing of schools or conversions from junior highs (7–9th grades) to middle schools (6–8th grades), yet there are few effective tools available for examining the quality of schools. Although there are many different grade combinations for students age 10 to 15 years, which have inhibited a dialogue about the purpose of schooling for this age group, the Middle Grades Assessment program (Dorman 1981) attempts to focus on what is known about early adolescent development.

With the aid of a checklist, teachers, citizen groups, or policymakers are guided through a procedure for interviewing, observing, and discussing ways and means for making middle schools more responsive to the developmental needs of young adolescents. This self-assessment process was employed in a number of schools that have reported changes in their school climate and curriculum.

Modifications included changes in student work patterns to allow groups physically to move more freely; increased display of student work; more use of student-made posters, murals, and bulletin boards; and a greater variety of teaching approaches that often required changes in the organization and layout of the classroom.

CLIENT

The Center for Early Adolescence works to increase the effectiveness of agencies and professionals who work with adolescents of ages 10 to 15 years. The Center also serves as a clearing house for information for professionals and volunteers working with young adolescents, and maintains a pool of consultants to assist agencies and institutions with specific planning and programming requests. As the Center became recognized as a national advocate and information resource, parents, policymakers, and citizens began to request help in making decisions about schooling for young adolescents. Hence, the idea of an assessment checklist based on the developmental needs of young adolescents was born.

PROJECT

The purpose of this project was to develop an approach for making teachers, parents, students, and policymakers aware of the appropriateness of their school environment for young adolescent students. The long-range goal of this project was to develop an action-oriented education and self-assessment process for school improvement. As an assessment tool, it was designed to take a comprehensive look at middle-grade schools to see how the academic and developmental needs of young adolescents are accommodated by the physical facilities, the school climate, and the teaching program.

An environmental design component of this assessment tool was created by North Carolina State's Community Development Group, to supplement the interviews and observations included in the Middle Grades Assessment Program (MGAP). A group-discussion process was developed whereby members of the community would examine the architectural character of spaces in school buildings, to assess how these spaces can enhance adolescent development and academic effectiveness.

PROCESS

In order to experience healthy development, adolescents require that certain needs be met. Young adolescents require diversity, which entails different opportunities for learning and different relationships with a variety of people. In a school that responds to its students' need for diversity, one would not find students all doing the same thing at the same time in similar rooms. One would not expect to see students sitting in neat rows of desks, all facing teachers who are lecturing or reading from textbooks. Instead, in responsive schools, students and teachers would be engaged in different learning activities in and out of the classroom. A variety of teaching methods including small-group work, lectures, learning by doing, individualized assignments, and learning centers, would be used.

Young adolescents need opportunities for self-exploration as they integrate the change of adolescence into a new sense of "self," and as they begin to think about future vocations and avocations. They need opportunities for meaningful participation in school and community. Not only can schools provide the structure and means for young adolescents to have a real voice in the running of their schools, but they should also have the opportunity to identify and carry out projects that will improve the school environment, such as building outdoor recreation and nature areas.

The rapid physical growth of adolescents is directly related to their high energy level, and the need for opportunities to vent their energy through physical activity. They need to build confidence and a sense of worthiness and opportunities to succeed. They also need the self-satisfaction that comes from knowing that they have done something well, and that it is recognized by others for its importance.

These and other needs form the basis for an assessment program that is basically a checklist, underscoring the ideal situation and questions to ask in order to discover the extent to which school is fulfilling these expectations. The checklist was designed to be used by educators, parents, citizens, and policymakers. It is a tool for observing and assessing, and making decisions regarding schools for young adolescents. It provides necessary information on early adolescence and on schools that can be used in planning to strengthen middle-grade schools. The program has many possible uses among which are staff use in accreditation self-study, school boards, citizens councils, and parent-teacher organizations, for their assessment of middle- or junior-high school quality and, most important, as a component for an evaluation designed to precede modifications to the school facility.

The checklist consists of a series of ideal statements and corresponding questions to be asked of the principal about his or her role, as well as about the curriculum, and interviews with teachers, guidance counselors, students, and parents (Figure 2-1).

In addition to interviews, an observation form was developed to gain a more comprehensive understanding of the school environment. Observations were required of the physical facilities (Figure 2-2), where such items as places for socialization, spatial flexibility, and opportunities for students to personalize their school, are noted. Observations of the classroom centered around the ability of students to direct their own studies, and modify the classroom to suit their needs (Figure 2-3). The Media Center or Library was also the subject for extensive observation, for recording the variety of areas for individual and group study, and for relaxation.

GROUP INTERACTION APPROACH

To stimulate more participation among school community members, design aids were developed to increase people's awareness of the architectural implications of the school environment. Unless a teacher understands why one room arrangement may be superior to another, all the physical changes in the world will have little or no impact on the nature of the learning process within the classroom (Weinstein 1979). It requires more than moving furniture. Room arrangements should reflect the educational purpose the teacher has in mind, and the educational process by which he or she proposes to achieve them.

Prior to planning and designing appropriate environments for adolescents, the objectives for that environment must be discussed, considered, and decided upon by the teachers, administrators, and students. The relationship among the activities students engage in, the places that accommodate those activities, and their relationship to the objectives, is the basis for designing. The objectives that are found in the educational literature describe concepts that are paramount to the development of the young adolescent. These objectives include personalization of the learn-

Interview with Student

Need	Ideal	Questions to Ask	Response
P	4. There is an established mechanism through which students are meaningfully involved in decision making.	Do students have a voice in making decisions and establishing rules in this school? **Yes:** How does that happen? If an individual or group of students wants to change something here, like a rule or one part of the schedule, is there a way to do that? **Yes:** Please describe it. Do students actually do this? How often? What are the results? Can you give me one example of something that has been changed as a result of this process? **No:** Then what do you do when you want something changed?	
S	5. Staff and students do not fear for their physical and emotional safety.	Are you willing to walk alone in the halls? Are you willing to go into the bathrooms? Do you worry a lot about getting beaten up, having things stolen from you, or being harmed by someone else here at school? Explain why or why not. Do you feel that you can express your ideas, concerns, and questions without being ridiculed or embarassed by someone else here at school? Why or why not? How much do you think adults here care about you?	
C	6. All students have an opportunity for success at something.	What is something that you are especially good at? How often do you get to do that in this school? Is there something else you are especially good at that you get to do at school?	
SE	7. There are opportunities within the regular curriculum for students to pursue questions and topics that interest them personally.	Do you have opportunities here at school to explore topics or questions that interest you personally? **Yes:** Please give an example. Do you get to suggest or select topics or questions for study that interest you personally? **Yes:** Please give an example. **No:** Would you like to have that opportunity? What would you do at this school if there were some topic you wanted to learn more about, like building a motor or making a pizza?	

FIGURE 2-1. Student interview schedule (Reprinted from the *Middle Games Assessment Program*. Copyright 1981 by the Center for Early Adolescence, University of North Carolina, Chapel Hill. Used with permission.).

ing environment, student control of movement, provision of adequate meeting and social gathering places, environmental flexibility to accommodate different student activities, and the ability for students to facilitate projects and studies in their areas of interest.

While there is agreement within the education profession that these objectives may be crucial to the development of young adolescents, there is a lack of agreement about the relationship of these objectives to the places in which they ought to occur, or to the variety of possible spatial arrangements. The interpretation and philosophy of an educational program has a significant impact on how the educational objectives are evidenced and realized in the learning environment. For example, "personalization of place" is an important objective because, as the educational literature points out, young adolescents need to have a stake in their environment (Sommer 1974). Personalization reflects persons' commitment to a place by reflecting themselves in their surroundings. Where personalization exists in the learning environment, it manifests itself in a number of ways. Prominent display of items of special interest to young adolescents is one way in which personalization is exhibited. The items displayed should identify who occupies and uses a particular place by reflecting their interests and personality, whether they are students or teachers. Space-use can reflect connections among home, school, and community, in addition to displaying student work. Another important aspect of personalized space is the presence of designated places where adolescents can gather, free from danger, to engage in stimulating activities, conversation, and exploration of ideas. Such places may take the form of outdoor courtyards, outdoor tables and benches, or interior places such as student lounges or corners of a larger room.

Observation Form

Need	PHYSICAL FACILITIES	Yes	No
C	1. Building is neat, clean, and in good repair. There are few, if any, signs of vandalism or graffiti.		
P	2. Student work is displayed on bulletin boards, walls, tables in classes and other areas throughout the building.		
SE	3. Pictures and displays depict various racial and ethnic groups.		
SE	4. Pictures, posters, and displays show both boys and girls engaged in a wide variety of activities, for example: girls as doctors, policewomen, construction workers; boys as nurses, social workers, secretaries; girls playing baseball and boys cooking.		
P	5. Announcements are posted by students and staff about activities and concerns.		
D	6. The building itself is flexible, including some large open spaces, some small rooms. Some spaces are multifunctional.		
D	7. Furniture throughout the school is movable.		
SE	8. There are quiet places for individuals, pairs, and groups of students to withdraw, relax, and think, such as student lounges or reading lofts.		
Phy	9. There are identified places where students can be noisy and engage in physical activity.		
Phy	10. There is plenty of room in corridors and classrooms for movement from one place to another.		
D	11. There is outdoor space for projects such as science gardens and building projects. It is being used.		
P	12. Students contribute to the upkeep and appearance of the school. For example, they may build furniture, clean their own tables in the cafeteria, pick up trash, decorate bulletin boards.		
SE	13. There are doors or curtains on the stalls in the bathrooms and dressing rooms.		

COMMENTS:

FIGURE 2-2. Physical facilities observation form (Ibid).

Observation Form

Need	CLASSROOM INSTRUCTION	Yes	No
	Student Behavior		
SI	29. Interracial groupings of students are present in the classroom.		
D	30. Students are often actively engaged in activities, manipulating materials and objects. They are not just listening.		
Phy	31. Students have some opportunities to move around, to shift positions, to squirm.		
P	32. Students are involved, paying attention, and participating.		
P	33. Students' facial expressions and body posture reflect alertness and interest.		
C	34. Students carry on with assigned activities when the teacher leaves the room.		
C	35. Students make references to topics the class has studied previously.		
S&L	36. Students understand the objectives of lessons and activities and make connections between class activities, objectives, and life outside the classroom. Ask students: What are you doing? Why are you doing this activity? Why is it important to know . . . (whatever is being studied, for example, prime numbers)?		
	Facilities		
SI	37. Seating arrangements vary, including small groups, pairs, individuals, and total group.		
D	38. Plants, pictures, displays, and equipment are used to reflect the teacher's and students' personalities.		
C	39. Student work is displayed throughout the room. Not all of it is "A" or excellent work.		

FIGURE 2-3. Classroom instruction observation form (Ibid).

OBJECTIVES

First, a set of educational objectives for the school is provided as the initial point of discussion. Although the objectives have been gathered from the educational literature, the list is not inclusive and may be extended as needed. Although all of the objectives may seem desirable, it is necessary for all participants to understand different points of view regarding the importance of the objectives. It is also necessary to begin the process by having each participant contribute equally and to continue to actively participate.

To begin the planning process, groups of three to five people should be formed comfortably around tables. Each group member, preferably unknown to the others, should review the educational objectives list and select four that seem to be the most important. Then the group must agree upon the four most important objectives. Each player is urged to forcefully support individual choices, even if other members of the group did not make the same choices. Decisions by consensus are more enduring than those made by voting, so it is necessary to allocate an appropriate amount of time for this first stage of the process. Record your group selections on the record sheet provided.

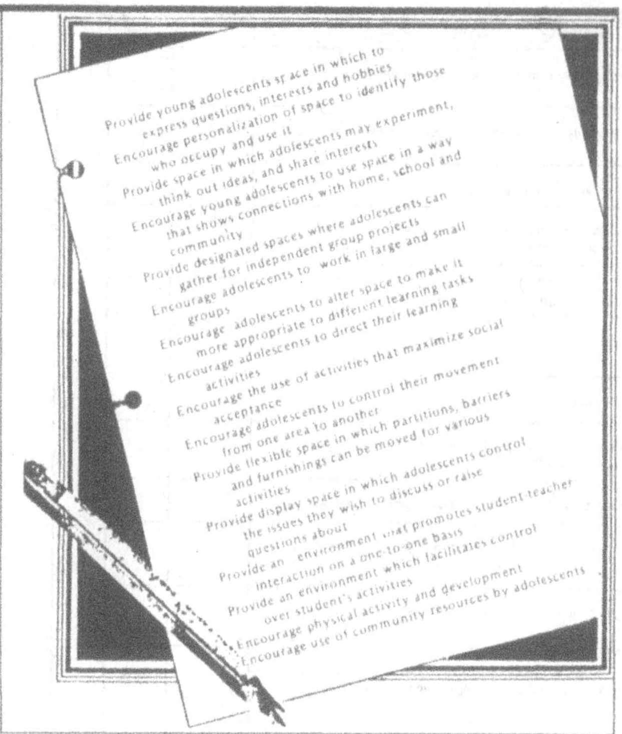

FIGURE 2-4. Typical objectives for a middle-grade school.

SCHOOL WORKSHOP

After recording observations, interviewing students and staff, the school-community members were ready to consider features of the physical environment, through small-group discussion sessions that stressed consensus decision making. The opening discussion was devoted to establishing commonly agreed-upon objectives. Group participants chose the most important statements from a prepared list compiled by the design evaluation team from the educational literature (Figure 2-4). This open discussion permitted different viewpoints to be heard with the possibility that participants could learn from each other. Once objectives were selected, they were matched to three photographs of school settings that satisfied the desired intentions (Figure 2-5). The photographs that were selected included typical school settings as well as unusual places and settings. Although the photographs represented the types of spaces that might occur in a middle school, the discussions revealed that there was not always a suitable match to the original objective. This factor contributed to an expanded discussion of spatial qualities and characteristics, and how particular environments might be altered to achieve the desired intention.

To further demonstrate the importance of architectural features each photographic image evoked, participants were asked to rate each photograph, using a prepared list of five descriptive words (Figure 2-6). The discussions resulting from the photographic ratings were extremely informative to the members of each group, since the participants were interpreting the meaning conveyed by each image. This factor helped to elevate the discussions from the more routine dialogue about school environments that usually focus on space requirements, ceiling heights, and seating arrangements to discussions about privacy, intimacy, and activity type.

IMPLEMENTATION

There are numerous middle-grade schools across the country engaged in school-improvement projects using the Middle Grades Assessment Program. The schools all vary in size, physical facilities, location, and sociometric makeup of the student body, yet these have not been deterrents if educators want to improve their schools. The thrust of the program is to help middle-grade schools marshal their own resources and deal effectively with self-improvement.

The self-assessment process is conducted by a team of 6 to 18 school staff and parents, usually selected by the principal. The results of the assessment process leads to an action plan, which includes conclusions

FIGURE 2-6. Rating images of school settings (Photo: Henry Sanoff & Tun Sing Chen).

drawn from the assessment, possible actions or behavioral objectives, responsible persons, time frame, and cost estimate. This plan is included in a report describing the assessment purpose and process. *Conclusions* are specific such as those developed by the Eual Landry Middle School (Delle, Gaubert, and Picard 1989) in Louisiana. For example: "ELMS will maximize the use of available space inside and outside of the school building." Possible *actions* include statements such as: "Teachers will be encouraged to vary their teaching sites depending on activities taught (use of commons area, gym, grassy area, etc.)" and: "Maintenance personnel will be requested to place built-in shelves in order to increase floor space in classroom." *Responsible persons* for completing the action are members of Central Office Maintenance. Another *conclusion* from this Louisiana middle school was that: "ELMS will provide quiet area for students to participate in quiet activities." Possible actions included: "The administration will set up a student lounge to reward students for appropriate behavior." and: "Teachers will establish an area inside the classroom for quiet activities."

Examples of other improvements reported by participating schools included in-service workshops on such topics as understanding early adolescent behavior, and alternative discipline strategies and student evaluation. In one instance, an assessment team that had observed 19 classrooms found the need for more student work to be displayed throughout their school. They also realized that most of the students were devoting classroom time to listening and writing. Teachers were not using a variety of teaching approaches, nor were students given opportunities to select alternative activities, or work with other students in small groups. The findings were instrumental in developing the school's improvement plan, which was put into immediate effect. To insure that the plan was carried out, specific days were set aside for training and planning sessions.

Another school, upon realizing that many young adolescent boys are just as desirous of privacy as are girls because of their changing bodies, immediately installed partitions in the boy's dressing room and restrooms. In a California school, a group of students participated in the assessment by interviewing the students.

While in the process of doing their assessments, different schools began noticing that spontaneous changes were occurring. For example, there was more positive interaction between teachers and students; more interest in the school among students, parents, and staff; and more specific behavioral objectives from teachers. The assessment gives teachers a more sanctioned method to participate in setting priorities for the school. As a result, staff members feel empowered to make their school a better place and are committed to reaching agreed-upon goals.

The current lack of participation by architects in the assessment process has underscored the need to emphasize the importance of the physical environment in achieving desired educational objectives. Architects can provide assistance in providing alternative interpretations to education standards and specifications that could facilitate a more flexible use of space. Also, an increased awareness of the way in which the school environment can be modified would encourage teachers to explore alternative learning methods.

Coyote Canyon Elementary School

Attitude Survey	
Charette Process	
Community Meetings	✓
Design-In	
Focused Interviews	
Fishbowl Planning	
Game Simulation	
Group Dynamics	✓
Public Forum	
Task Force	
Training	
Workshop	

SUMMARY

The Central School District of Rancho Cucamonga, California, was an outgrowth of the Cucamonga School District, petitioned by ten families in 1870. In its early days, the area was inhabited by the Tongva Indians, later was a portion of the Spanish Land Grant, and from the late 1800s to the mid-1900s was a thriving vineyard area. From a one-room schoolhouse in 1890, limited growth up to the 1970s had caused the district to add classrooms on a piecemeal basis through the purchase of portable classrooms. An upswing in home construction that began in the mid-1970s because of its close proximity to Ontario Airport and two major freeways, caused the Central School District population to expand rapidly. Since incorporation in 1978, the City has placed strong emphasis on controlling development and the quality of construction and design. The Central School District believed that if they involved those who teach, maintain, administrate, attend, and visit their schools, their designs would be much stronger and responsive to the needs of users. To this end, the architectural firm of Wolf, Lang, Christopher was retained to design the new Coyote Canyon Elementary School. This architectural firm's decade-long history of participatory design was influential in the District's decision in the selection process. In addition to the local School Board, a design committee was formed to help shape the educational program as well as the design of the building. The rich and varied history of the community was a strong influence on the design of the building, which features four theme courtyards, each reflecting four major periods in the history of the city.

CLIENT

The School Board of the City's Central School District appointed a principal designated for the new campus to chair a newly formed community design committee. Membership was composed from the community and district-at-large through a charter, and included parents, teachers, and administrators. The committee was responsible for soliciting input from parents, community members, City of Rancho Cucamonga officials, community groups, certified and classified staff, and other individuals or groups who wished to represent their ideas to the committee. They were responsible for considering design alternatives presented, and for making recommendations to the Board of Trustees regarding preliminary designs and final plans. While this community design committee served in an advisory capacity, none of the committee's decisions was overridden by the School Board or District Administration.

Early in the process, committee members visited and videotaped eight existing elementary schools within the District. Each of the schools was different in its organization and design, including courtyard schemes as well as schools where access occurs through the use of interior corridors. Some of the major features that were compared during the walk-through evaluations were building image, circulation, use of windows, and climate control. The results of the walk-through visits enabled the committee to generate desired characteristics, which included sense of entry, well-defined circulation, individual climate control, and exterior courtyards. These characteristics helped shape the goals for the school.

PROJECT

The planning process initiated by the Central School District of Rancho Cucamonga stems from its nonauthoritarian management structure which mandates public participation in the planning and design of district schools. A community design committee, drawn from the community at large, has a charter established through bylaws, which outlines its procedures and responsibilities. The selection of an architect for this elementary school was based on the School Board's familiarity with Wolf, Lang, Christopher's ability to work effectively in a participatory mode. The design committee consisted of 14 community members, 10 staff members, with several others representing the City and the adjacent residential area. A principal, designated for this new campus, came from the adjacent elementary school, and served as a facilitator. The meetings were conducted informally, with most decisions being reached by consensus. In general, the planning process included the following:

- Brainstorming and goal setting
- Information gathering and exploration, including visits to numerous unique elementary schools
- Development of goals and objectives
- Development of an educational program
- Review of master plan and classroom alternatives

An example of the 21 program goals included:

- The school should have a sense of tradition
- The school should be inviting and friendly
- The design should provide for natural daylighting
- The design should incorporate elements from winery or historical Spanish designs
- The school environment should facilitate learning
- The design should foster a positive attitude among students, staff, and parents
- The school should be designed for children
- The interior environment should be inviting, incorporating warm colors and natural light

Based on the program goals, the design team provided several alternative schemes for discussion. The three major concepts proposed were ideas exhibited in the schools visited; they were a courtyard scheme, an internalized scheme, and a scheme that integrated both of these concepts. One option was selected with a recommendation to incorporate several of the positive features of other options that were explored. The scheme selected featured an internal administrative cluster that included the media center, multipurpose room, and lobby with an internal corridor connected to the classroom courtyards. This solution satisfied the goal of providing student access during inclement weather and high winds, while allowing the use of courtyards during pleasant weather. While the design

FIGURE 2-7. Native American village featuring a wickiup (Photo: Fred Daly).

FIGURE 2-8. Mission style courtyard (Photo: Fred Daly).

FIGURE 2-9. Interactive display station (Photo: Fred Daly).

committee discussed each area of the school in general, detailed discussions were conducted with people having particular expertise in the area. For example, the food services coordinator and district librarian discussed the kitchen and media center, accordingly.

The design team proposed a scheme that symbolized the rich and varied history of the community. The initial desire was to create a school that emphasized the community's Spanish heritage. However, as the idea developed, the design took on much more significance by identifying the four major periods of history. Consequently, four theme courtyards have been incorporated into the design to reflect Rancho Cucamonga's early history. The idea of the historical courtyards came from a desire to give new students who have recently moved to the community a sense of their local heritage. The design of each courtyard was the result of ideas generated by a Community Liaison Committee, a group of people with a keen interest in Rancho Cucamonga's heritage, consisting of parents, staff, historians, architects, and a descendant of the local Native American tribe. It was established in order to provide more appropriate, sensitive, and authentic design input for the courtyards. The courtyards represent four major periods in the history of the city starting with the Native American's courtyard, the focal point for the kindergarten and first-grade classrooms. A traditional village is simulated to include a wickiup and dry river rock bed (Figure 2-7). The Spanish-Mexican courtyard, for the second and third grades, consists of a five-foot Aztec pyramid, which also serves as a sitting area where adobe planters accent the outdoor learning environment. A third courtyard, adjacent to the third- and fourth-graders, represents the Mexican/Spanish rancho period of early California, with mission style focal elements, such as a mission bell, and wagon wheels embedded in the pavement (Figure 2-8). The fourth courtyard, planted with grape vines, will remind the students of California's first vineyards located within the city before it became a residential area. This courtyard is accented by a grape arbor that will eventually shade a seating area as it matures.

A main hallway, or central spine, serves as a historic gallery where pictures depict the early residents and buildings and sites important to the area. The gallery will also include interactive displays to acquaint students with a variety of professions, as well as to display student work (Figure 2-9). The gallery allows all students access to classroom areas as well as access to the courtyards.

Some of the significant decisions that were made as a result of this participatory process included the establishment of the central corridor or gallery space, the historic courtyards, the science and nature area, and the compact design of the support services, which included the media center, the multipurpose room, and the administration section (Figure 2-10).

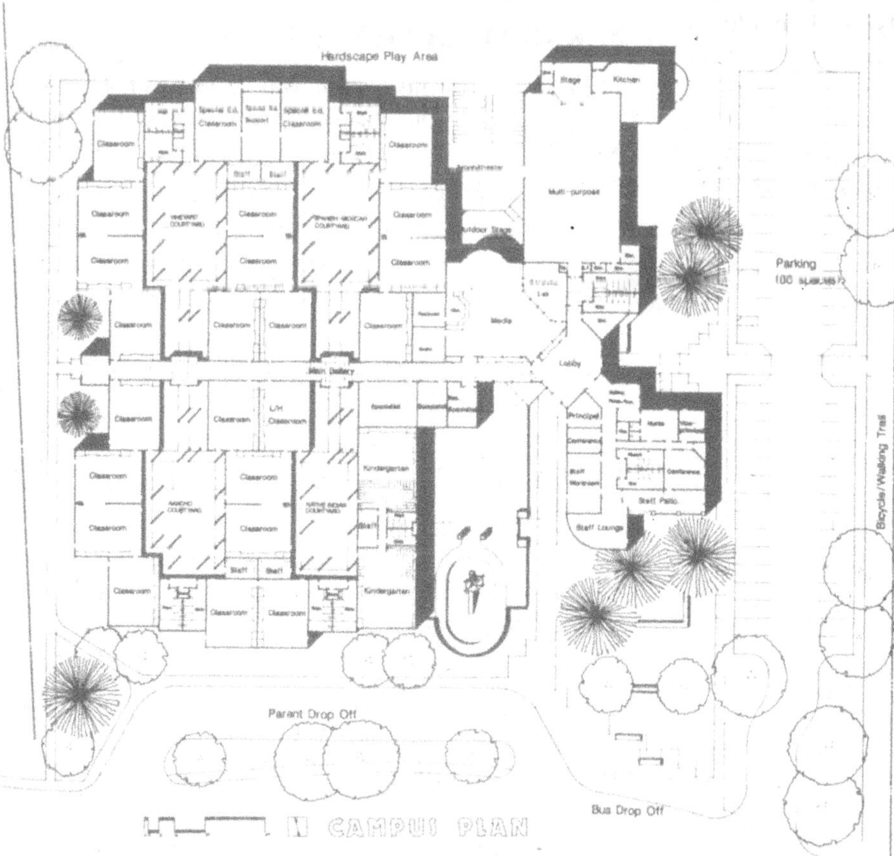

FIGURE 2-10. Plan of building (Drawing: Wolff, Lang, Christopher).

AFTER-OCCUPANCY RESPONSES

In an article in the city's newspaper, the *Daily Bulletin,* students of Coyote Canyon were reported to have built an Indian court. The children bent willow poles, tying them tightly with string just like the Tongva Indians, 200 years ago. Besides the wickiup (a small dwelling), the Native-American court has a grinding stone for acorns and a loom used to weave rabbit capes and blankets. The project is part of a unique plan to create a living-history curriculum at the newest school in the Central School District. Native-American community leaders were "pleased that they wanted to depict the Gabrieliano (or Tongva) people in the proper way." Barbara Drake, secretary to the Gabrieliano tribal council, commented that "The kids are so excited. The whole school is in an uproar. Everyone wants to come over and see it." A teacher, Darlene Carlmark, sees a longer-term goal for the project. "By the time a child comes into kindergarten and leaves after fourth grade, they'll have an enormous background about the history of this area. Understanding your own history helps you to understand other cultures."

Staff members responding to a survey of best-liked and least-liked features unanimously endorsed the courtyards as an important design idea that encouraged teachers to explore and experiment with new approaches to teaching. The outdoor areas encourage small-group activities, as well as opportunities for planting and gardening. Accessibility to the outdoors was seen as an important aspect of creating a variety of learning places.

The science and nature laboratories were also cited by teachers as features contributing to their exploring new teaching ideas, particularly more "hands-on" experiments. Generally, the overall aesthetic quality was clearly a source of pride among the respondents, particularly by the principal, who was appointed to open the school (Figure 2-11). The principal designated for the new campus, who chaired the community design committee, was reassigned as a result of the State's year-round requirements. The superintendent and new principal pointed out, however, that participants in the committee may not be the occupants once the facility is complete. They therefore suggest the necessity for considering the generic functions that continue for the life of the building. They both comment on the poor location of the kitchen not being adjacent to the student eating areas. Teachers, on the other hand, express different concerns.

Their remarks were consistent and referred to the small size of the classroom. The most common annoyance, though not a building feature, was the loudness of the bells, which cause the students to react as though there were an emergency. Other features appeared to be more focused on particular aspects of the building such as heavy doors or the inability to control the temperature in some of the classrooms. Generally, the teachers' responses are related to their previous experiences, though the feeling of openness, the use of daylight, and the color scheme were those features that were regarded as particularly unique to this school building.

ACKNOWLEDGMENT

The material for this section was in the form of written comments generously provided by Gaylaird Christopher, minutes from committee meetings, and newspaper articles.

FIGURE 2-11. Building exterior (Photo: Fred Daly).

Davidson Elementary School

Attitude Survey	
Charette Process	✓
Community Meetings	✓
Design-In	
Focused Interviews	✓
Fishbowl Planning	
Game Simulation	✓
Group Dynamics	
Public Forum	
Task Force	
Training	
Workshop	✓

SUMMARY

Davidson, North Carolina, is a small, active community that has taken an interest in its facilities and their appearance. As a result of Davidson's activism, its outmoded elementary school is being replaced as a result of a recent bond issue that provided funds for a new 600-student elementary school. In anticipation of their new building, the Davidson teachers had organized, and began discussions about educational changes they would like to see occur. Recognizing the community spirit and interest in this project, the county school planning administration awarded the contract for the new school to the Adams Group architects, because of their past experience in working effectively with community groups.

The community involvement process initiated by the Adams Group and consultant, Henry Sanoff, consisted of several workshops oriented toward students, teachers, parents, community members, and school-planning representatives. The intent of these community events was to build consensus for the educational objectives of the new school in order that the building would complement and support those intentions.

CLIENT

The school district located in the Charlotte-Mecklenburg area of North Carolina is undergoing educational reform that can have a substantial effect on the design of school buildings. The results of numerous workshops and teacher in-service training programs in 1991, has been to create a climate conducive to team teaching in the county's elementary schools. The growing population and inadequacy of older schools in the area have prompted the school administration to construct four new elementary schools in 1992, on four different sites. The Davidson site is the only one containing an existing school building, located in a well-organized community, with an appearance commission, an historic district commission, and an active citizen's group. The School Planning Board selected the firm of Adams Group architects because they had experience producing effective results, working with a variety of community groups, and a previous award-winning elementary school addition. Davidson Elementary School already had a committee structure examining excellence in education, and a group of teachers and parents anxious to be involved in the process of designing their new school.

PROJECT

The Davidson Elementary School was designed to accommodate the teachers' and parents' vision of an appropriate environment for kindergarten through 5th grade. It was also a goal of this project to reexamine the use of educational specifications (ed specs), and to assess their intentions through reactions of the users — the teachers, the parents, and the students. It was equally important to evaluate the ed specs in view of the pedagogical changes proposed for the school district. In addition to a new elementary school building designed in collaboration with the school community, the ed specs were reevaluated. This assessment process occurred through the use of extensive interviews with teachers at each grade level, as well as through workshops aimed at identifying educational objectives for different grade levels, and the complementary teaching methods for achieving those objectives.

PROCESS

The process began by an introductory meeting with the Davidson Elementary School Principal, Dr. Eugene Davis, to outline a strategy for parent, teacher, and student involvement. The first step consisted of individual interviews with each of the teachers to review the educational specifications provided by school planning. The specifications consist of a quantification of spaces, and a listing of classroom equipment for each grade level. The obvious limitation of the ed specs is that they presume a set of educational objectives and a style of teaching. During the interview process, many discrepancies were found between teachers' requirements and the ed specs, such as the location of teachers' workrooms, location of counselor's office, and general requirements for proximity between academic and administrative areas. Teachers preferred several small workrooms to be adjacent to their classroom to allow for parent tutoring and sharing ideas with other teachers, rather than the required work area designated for clusters of classrooms that would be remote from the individual classrooms. The teachers also discussed teaming, and the opportunity for teachers to collaborate more effectively. In respect to spatial concerns, they were fearful that the long noisy corridors in their present school might be repeated.

The interviews were followed by a walk-through evaluation by the teachers of the existing two-story school building. The walk-through revealed many negative features of their building, such as noisy corridors, desks located in the corridors for tutoring purposes, and play areas separated by parking.

The combined interviews and walk-through evaluation disclosed the features of the building that were valued, as well as giving voice to the aspirations for the new building. A parent-staff-teacher workshop followed the more individual activities that occurred on the previous days. This workshop was intended to create a dialogue among teachers: about their educational objectives, the variety of teaching methods generated from those objectives, and the types of physical settings that would be supportive. This workshop was designed to prepare the participants for the second meeting that would engage them in the site design of their new school building.

The teachers were divided into small groups based on their teaching focus. They selected objective statements from a prepared list generated from the educational literature. They were asked to make their decisions based on group consensus to insure that all voices were heard in the deliberations. In addition to work groups clarifying their ideas and intentions about classroom education, there was strong support for the school's interaction with the Davidson community. Developing a sense of community emerged as an important focus for the teachers.

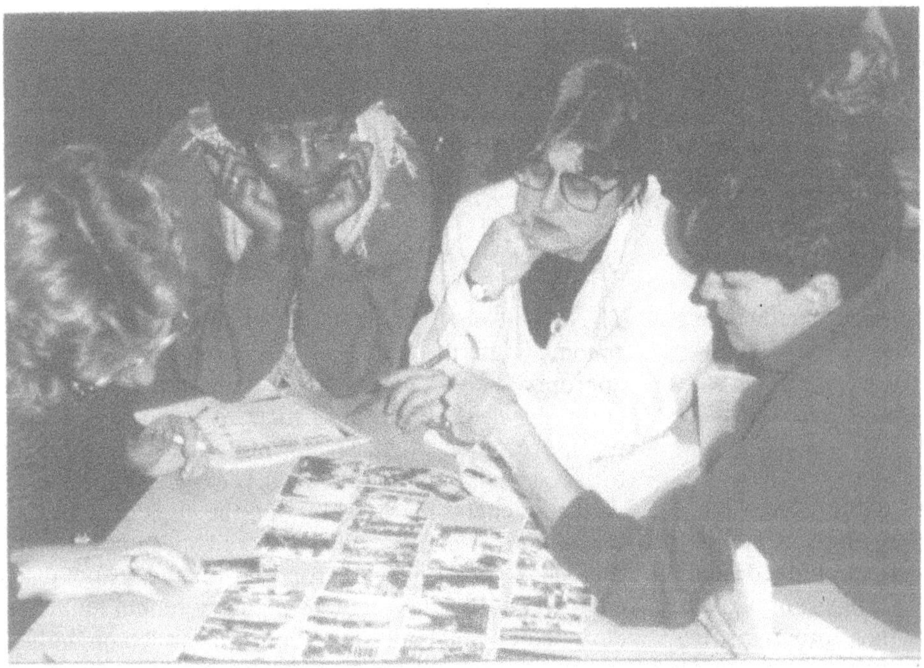

FIGURE 2-12. Participants organizing photographs of settings to correspond to teaching methods.

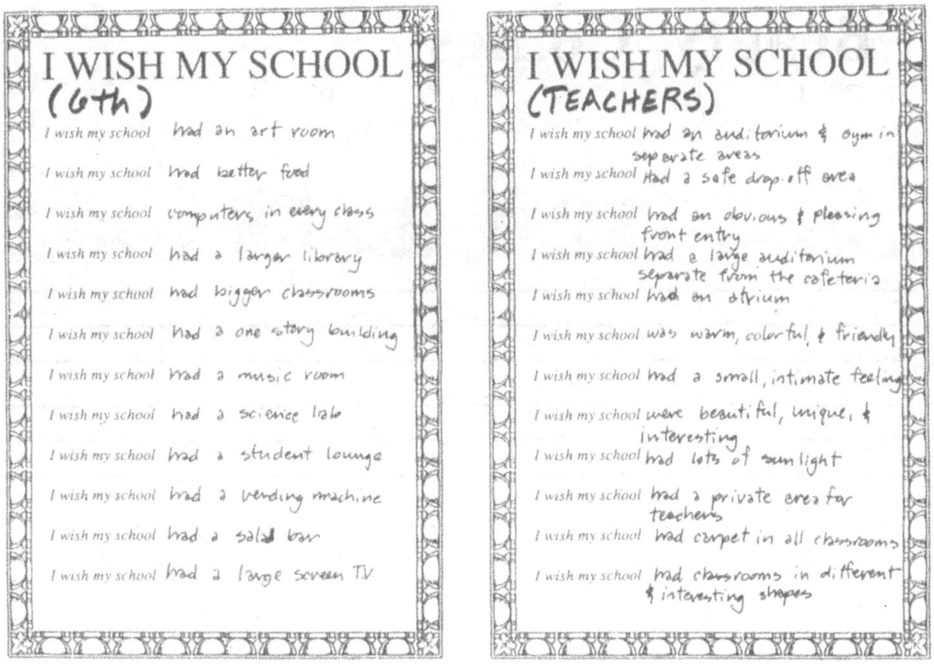

I WISH MY SCHOOL
(6th)

I wish my school had an art room
I wish my school had better food
I wish my school computers in every class
I wish my school had a larger library
I wish my school had bigger classrooms
I wish my school had a one story building
I wish my school had a music room
I wish my school had a science lab
I wish my school had a student lounge
I wish my school had a vending machine
I wish my school had a salad bar
I wish my school had a large screen TV

I WISH MY SCHOOL
(TEACHERS)

I wish my school had an auditorium & gym in separate areas
I wish my school Had a safe drop-off area
I wish my school had an obvious & pleasing front entry
I wish my school had a large auditorium separate from the cafeteria
I wish my school had an atrium
I wish my school was warm, colorful, & friendly
I wish my school had a small, intimate feeling
I wish my school were beautiful, unique, & interesting
I wish my school had lots of sun light
I wish my school had a private area for teachers
I wish my school had carpet in all classrooms
I wish my school had classrooms in different & interesting shapes

FIGURE 2-13. Children's and teachers' wish poem.

The ability to link teaching methods to physical settings was a new experience for the teachers, since their teaching methods were always constrained by the existing classroom. The use of photographs corresponding to the physical settings allowed participants to explore and discuss a wide range of traditional and nontraditional settings used to accommodate various teaching methods (Figure 2-12). The opportunity to use the outdoors for a variety of different activities — for small- or large-group activities, for reading, art, eating, and gardening — expanded the teachers' awareness of new opportunities for their new school building. This discovery found its way into the building design in the form of outdoor areas adjacent to each classroom, covered porches, and a variety of different courtyard spaces.

Children, too, were involved in offering their ideas and perceptions about the new school through their art and through poetry. The art teacher and office staff of the Adams Group met with all the students in the school, for two successive days, through an art exercise where the students were asked to draw a picture of their ideal or dream school. The students made different types of drawings including floor plans, sections, and elevations. Images such as towers, clocks, and clerestory windows all appeared in the students' drawings. One of the interesting ideas that emerged from these sessions was that the media center could open to the outdoors, a feature that was included in the building design. The students also stressed the need for daylight in the classrooms, and other areas of the building.

In addition, teachers, parents, and students were asked to write a wish poem, stating their desires for their new school. All participants were asked to complete the phrase, I wish my school . . . (Figure 2-13). The results of the wish poem, students' drawings, and all subsequent work was on exhibit in the school, as an ongoing record of events, as well as serving to inform those who were not participating of the events that had occurred.

The final workshop consisted of a building-image study, and site-planning exercise, in which 35 teachers, parents, and school-planning officials worked collectively. The building-image study began with a slide show depicting ten different school buildings, each representing different regional characteristics and design features (Figure 2-14). Each building was rated by the participants, and an overall priority list was established. The purpose of this exercise was to increase the participants' level of awareness to the possible variations in the visual character of school buildings. In effect, the exercise intended to expand their vision of building images beyond their everyday experiences with school buildings.

The final event was the site-planning exercise where participants were given a scaled drawing of the new site, located several blocks from their present school, and scaled building components representing all the spaces in their school building (Figure 2-15). All components had labels fastened to the styrofoam components. Each of the six groups was asked to develop a building plan located on the site, considering bus drop-off, parking, soccer field, cluster patterns of class-

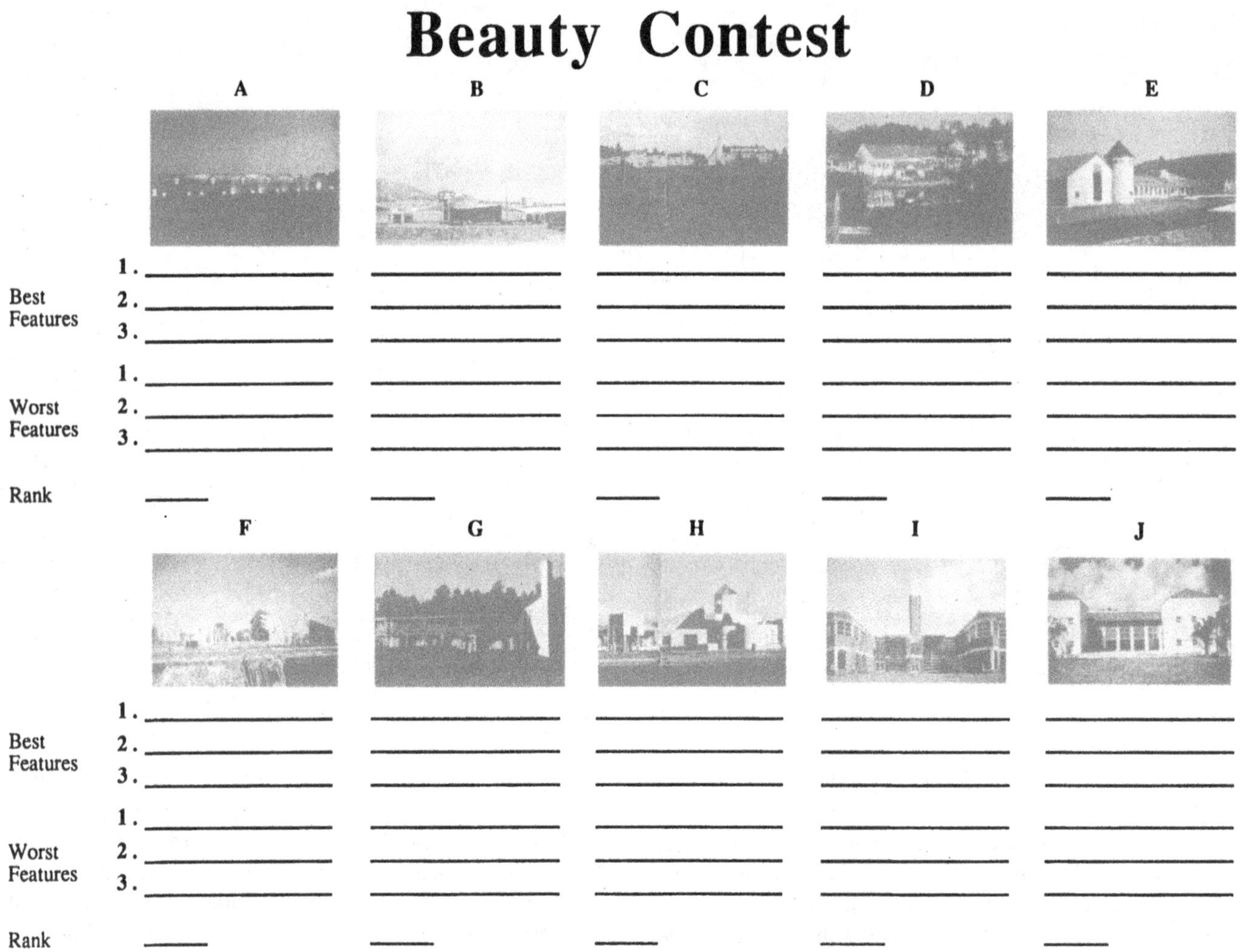

FIGURE 2-14. Beauty Contest: Evaluating images of school buildings.

FIGURE 2-15. Site-planning workshop (Photo: Henry Sanoff).

FIGURE 2-16. Display of solutions at site-planning workshop (Photo: Henry Sanoff).

rooms, outdoor space, and appropriate orientation and daylight. At the completion of the two hour exercise, representatives from each team presented their solution for discussion and debate. All of the solutions were then displayed for review by the participants (Figure 2-16).

Similarities among solutions occurred in the deliberate use of open space and courtyards, and the clustering of kindergarten, 1st-, and 2nd-grade classrooms, separated from the 3rd-, 4th-, and 5th-grade classrooms. Team teaching appeared to guide many of these design decisions.

While group members had some dissatisfaction with their solutions, they all agreed that they had a better understanding of the complexity of issues that required simultaneous consideration. They readily admitted being more sensitive to the role of the architect, and were willing to leave the resolution of the problems to the architect.

The Adams Group met after the workshop to synthesize the workshop results and to arrive at several alternative concepts that would satisfy the requirements developed through the interviews and workshops (Figure 2-17). After considerable design deliberation, one scheme was developed and proposed to the client group. This was accomplished by posting large-scale drawings in key locations in the present school building, and a request for teachers to write comments, directly on the drawings, about positive and negative features (Figure 2-18).

After several days of allowing the teachers to discuss the proposal and to comment, the drawings were retrieved and reviewed by the design team, only to find the comments very minor in detail. All the teachers seemed to identify elements of their design ideas in the architect's submission. At this point, and until preliminary drawings were completed, the involve-

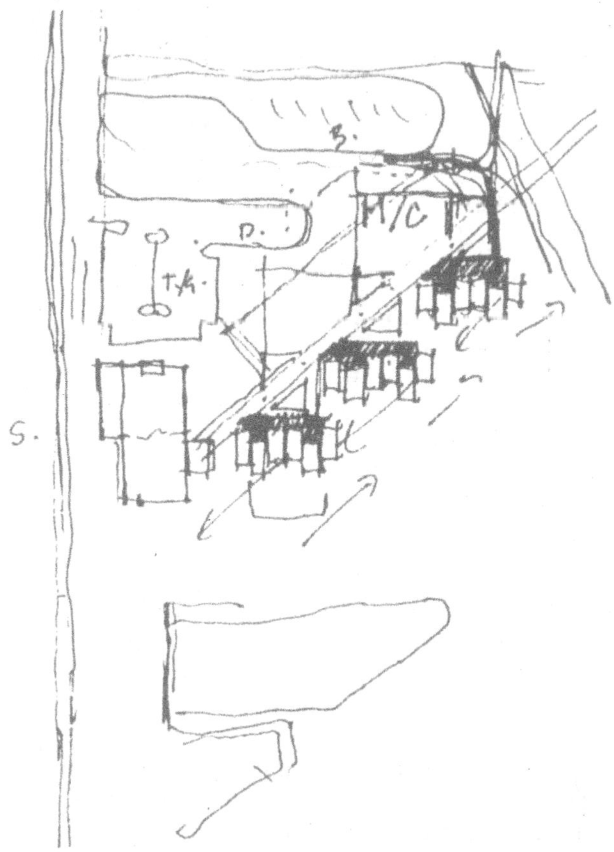

FIGURE 2-17. Initial sketch of building design (Drawing: Henry Sanoff & Graham Adams).

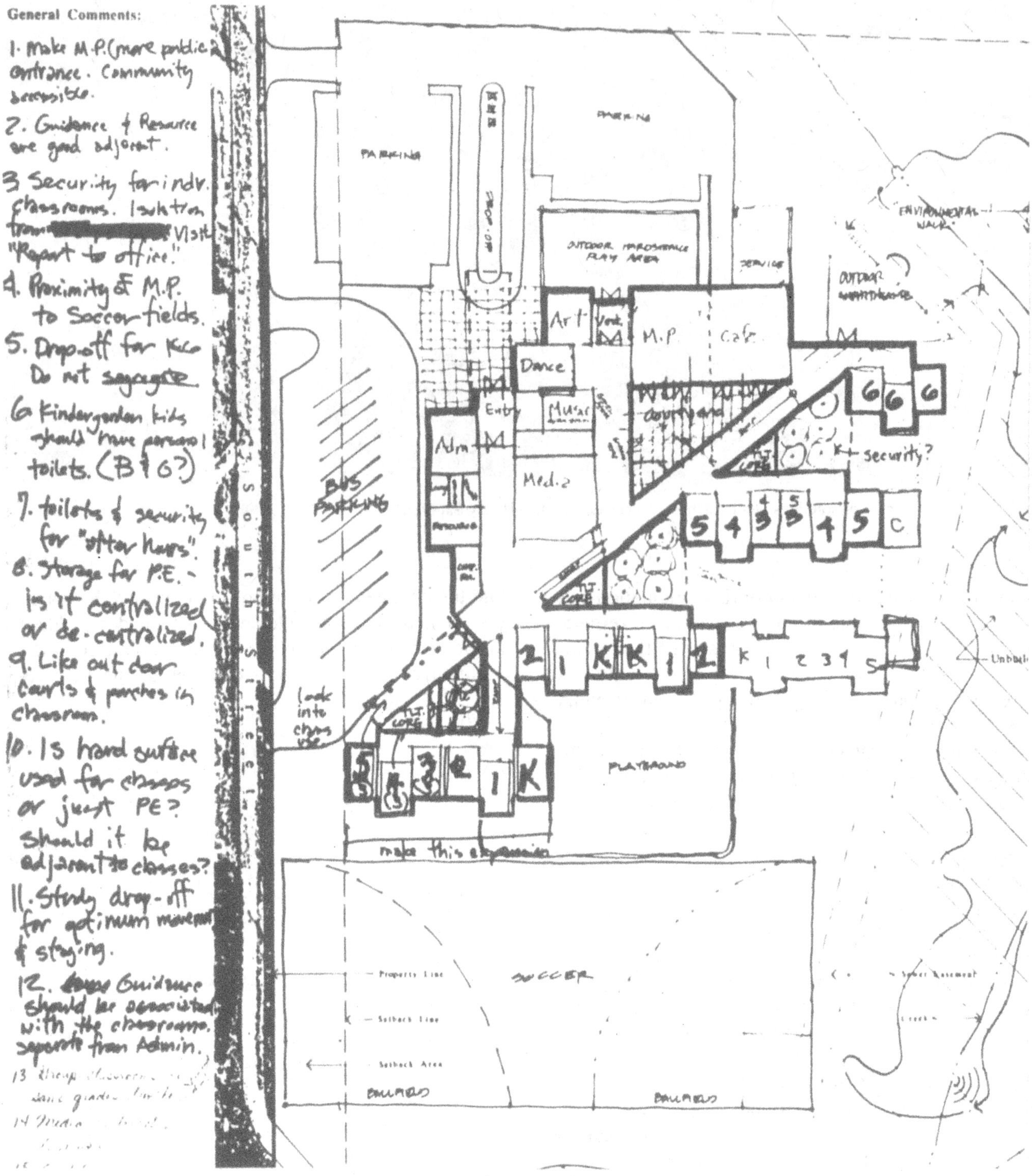

FIGURE 2-18. Preliminary plan of school (Drawing: Adams Group).

ment of teachers was limited to personal interviews clarifying details of classroom design.

The building design contained features that were not typical of traditional schools in the area: namely, grades K, 1, 2 and 3, 4, 5 clustered classrooms to facilitate team teaching and nongraded classes corresponding to the curriculum changes occurring with all Charlotte-Mecklenburg schools, single-loaded corridors with classrooms oriented toward the south, and outdoor play areas for each classroom (Figure 2-19). This arrangement allowed each classroom to have a relatively private outdoor area.

A plan review conducted by the North Carolina State Department of Public Instruction raised questions about these and other unusual design features, some of which might increase the operating cost of

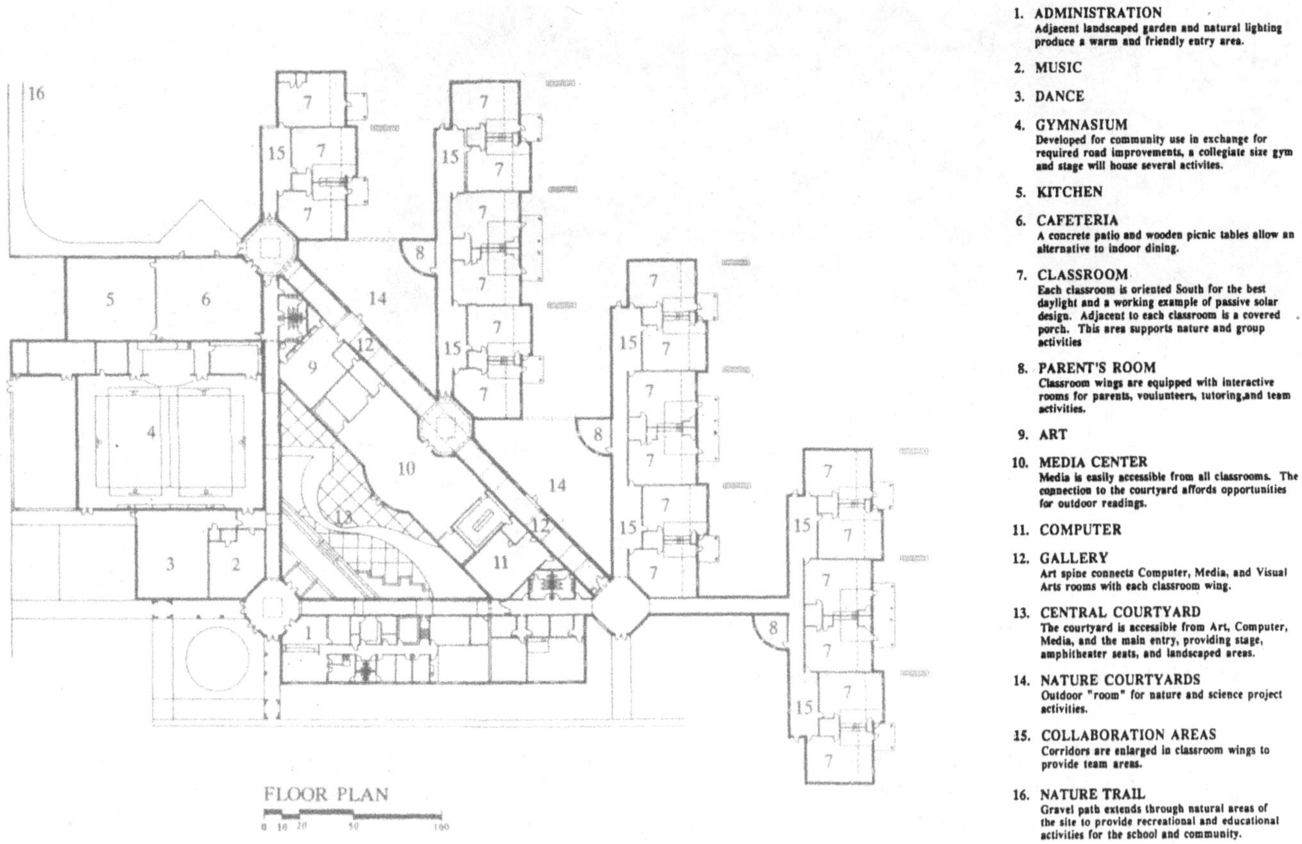

FIGURE 2-19. Final plan of school (Drawing: Adams Group).

the building. The Davidson School proposal was very different from any other school plan that they reviewed. Since the original intention of this project was to create a building that satisfied the needs of the teaching staff and administration, as well as the historic concerns of the community (Figure 2-20(a)), it was agreed to allow the community to make the final decision. To this end, several alternative design solutions were prepared that included the more traditional double-loaded classrooms. A review with the teachers and principal indicated strong support for the K, 1, 2 arrangement and the opportunity for greater teacher collaboration. The Superintendent's office, too, supported the building concept and believed it would enhance their curriculum goals. Adams' comment: "If the teachers and administrators had not been involved in the process, it is pretty clear that the State and County plan reviewers would have been very forceful to have the architects change the plan. It was only through the intervention of the teachers and administrators, and the arguments they made for the curriculum, that allowed the slightly higher cost for heating to be overpowered by the gains of the curriculum."

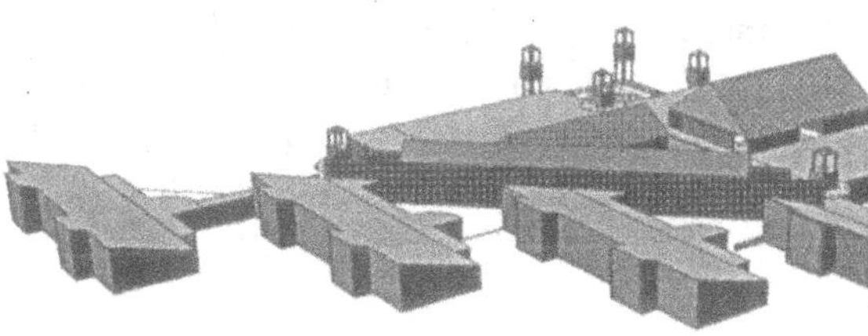

FIGURE 2-20(a). Computer drawing of school (Drawing: Adams Group).

DESIGN INTENTIONS

The design of this building was driven by the integration of classroom objectives, of experiences planned, and of teaching methods, where team teaching and group activities were the most influential educational features. Another critical factor that emerged from the participatory process was the consideration of outdoor areas as rooms, requiring similar attention to detail as the indoor rooms. Above all, there was the common concern by teachers and students for a building that considered their special needs, that created niches for privacy and alcoves for chance encounters, and that conveyed an image of smallness.

To this end, the central concept of the building was to provide the students with a clear sense of their domain, differentiated from that of the administration. This concept was realized by the creation of an art

FIGURE 2-20(b). Building during final stages of construction (Photo: Tom Weiland).

spine or gallery (12) which connects visual arts (9) and media (10) with each classroom wing. At the intersection of the classroom wings and the gallery are social centers providing opportunities for students and teachers to meet. Also connected to each classroom wing is a parent/resource room (8) for counseling, tutoring, and small-group activities. Enlarged corridors flanking classroom wings create special places for small groups. Nature courtyards, formed by the confluence of classroom wings, provide opportunities for science projects, as well as outdoor group activities. The natural part of the site with large trees and a stream was preserved for a nature trail and natural habitat. The nature trail connects each classroom to outdoor space. The central courtyard is visible from the main entrance, and has equal access through the art and media areas. This area also provides amphitheater seats and a stage for outdoor performances. A gymnasium was also provided so that the entire school population can assemble at one time, as well as a place to serve as a community recreation center.

The Davidson School is presently under construction, and was expected to open in September 1993 (Figure 2-20(b)). It is particularly noteworthy that while the three other elementary school projects were awarded at the same time, they are in the same stages of construction. They were designed in a traditional manner and without the involvement of the future occupants of the building. The other schools also followed a more traditional pattern of double-loaded corridors, and age-grade group clustering. Consequently, a comparative evaluation is planned after six months of occupancy, and annually thereafter, to assess the impact of the participation process on student and teacher attitudes, performance, academic innovation, and to user reactions to each of the school buildings.

CONCLUSION

The intent of this project was to narrow the gap between what we know about the education of young people through the literature, and what we observe happening in everyday school environments. Observations of school buildings and classroom behavior have provided some insight into space use, which often denies the existence of variations in types and styles of learning. Also, buildings produced without the involvement of those who will use the building can further exacerbate the rising alienation found in many schools. It is evident that having a sense of ownership, achieved through participation, can have far-reaching positive effects, especially in terms of confronting the viability of traditional school building standards.

The techniques employed in the participatory stages of this project have been used in a variety of different school projects by this author and independently by the Adams Group. They are well documented in the publication, *Design Games* (Sanoff 1984).

First Ward Elementary School

Attitude Survey	
Charette Process	
Community Meetings	✓
Design-In	
Focused Interviews	✓
Fishbowl Planning	
Game Simulation	✓
Group Dynamics	
Public Forum	✓
Task Force	
Training	
Workshop	✓

SUMMARY

A unique activity took place at Charlotte's oldest active urban public school — First Ward Elementary. A group of PTA parents, teachers, school staff, and community leaders, working together, brought to fruition many new ideas and a long-term strategy to improve First Ward Elementary and to restore its former stature and prominence in one of Charlotte's oldest uptown neighborhoods.

The teachers initiated the idea of organizing the energy and talents of a dedicated parent organization to participate in the planning process for a school renovation project. The Charlotte-Mecklenburg Schools showed confidence in this group by offering First Ward School the opportunity to conduct the entire planning process.

The success of this project has demonstrated that teachers with the support of a well-organized parent group, working along with architects, can be an effective guiding force in planning and designing educational spaces to meet the needs of students and the surrounding community. In 1989 this school received the Department of Education award for excellence.

CLIENT

The need to renew First Ward School began as a dream of nine teachers who focused their graduate studies on the improvement of their inner-city school. They were backed by the Metrolina Consortium, a partnership of the Charlotte-Mecklenburg School System, the University of North Carolina at Charlotte, and the University of North Carolina at Chapel Hill.

Demonstrating expertise as classroom teachers required certain changes in their school: they would have to unite diverse parent populations behind First Ward, and broaden the support base by recruiting business, civic, and religious leaders. At their urging, the principal formed the Friends of First Ward, a broad-based community support group to help chart the school's road to academic excellence and community leadership. They agreed that replanning the school would serve as a rallying point for both "Friends" and parents from the diverse neighborhoods the school serves.

PROJECT

This is a four-to-six grade elementary school that serves First Ward, Fourth Ward, Piedmont Courts, and Lansdowne neighborhoods. In its original condition, the school was conspicuously disoriented from the neighborhood. Entrances were particularly in need of definition. In addition, the school had a negative appearance because of a mismatched collection of permanent and temporary buildings. A large asphalt area that edged East Ninth Street presented an uninviting face to the community. A lack of trees and landscaping added to the sterility of the campus.

Conflicts also existed among bus loading and unloading, staff parking, walk-in traffic, and automobile drop-off and pickup. Since the school campus comprised less than six acres (compared to 15 acres for a typical elementary school), it was imperative that the site be carefully utilized for resolving building, circulation, and recreational needs.

First Ward Elementary was always considered to be a unique resource within the Charlotte-Mecklenburg School System. The experiment of involving both faculty and parents in a collaborative planning process reaffirmed this long-time claim. Because of an upcoming bond referendum, and through funding by the School Board, parents and faculty were able to interview and select their own architect. This response to "grass roots" participation represented a major breakthrough for the local school system. When it came time to make the selection, the major characteristics the teachers and parents were looking for was the willingness and ability of the architect to involve them — as well as parents and students — in the design process itself. They ended up choosing a collaborative team consisting of principals from two firms, The Adams Group (formerly Morgan Adams Group) and Murray Whisnant Architects.

Activities commenced with members of the College of Architecture, University of North Carolina at Charlotte, led by Ken Lambla, who initiated a workshop involving the children in drawing, painting, planning, and dreaming about the future possibilities of the school (Figure 2-21). Simultaneously, teachers met with parents at neighborhood coffee klatsches, gathering long lists of needs and suggestions. Culminating these activities was a full day of "programming sessions": at breakfast with the Friends of First Ward,

FIGURE 2-21. Children's drawings.

after school with the faculty, and that evening with the parents. The results formed the basis for a two-day design workshop conducted by the architects. The workshop consisted of a general discussion about the value of the school as a resource for the school system and the city. More specific discussions pertained to the expansion of the current programs in art and dance as well as to provide a new media center. An important by-product of the workshop was a poster that communicated the participatory process and the design ideas to the School Board. As a result, the School Board included First Ward School in the Fall 1987 Charlotte bond referendum. Because of higher priorities, First Ward School was not approved for renovation until the following fall. The architects were selected by the teachers, a first-time occurrence in the school system, and the participatory process begun a year earlier was continued.

The project presented the architects with a unique challenge. To begin with, they were dealing with people who were not used to making design decisions. And because of funding deadlines, a final plan and projected construction costs had to be prepared in less than six weeks. After six weeks of intense workshops and planning activities, parents and staff had completely redesigned the campus, which sits at the edge of Uptown.

The architects conceived of a step-by-step framework within which participants could make decisions. It was their belief that the school community needed to be presented with clear choices in order to feel comfortable in making decisions. Consequently, a variety of methods were utilized to allow people to respond and to provide the type of information needed by the architects.

Background research was done, exploring current design trends, as well as evaluating other schools using the "walk-through" process, which consisted of guided visits, and meetings with teachers and staff. The architects also placed a great deal of emphasis on behavioral design research, a growing body of scientific knowledge that uses architecture, psychology, and the behavioral sciences to analyze how buildings affect people's behavior — and this means going directly to the people who use the building. "You need to discover people's frustrations as well as their dreams," Adams explains.

The first step that the design team took was to meet with both students and teachers to discuss their aspirations; this included asking students to make up "wish lists," or dreams and fantasies of what they wanted in their school. Answers ranged from no homework to skylights in the gym. They were then asked to draw pictures of their ideal school. What emerged ranged from images of the school mascot to simple floor-plan diagrams.

Next, came a meeting with more than 30 teachers and community leaders. Adams organized the session into problem-solving games with six small teams. Each team was asked to list goals for the school, rank the goals by importance, and identify the learning activities that supported each goal.

Their next task was to choose a location on the campus for the proposed activities. A group of 32 photographs was then supplied by Adams. The photos were pinned on a site plan to indicate where teachers felt their proposed activities best fit (Figure 2-22). Finally, each team made a stand-up presentation of their proposed site plans, and explained the rationale for their choices.

"For me, these sessions represented the meat and potatoes of the process. The building design then logically followed and, you might say, was the dessert," Morgan notes. "To create the design, we reviewed all the information from the many sessions and looked for areas of consensus. We kept the points of consensus as constants for utilization in our designs (such as a new entry and image to the community). Where there was conflict, we developed new design options and worked our way back to consensus." Areas of conflict included the location of the media center, community access versus school accessibility of art, dance, gym, and meeting areas, and the office location with respect to teacher or visitor convenience. Five alternative site plans and models were prepared for discussion with the teachers, who were asked to record their likes and dislikes on a visual rating scale. The final result was a preferred alternative, which was

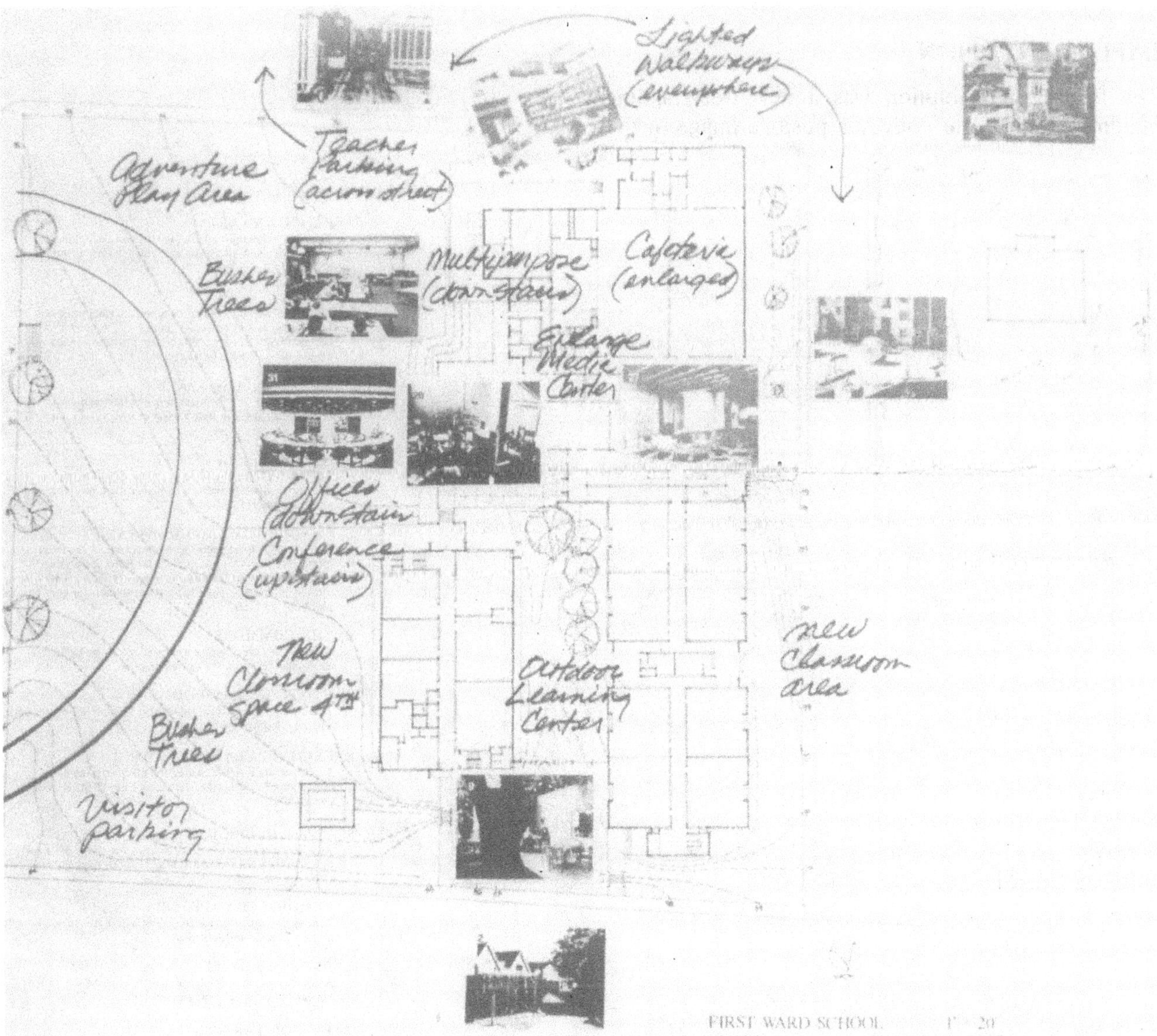

FIGURE 2-22. Workshop results showing location of preferred settings on existing floor plan (Drawing: Adams Group).

subsequently revised to include the positive features of the other alternatives. It included an outdoor covered area or courtyard for school events, surrounded by special places for art, dance, and meeting areas which varied in form by the use of light and changing volumes. This concept was referred to as the village scheme where all activity areas were connected by covered walkways and each had a direct outdoor connection.

Difficult decisions and painful compromises had to be made on several issues: conflicts between car and bus traffic, the need for security versus the desire to be open to the community, and budget restraints versus design expectations. Each decision and every compromise was reached by consensus, a slow and complex process, but a critically important one. There were no losers, only winners — a natural by-product of creative collaboration.

IMPLEMENTATION

The final design solution was a new free-standing building proposed to convey a positive image to the community, while also being available for various community activities (Figures 2-23 and 2-24). The "hard surface" play area serves students while also functioning as a formal entry plaza facing Uptown Charlotte. The covered gathering area for school and community events has affectionately been called "the Terridactile." The multipurpose building is oriented toward the city to serve a variety of community and school needs. Serving as the focal point for the whole school, the environmental courtyard offers imaginative barnyard sculpture, and opportunities for artistic displays by the students. Clay tiles are displayed on the buildings that face the courtyard. The tiles were the product of a "tile workshop" conceived by the architects as a way for parents, teachers, and students to personalize their building by producing the 85 tiles that became a permanent part of the building (Figure 2-25).

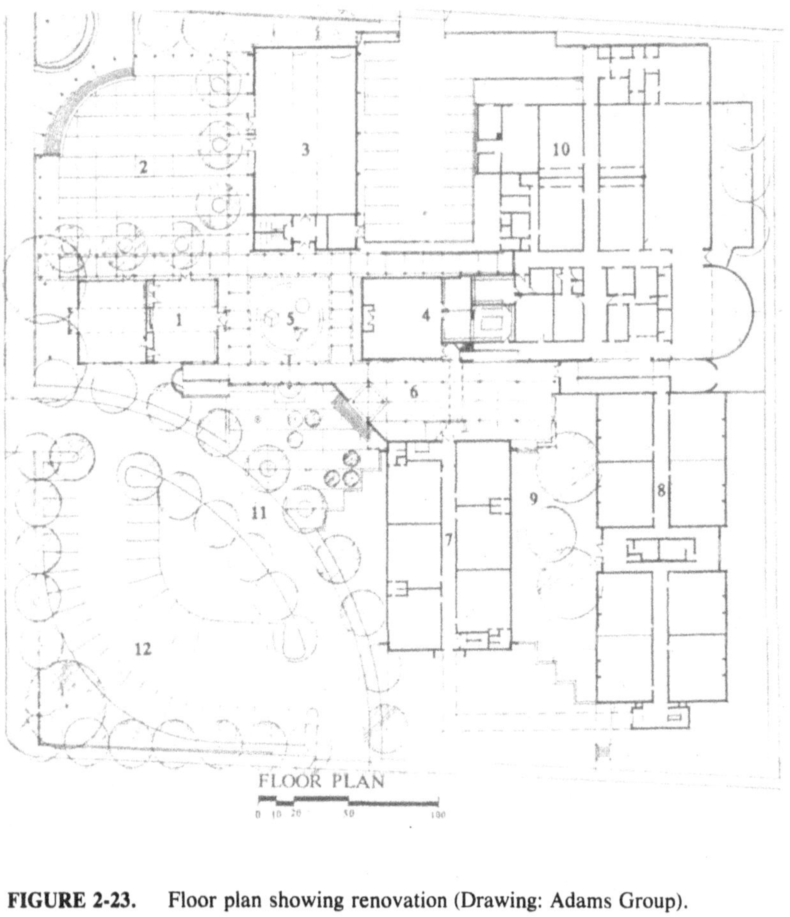

1. DANCE AND ART
   This new free standing building offers an active image to the community while also being available for various community activities.
2. PLAZA
   This "hard surface" play area serves students while also functioning as a formal entry plaza facing uptown Charlotte. Landscaping and edge trellis system provides a much needed image change for the school.
3. MULTIPURPOSE SPACE
   Oriented to the city for maximum exposure and use, this building serves a wide variety of school and community needs.
4. ADMIN./ MEDIA CENTER
   Located as the first building to be seen off the entry courtyard, this area houses the school's administration, reception and various support functions.
5. ENVIRONMENTAL COURTYARD
   Serving as the focal point for the whole school, the courtyard offers very singular opportunities for water features and artistic displays by the students. This area became not only visually interesting, but also serves as an oasis for both visitors and building users.
6. THE COMMONS
   This recycled area became a covered spine which doubled as circulation space and exhibition areas.
7. EXISTING CLASSROOMS
   This structure is reorganized to serve as improved classrooms with new mechanical systems
8. EXISTING CLASSROOM WING
   This structure received modest modifications; the most important of which is the new access doors to the outdoor garden area.
9. CENTRAL GARDEN
   An existing space between the two existing classroom structures, this grass and weed area was heavily landscaped and secured along the south edge with a new wall.
10. REMODELED CAFETERIA
    The existing cafeteria/ meeting room was altered to accommodate music rehearsal and arts room.
11. DROP OFF DRIVE
    A new circular drive designed to emphasize the separation between bus and drop-off pick-up activities
12. VISITOR PARKING
    New on-site parking designed to avoid conflicts with drop-off zone.

FIGURE 2-23. Floor plan showing renovation (Drawing: Adams Group).

FIGURE 2-24. New addition: Media (right); Multipurpose (center); Art/Dance (left), taken from entry courtyard (Photo: Alan McGuinn).

AFTER-OCCUPANCY RESPONSES

Three years after occupancy, the staff that participated in the First Ward School Renovation process were asked to comment on the design features they liked and those they disliked. In addition, Pat Holleman, the principal, responded by noting the changes she observed in the attitudes and behavior of staff and students. The most important change, she observed, was the "closeness of the staff," that resulted from the participatory process. The teachers' morale showed marked improvement, since there was a "can do" attitude resulting from working together to challenge the bureaucracy. Positive, marked changes were also noted in the spirits of the students, resulting from their involvement. Attendance records improved and CAT scores went up by ten points in three years. Parents, too, remarked that First Ward Elementary no longer looked like a school, but was inviting. People generally felt better about bringing their children to school. Neighbors were equally positive about the new image of the school and its openness to the community.

FIGURE 2-25. Tile workshop with teachers, parents, and children (Photo: Alan McGuinn).

The majority of staff members found the building's overall appearance to be the most-liked feature, which was further qualified to include the interior and exterior appearance. One of the most favorable characteristics of the interior was the feeling of openness achieved by the introduction of daylight. The addition of the art, dance, and media center were described as pleasant places in which to teach (Figure 2-26). The gymnasium, which doubled as an assembly area — often referred to as a multipurpose area — on the other hand, was seen to be less satisfactory. The capacity of the assembly area was established in 1989, by the County Public School System and the architect. During the three years after occupancy, several mobile units were added due to the increase in enrollment. As a result, the entire student population can no longer assemble together in the multipurpose area, which has

FIGURE 2-26. Dance and art addition with view of the city (beyond) taken from covered bridge (Photo: JoAnn Seiburg Baker).

The Charlotte Observer

ROLFE NEILL, Chairman and Publisher
RICHARD OPPEL, Editor — JOHN LUBY, General Manager
ED WILLIAMS, Editor of the Editorial Pages — DOUGLAS CLIFTON, Managing Editor
JACK CLAIBORNE, TOM BRADBURY, JERRY SHINN, Associate Editors
Monday, April 23, 1990

Editorials

A Well-Earned Honor

Expansion Of First Ward School Wins Design Award

It's rare that the design of a public school wins an honor award in the annual competition of the N.C. chapter of the American Institute of Architects. It's even rarer for a school renovation to win. That's why it was especially cheering Friday night to see the Morgan-Adams Group and Murray Whisnant/Architects cited at the N.C. AIA awards banquet for their design of Charlotte's First Ward School expansion.

Even more rewarding was the grassroots process Ron Morgan, Graham Adams and Murray Whisnant followed in designing that expansion. They consulted and then followed the wishes and recommendations of First Ward teachers, parents and students. Their final drawings were the culmination of a long series of meetings in the First Ward neighborhood, in the homes of parents and in the offices and libraries of the school's principal and faculty.

That procedure consumed many additional hours and added frustration to what was already a complex project. But it paid off in both tangible and intangible results. It helped inspire a faculty and unite a school community, and it produced an expansion that has not only increased the school's physical space, but has also helped to build collegial pride and a spirit of adventure that are being reflected in the school's award-winning instructional program.

In literal and figurative ways, it turned the school around. Take a bow, gentlemen.

First Ward's Winning New Look.

FIGURE 2-27. Newspaper editorial announcing design award.

also been used as a theater and for viewing films, activities not originally discussed in the development of the program.

The building received an honor award from the North Carolina Chapter of the American Institute of Architects (Figure 2-27).

ACKNOWLEDGMENT

Comments by Graham Adams, Architect, and observations by Pat Holleman, Principal of First Ward, served as the basis of this case study.

East Orange Middle School

Attitude Survey	
Charette Process	
Community Meetings	✓
Design-In	
Focused Interviews	✓
Fishbowl Planning	✓
Game Simulation	
Group Dynamics	
Public Forum	✓
Task Force	
Training	
Workshop	

SUMMARY

The East Orange Middle School (EOMS) was designed with full community participation and opened in 1975. The designers achieved this involvement by using a storefront on the city's main commercial street as a studio whose door was always open to passersby. The architectural firm of Uniplan, located in Princeton, New Jersey, set up the design center to directly confront the problems of school planning in another city. The East Orange School Design Center (EOSDC) was an informal way of involving citizens and officials in planning and design. It allowed people to walk in off the street at any time to observe, inquire, and even assume a task.

CLIENT

The Board of Education of East Orange, New Jersey, selected the firm of Uniplan to design the new middle school. East Orange was, in 1970, a city undergoing rapid social change. The population was about 50 percent black — relative newcomers and young people who came from socially troubled cities such as Newark and Philadelphia. The white population, in contrast, was aging. As a result, the schools were 90 percent black, and did not necessarily reflect the city's racial composition.

The educational specifications for EOMS called for a capacity of 1,800 students in grades six through eight, and emphasized educational principles which allow for personal growth according to life style. The site proposed for the new middle school was a tract of less than four acres in an area surrounded by one- to four-family houses. The restriction of site size posed such problems as the accommodation of the necessary playground area, and parking for 150 cars.

PROJECT

Uniplan decided that the approach for design of this project was through community involvement. With the support of a grant from the Educational Facilities Laboratory (EFL), the concept of a design center was proposed. The EOSDC opened in 1970 with a public celebration. The street was closed to traffic, the Mayor of East Orange cut the ribbon, and the Center began its work. The objectives of the Design Center were:

- To draw people into the design process and make them equal partners
- To overcome the lack of constructive focus and act as a catalyst for community vitality
- To help people understand each other through involvement
- To stimulate and cross-fertilize ideas
- To identify community hopes and ideals, and measure them against the realities of economic and technical constraints
- To assure that the physical needs of the children and adults of East Orange will be met

PROCESS

The process was initiated by identifying some 30 community organizations, and several evenings every week were devoted to meeting with these groups to get their perceptions and recommendations. The children from

FIGURE 2-28. Children's drawing reflecting the spirit of the design process.

East Orange schools expressed in drawings and paintings what they thought a school should be (Figure 2-28). The Center's open door attracted the collaboration of the community, particularly young people, whose involvement was influential, even though they had no prior training in design. The Center's director for Uniplan, Larry Goldblatt, an architectural student from North Carolina State University, and two young people from the community in particular, Stefanie Wilson and Larry Goldstone, organized other youths to work in teams. A human resources map was prepared showing where everyone lived, their interests, needs, and goals.

The process was divided into several phases beginning with the introductory phase, which produced impressions of the community. Here the design team and community members exchanged views and established mutual trust. In the second phase, program needs, goals, and aspirations, as well as constraints, were explored. Since the community participants requested that the gymnasium, pool, and library would be planned to serve the entire community as well, considerable interest was generated for their solution. Students and community members built study models and eagerly expressed their viewpoints. The final phases produced seven study schemes, and a final scheme, respectively (Figure 2-29). Community members, participating in these phases, were given an opportunity to see how architects work, and to understand the advantages or disadvantages of their contributions (Murphy 1972).

At the design center it was learned that there was a desire of the community for a close relationship between the learning areas and the outdoors. This wish posed some difficulty if the entire site was covered with a building. After considering scale and ground coverage, the architects proposed that the entire roof be used for play space for students and a park for the community (Figure 2-30). The rooftop park would be reached by public ramps when the school is closed (Figure 2-31). It also became evident that students would enter the school from many directions, and a "main entrance" would be of use to only one approach.

The building, which opened in 1975, is in the form of three blocks connected by an internal "street" at the lowest level, with a variety of configurations along the way. Each block contains a "house" consisting of

FIGURE 2-29. Several study schemes displayed in design office (Photo: Larry Goldblatt).

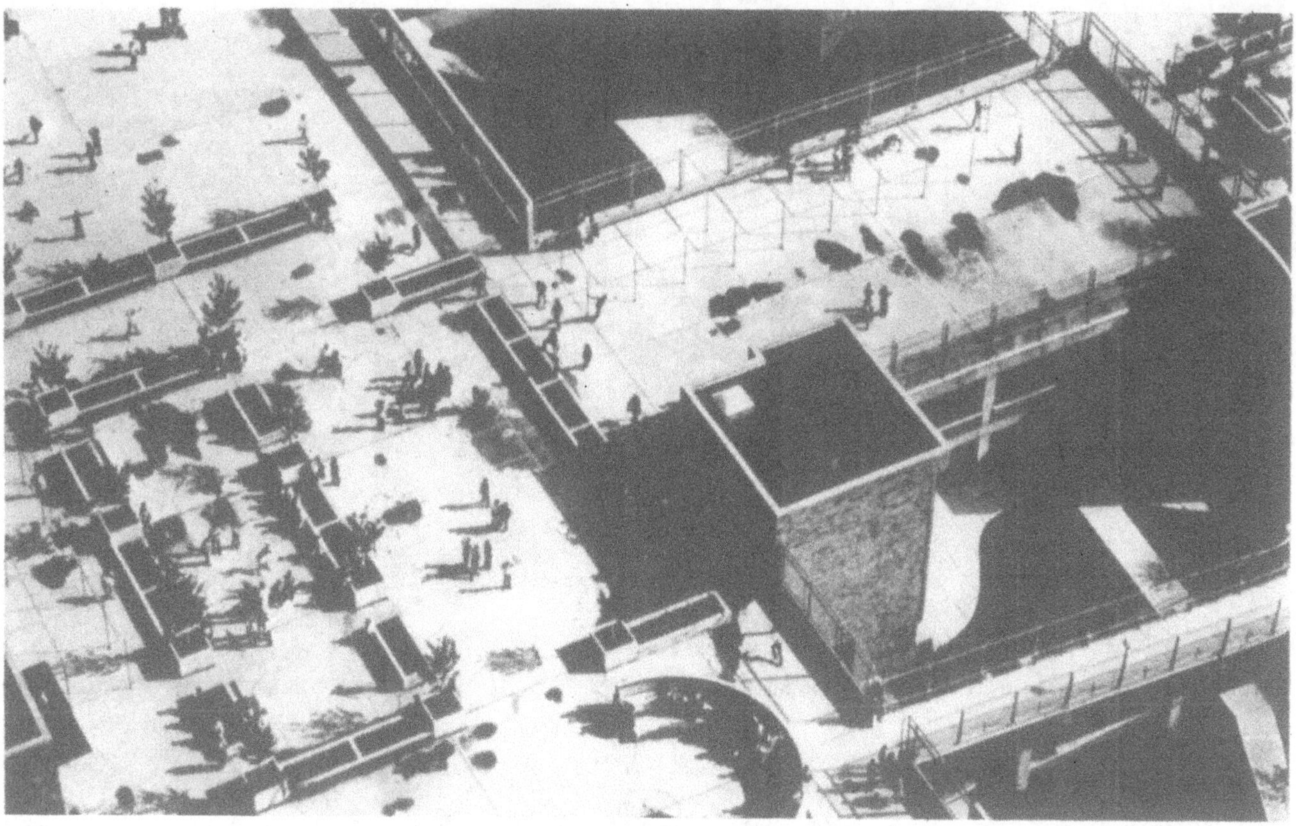

FIGURE 2-30. Photo showing roof play area (Photo: Matt Sinclair).

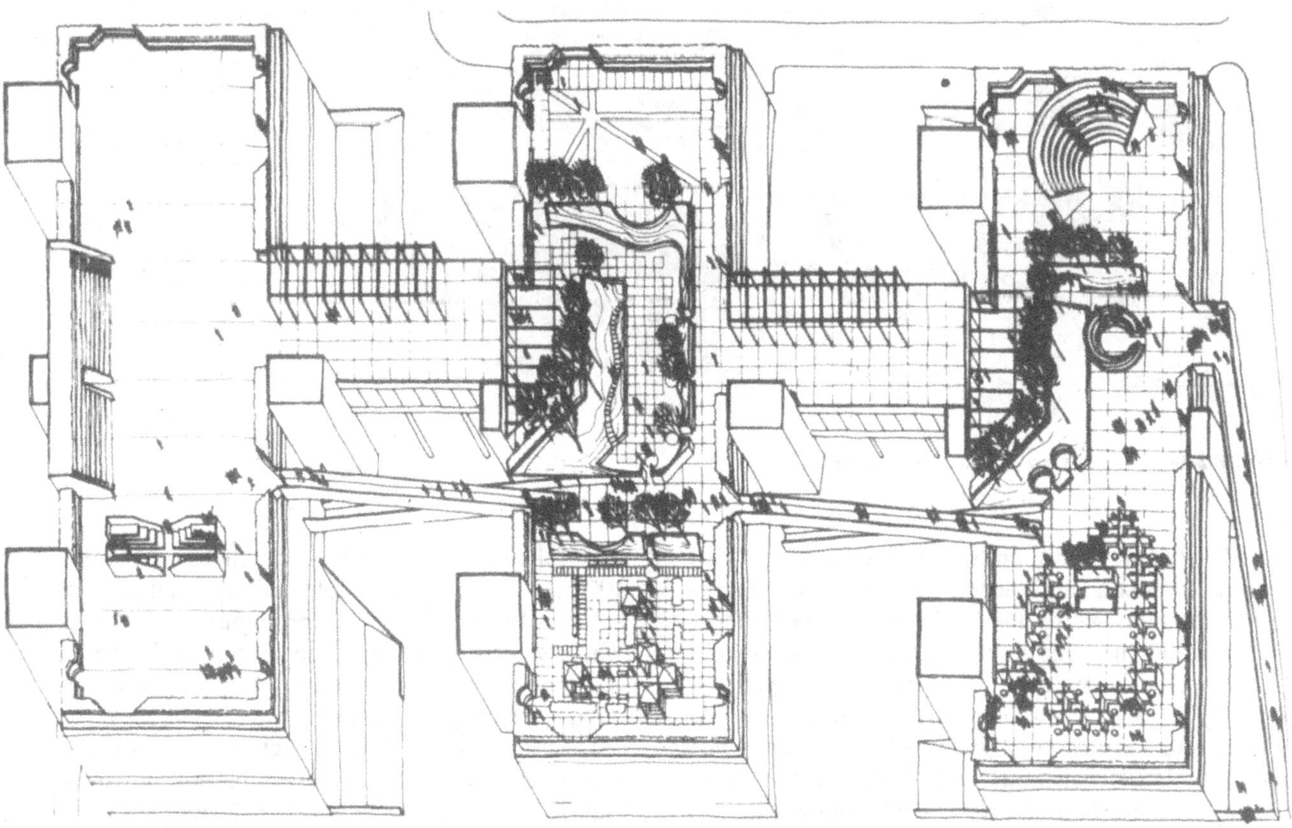

FIGURE 2-31. Roof plan of building showing ramp from the street connecting to the public park (Drawing: Uniplan).

FIGURE 2-32. Students' activity area (Photo: Matt Sinclair).

FIGURE 2-33. Aerial view of school (Photo: Larry Goldblatt).

two 300-student family units, where each family unit operates almost as an independent school, but shares certain facilities within the house such as performing arts, homemaking, and industrial and fine arts (Figure 2-32). This is a manifestation of the school's philosophy of giving students an educational plan to complete at their own rate of speed within a "family" unit. The upper levels of each house are identical, with high-ceiling loft classroom areas for each family. The loft areas are meant to be manipulated by the students to correspond to their activities.

A follow-up, one year after construction (Murphy 1976), revealed considerable activity in all parts of the school (Figure 2-32). The prominence of the ramps was a clear expression of community use. Access to the school from all directions was successful, and no entrance hierarchy existed or was intended (Figure 2-33). In a recent interview, Architect Larry Goldblatt comments that: "The citizen/parent involvement clearly beneficially affected the design process. The building would not have been built as designed had it not been created in the community based setting."

Ligon Middle School

Attitude Survey	✓
Charette Process	
Community Meetings	
Design-In	
Focused Interviews	✓
Fishbowl Planning	
Game Simulation	✓
Group Dynamics	
Public Forum	
Task Force	
Training	
Workshop	

SUMMARY

In response to the growing concern for more student involvement in school planning decisions, this project was conducted to develop a procedure for utilizing student experiences to contribute to the design decision-making process. Through the use of a questionnaire directed at assessing their present school environment, it was found that junior high-school students favored the educational program, yet were critical of the inflexibility and dullness of the physical environment.

To complement the student responses, additional reactions about the day-to-day operations of the school were sought from teachers and staff members through the use of structured interviews. These findings provided a basis for developing a conceptual layout for a new school building.

CLIENT

The Wake County School System is continuously involved in building and programming modifications to their constituent schools, of which Ligon Middle School was a prime candidate, since they had undergone programmatic changes without any alteration to the building. The principal and teaching staff were anxious to participate in a process that would enable open discussion and critical commentary in order to present an approach to school boards that would stimulate more innovative school buildings and programs. Although the teaching staff had been involved in a self-assessment of their educational program, their focus was the responsiveness to the needs of adolescents, teachers, and parents. It was apparent that their approach did not consider ways in which the physical environment could enhance educational goals.

PROJECT

Ligon Middle School in Raleigh, North Carolina, a typical 1950s building, consisting of a series of self-contained classrooms arranged along a double-loaded corridor, was the subject of a student assessment. Students were questioned about attitudes toward their school and community, about their classroom, library, and outdoor areas, and about their preferred learning style. A questionnaire was administered to 80 students, representing the various grade levels contained in the school. From the results of the questionnaire, a student profile was developed that characterized their likes and dislikes.

This information was used to supplement the results of teacher and staff interviews that provided the source for the development of a building program. The overall results of the assessment pointed to the need for a new building, particularly if the information gathered would be influential in shaping new places for learning. This information became the foundation for the program which described the characteristics of all building spaces and their appropriate relationships.

PROCESS

The research team had made frequent visits to several junior high schools. These visits included "walk-throughs" and informal observations of students engaged in a variety of activities. The walk-throughs

learning style

The following questions will try to find out how you feel about the way you work and learn in school.

1. Do you have any classes which have more than one teacher?
   [ ] Yes
   [ ] No
   If so, what kind of class is it? ______

2. What do you prefer, a class with one teacher or a class with more than one teacher?
   Why? ______

3. Does the school promote student-teacher interaction on a one-to-one basis?
   [ ] Yes
   [ ] No

4. Do you work in small groups?
   [ ] Yes
   [ ] No

5. Do you work in large groups?
   [ ] Yes
   [ ] No

6. Do you direct some of your own projects and learning activities?
   [ ] Yes
   [ ] No

7. How do you most often work at school?
   [ ] Independently
   [ ] In small groups
   [ ] In large groups
   [ ] With the entire class

8. How do you prefer to work at school?
   [ ] Individually
   [ ] In small groups
   [ ] In large groups
   [ ] With the entire class

school & community

The community that sends its young people to a school can also have an effect on the learning that happens in that school. Therefore it is important to find out how you feel about community involvement in the school program.

1. How many students at your school do you know by sight?
   [ ] Most of the students
   [ ] Some of the students
   [ ] Few of the students

2. How many students at your school do you feel you know by name?
   [ ] Most of the students
   [ ] Some of the students
   [ ] Few of the students

3. How do you feel about the number of people attending your school?
   [ ] Too many
   [ ] Too few
   [ ] About the right number of people

4. Do you prefer to attend a school that is close enough for you to walk from home, or do you prefer one that is farther away so you can meet people that live in other communities? ______

5. Do any people from your community teach special classes at your school or become involved with students in the school in other ways?
   [ ] Yes
   [ ] No
   If so, what kinds of things do they do? ______

   If not, how important do you feel it is for people from the school community to play an active part in your school program?
   [ ] Very important
   [ ] Important but not essential
   [ ] Not important at all

6. What three things do you like most about your school?
   a. ______
   b. ______
   c. ______

7. What three things do you dislike most about your school?
   a. ______ Why? ______
   b. ______ Why? ______
   c. ______ Why? ______

8. What three things would you most like to change about your school? How might you change them?
   a. ______
   b. ______
   c. ______

9. Name three places in the school where you spend most of your free time. Why do you go there?
   a. ______
   b. ______
   c. ______

10. What activities do you enjoy most when you are not in school? (Please list in order of importance.)
    ______

SCHOOL: ______
DATE: ______
TEACHER'S NAME: ______
GRADE: ______
AGE: ______
SEX: ______

student areas

Student areas are places in the school that are used mostly by students for various kinds of activities.

1. Are there special places in your school that you feel "belong" to you where you can talk about ideas and share interests?
   [ ] Yes [ ] No
   If so, where are these places? ______

   How important do you feel it is for students to have places in their school that "belong" to them?
   [ ] Very important [ ] Important [ ] Not important

2. Where do you go when you want to be alone? ______
   Why? ______

3. Where do you go to work with other students? ______
   Why? ______

4. Where do you go to work on group projects? ______
   Why? ______

5. Do you have a place(s) in which to display personal work?
   [ ] Yes [ ] No
   If so, where is student work displayed? ______

6. Who decides what is displayed and where it is displayed?
   [ ] Students
   [ ] Teachers
   [ ] Assistants or aides
   [ ] Administrators
   [ ] Clubs
   [ ] Other ______

outdoor areas

There are many outdoor areas in schools that may be used by teachers and students. These may include playgrounds, playing fields, courtyards, and other places that you may think of.

1. Do you use any of the outdoor areas at your school?
   [ ] Yes [ ] No

2. When do you use these outdoor places?
   (Number from 1 to 4 with 1 = most often
   4 = least often
   [ ] During scheduled school times
   [ ] Free time during the school day
   [ ] Free time after school, weekends
   [ ] Other times

3. What kinds of things do you do in the outdoor places that you use?

4. What kinds of outdoor places would you like to have that you don't now have?

library

1. How often do you use the library? (Check one)
   [ ] Several times per month
   [ ] Several times a week
   [ ] Everyday

2. Are your visits to the library usually:
   [ ] Mandatory
   [ ] Voluntary

3. For what purpose do you use the library? (Number from 1 to 6
   where 1 = most often
   6 = often
   [ ] Reading for enjoyment
   [ ] Homework or studying
   [ ] Gathering research for assignments
   [ ] Working on independent projects
   [ ] Meetings for group projects
   [ ] Other ______

furnishings

1. Do you move the furniture, desks, chairs or partitions in the classroom when you engage in different activities?
   [ ] Yes
   [ ] No
   If you do move the furnishings, what changes do you normally make? ______

   If you do not move the furnishings in the classroom, why don't you? (Check one)
   [ ] Not permitted to make changes
   [ ] Don't want to make any changes
   [ ] Like the room the way it is
   [ ] Not enough time to make changes
   [ ] Don't have any preferences about arrangement

2. How important is it to be able to move desks and chairs to suit various tasks?
   [ ] Very important
   [ ] Important
   [ ] Not important at all

3. Are you permitted to leave the classroom if you want to?
   [ ] Yes
   [ ] No

4. Are you permitted to move from place to place in the school freely?
   [ ] Yes
   [ ] No

5. Would you like to have more places in your classroom in which to do different kinds of activities?
   [ ] Yes
   [ ] No
   If so, what kinds of places would you like to have? ______

6. Name two things you like about your classroom.
   a. ______ Why? ______
   b. ______ Why? ______

7. Name two things you dislike about your classroom.
   a. ______ Why? ______
   b. ______ Why? ______

FIGURE 2-34. School evaluation questionnaire.

were usually guided by administrative staff, who were asked to respond to questions about building performance. The observations, which reveal the complexity of student and staff activities, were a necessary complement to plans of the buildings being assessed. This preliminary investigation was necessary to determine the assessment strategy, particularly since the limited amount of time available to conduct the study was a critical factor. A questionnaire was the format for the conduct of the study because it would yield the greatest amount of information in the shortest period of time.

The study began with a survey of Ligon students, who were asked to evaluate particular aspects of the school environment based on their personal experiences. Information was obtained about existing conditions as well as the desired environmental conditions. A 50-item questionnaire was administered during class time to 80 students, ranging between seventh and ninth grade (Figure 2-34). The questionnaire attempted to target students' feelings about their school environment and their educational program. An important category of information contained in the questionnaire pertained to the physical characteristics of the classroom, where students spend a considerable amount of time (Figure 2-35). When asked about the quality of light, for example, a majority of students indicated that the combination of daylight and incandescent or fluorescent light produced "adequate" light levels, while nearly half of the students preferred daylight exclusively.

When asked about classroom-activity use, students indicated that the majority of classrooms were not typified by simultaneous activities occurring during class time. Less than half of the students indicated that furnishings were moved to accommodate different activities. The majority of changes reported involved repositioning of desks for greater visibility, with no cabinets or partitions being moved. Those who occupied classrooms where there were no changes, indicated that it was due to a lack of time, that they were not permitted to make changes, or that they preferred

classrooms

Classrooms are very important places in the school because teachers and students spend so much time there. We think it is especially important to look at how you feel about them and how you might change them.

Lighting:

1. What type of lighting is used in your classroom primarily? (Check one)
   [ ] Daylight
   [ ] Artificial light
   [ ] Daylight and artificial light
2. What type of light do you prefer to work by?
   [ ] Daylight
   [ ] Artificial
   [ ] Daylight and artificial
   [ ] No preference
3. How would you describe the daylighting in your classroom?
   [ ] Good
   [ ] Adequate
   [ ] Inadequate

Acoustics/Distractions:

1. Do several activities occur simultaneously in your classroom?
   [ ] Yes
   [ ] No
2. Do students move about during class from one activity area to another?
   [ ] Yes
   [ ] No

   If so, does the movement of students in the classroom distract you from your work?
   [ ] Very much
   [ ] Occasionally
   [ ] Not at all

   How disturbing do you find it when two or more activities occur in a classroom at the same time?
   [ ] Very disturbing
   [ ] Occasionally disturbing
   [ ] Not disturbing at all

Very Large — Somewhat Large — Neither Large nor Small — Somewhat Small — Very Small

Attractive						Unattractive
Bright						Dark
Changeable						Unchangeable
Cheerful						Gloomy
Comfortable						Uncomfortable
Modern						Traditional
Drafty						Stuffy
Exciting						Unexciting
Rigid						Flexible
Friendly						Unfriendly
Imaginative						Unimaginative
Interesting						Boring
Repelling						Inviting
Pleasant						Unpleasant
Quiet						Noisy
Relaxed						Tense
Secure						Insecure
Intimate						Distant
Like						Dislike

Existing

Very Large — Somewhat Large — Neither Large nor Small — Somewhat Small — Very Small

Attractive						Unattractive
Bright						Dark
Changeable						Unchangeable
Cheerful						Gloomy
Comfortable						Uncomfortable
Modern						Traditional
Drafty						Stuffy
Exciting						Unexciting
Rigid						Flexible
Friendly						Unfriendly
Imaginative						Unimaginative
Interesting						Boring
Repelling						Inviting
Pleasant						Unpleasant
Quiet						Noisy
Relaxed						Tense
Secure						Insecure
Intimate						Distant
Like						Dislike

Alternative

FIGURE 2-35. Classroom evaluation questionnaire.

the classroom the way it was. It was perceived by the students, however, that such changes would be important. Many students also indicated that increasing classroom activities and noise levels would not necessarily be a source of disturbance. The nature of the activity areas that could be incorporated into the classroom were reported to be either special-interest support areas or individual study areas. This desire for increased activity areas suggests the need for greater classroom organizational flexibility.

When asked for their likes and dislikes about their classroom, students reported that the best-liked features were the classroom size, the teachers, and the presence of their friends. The features of the classroom that were most disliked were inflexible seating arrangements, uncomfortable furnishings, and poor ventilation; other students described the classroom colors as depressing.

Student reactions to their visual environment was also an integral component to the school assessment. The approach used was to compare a typical classroom with one having different physical characteristics. Two photographs were selected (see Figure 2-35), depicting alternative classroom environments. Students evaluated each using a list of opposite pairs of descriptors. The photograph on the left in Figure 2-35, which depicts a typical Ligon classroom, generally elicited unfavorable responses. The alternative classroom (the photograph on the right in Figure 2-35), evoked more extreme and positive feelings, such as "friendly" and "cheerful." Figure 2-36 shows the comparison of the two profiles.

Another major subject area included in the questionnaire was that of places exclusively designated for

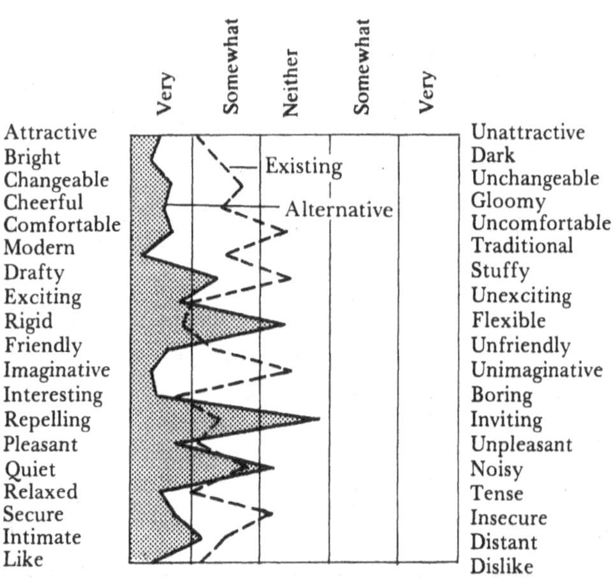

FIGURE 2-36. Profile comparing existing and alternative classrooms.

student use. While the vast majority of students indicated the importance of having places that "belonged to them," over half suggested that no such place existed at Ligon. Main areas identified as belonging to students, by those who felt that such areas did exist, were the play area behind the gym, the cafeteria, the corridors, and the counsellor's office. Looking further for insights about places students chose to go to be alone, work with others, or work on group projects, the general indication in all three cases was a perceived lack of appropriate places in the school which support individual or small-group activity, or provide the option for privacy. Generally, students indicated that the only places they could go for privacy were the restrooms, the library, or nowhere. When asked about a place to work with others, many students cited the use of classrooms, due to convenience, or due to the lack of other available choices. Some students selected the library to work with others because of the availability of resources and the privacy. Working on group projects was also conducted in the library or classrooms because of the resources and the quiet atmosphere. Personalization opportunities were typically in evidence by display of student work, or items of special interest, located on bulletin boards in classrooms, in the library, in the lobby, and in the corridors. Many of the students, however, indicated that such displays were controlled by teachers and administrators, not by the students.

Outdoor areas, another important component of the school environment, were indeed used by a majority of the students. The most frequent use occurred during scheduled school hours in the athletic field, and less frequently after school, since many students do not reside in the neighborhood and are bused to school. Generally, outdoor activities included team sports, conversation and socializing, and observing. Student desires for additional types of outdoor activities ranged from eating to studying areas.

The importance of community–school interaction to the enrichment of the students' educational program has long been recognized by the County School System. While over half of the students felt community involvement was important, the same number felt there was no active community participation program in the school.

It appeared that those features about the school that students felt most positively about were programmatic in nature. They liked the strong academic program, and had good rapport with the teachers and the administration. The students believed that the recreation facility and the resource center were very good. Overall, the school was judged to have numerous programmatic options available to the students, and the learning atmosphere was considered to be warm and friendly. On the other hand, the features disliked most

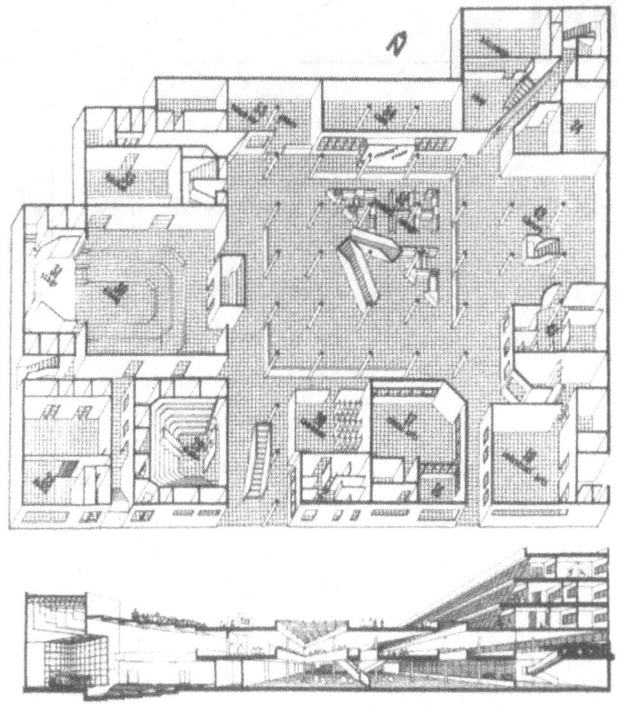

FIGURE 2-37. Plan of proposed school (Drawing: Cheryl Walker).

by the students pertained to the physical environment. Those features were ventilation and heating, lack of visual appeal, dull interior colors, and uncomfortable furnishings. They also suggested the development of outdoor areas for dining, studying, and conversing.

To complement the extensive student survey of reactions to their school environment, interviews were conducted with the teaching staff of Ligon. The purpose of the interviews was to assess the adequacy of the present environment and to discuss the necessary and desirable changes. An activity data sheet was developed on which to record information pertaining to the primary subject area, supporting activities, and their spatial requirements. This information-logging process required teachers to examine critically their present working environment in order that proposed changes have a realistic basis. All activities were coded by desired group size and privacy requirements. This information was combined with adjacency requirements between learning and support areas in the school. Teachers participated in the clarification of adjacency decisions, which were made on the basis of such factors as shared equipment, frequency of student and teacher interaction, and movement patterns, such as traffic flow and circulation. The results constituted an assessment of the present school building as well as a program for modification, or for a new facility.

From the information gathered about spatial activities and their requirements, it was possible to generate use patterns for daily, weekend, and evening occupancy. The occupancy analysis revealed the need for separating and controlling the publicly used areas such as the library, the gym, the cafetorium, and the unified arts area from other learning areas.

It appeared that modifications to the existing building, based on the new program, would be extensive and difficult to achieve. As a result, it was agreed that a proposed design solution would better serve the Ligon community and the School Board, as a model of what ought to occur. The concept that emerged from discussions with students and with teaching staff consisted of a building organized into three distinct types of learning areas:

Open learning: This area would require places for language arts, social studies, and foreign language.

Unified arts: This area would require lecture and laboratory spaces for science, shops, and studios.

Performing arts: This area would require space for theatrical productions, scenery construction, and rehearsal areas for the choir and the band.

Each type of learning area was clustered around its own common area. Performing arts and unified arts were directly associated with the cafeteria, while the quieter learning areas were connected to the library resource center. The major public areas, such as the library and cafeteria, were linked by an exhibition area to the entrance, since they would be used by the community, the students, and the faculty (Figure 2-37). Other more technical information was also integrated into the program. Consideration for thermal comfort and daylight were the most important physical factors that influenced the shape of the building.

Nantucket Elementary School

Attitude Survey	
Charette Process	
Community Meetings	✓
Design-In	
Focused Interviews	✓
Fishbowl Planning	
Game Simulation	
Group Dynamics	
Public Forum	
Task Force	
Training	
Workshop	

SUMMARY

Nantucket Island, off the southern coast of Massachusetts, once flourished through its whaling industry during the seventeenth and eighteenth centuries, when it was the world's whaling capital. During that time, many fine buildings reflecting the New England style were erected. The scarcity of wood on the island, and difficulty of transporting materials to the island, created the need to preserve the existing buildings. By the early 1900s, Nantucket experienced a depression resulting from the decline of the whaling industry. It was not until that time that "off-islanders" began to buy these historic buildings with the intent of preservation. In 1936 the State passed legislation establishing historic districts. Thus, the Town of Nantucket established a Historical District Commission to protect the architectural legacy of its whaling past. Its sole purpose was "to maintain the fundamental harmony of the historic community by having the decision-making authority on all new and renovated structures on the island in reference to its architecture so that the strong influence of existing architecture can be harmoniously blended into the new structures, thus preserving the traditions of the era of 1846." This factor influenced the design of new buildings on the island.

The design of the Nantucket Elementary School by Earl R. Flansburgh and Associates Inc., adapts traditional architectural features to shape an innovative building in harmony with the existing setting. The distinctive materials, proportions, and stylistic characteristics of the residential vernacular is appropriately translated into a large, public structure. In addition to the dominant architectural and historical environment, this 600-student building had to satisfy the programmatic needs of a contemporary educational facility.

CLIENT

The overcrowding of Nantucket's schools and the need for diversified facilities were issues confronting the town's School Building Needs Committee. This committee was composed of seven members with representation from local government, finance, education, and other town committees. The architect, working with the School Building Committee, studied numerous options, including the evaluation of the renovation of existing elementary schools which was considered not to be an appropriate path to follow. The high cost of renovation and the substantial amount of deferred maintenance influenced the town's decision to build a new elementary school, and to abandon the existing elementary facility. A large sandy site covered with low level shrubs and small pine trees was selected. The island, being uniformly flat overall, influenced the low silhouette of the new facility.

The building program was established by the School Administration and by the architects' collaboration with the administration, teachers, students, and the Building Committee.

PROJECT

The design process for the development of this school consisted of a series of meetings between the architectural and interior design staff, the school administration, and the teachers. In developing the architectural character for this building, the Architect took a wide variety of slides of existing architecture on Nantucket Island and presented to the Building Committee a survey of this architecture and the dominant forms it represented. The meetings of the Building Committee consisted of informal discussions with the Architect about design issues. The Architect, however, often met independently with the teachers and representatives of the Committee. The issues that were discussed at these sessions were as follows:

1. *The character of the classrooms.* The classroom character that was analyzed included the height and positioning of sinks, the location of wardrobes, the type of exterior access, and the desirability of painting exposed utility lines bright colors.
2. *The facilities in the project rooms.* In project rooms there were lavatories at adult and student height.
3. *The location and function of the library.* It was determined that the best location for the library was in the heart of the clusters of classrooms. The library floor is depressed two feet below the main floor of the school, providing a separation between classroom circulation and library seating. In addition, the library has a story-telling area that is sunk into the floor.
4. *The character of the kindergartens.* The kindergarten classrooms are located at the front of the school to allow for easy pickup by the parents. In order to achieve a domestic scale to the kindergartens, the toilets were accommodated in small structures giving the appearance of little houses.
5. *How the lunch servings would function.* The lunch-serving area is located adjacent to the gymnasium-cafeteria, which also functions as an auditorium. Circulation to the auditorium is possible without going through any other part of the school.
6. *Outside play space.* There is outdoor play space of a general nature for the entire school, with a special outdoor place for the kindergarten.

The teachers were very interested in a library facility at the center of the school to display the importance of books, as well as to provide a symbolic center for the school. Other ideas generated from their discussions was the location and character of the music room, and the design of the toilet-room roofs. The preliminary designs were reviewed by the teachers and by the School Building Committee. The School Building Committee was responsible for overseeing the design, and their approval was necessary before proceeding (Figure 2-38).

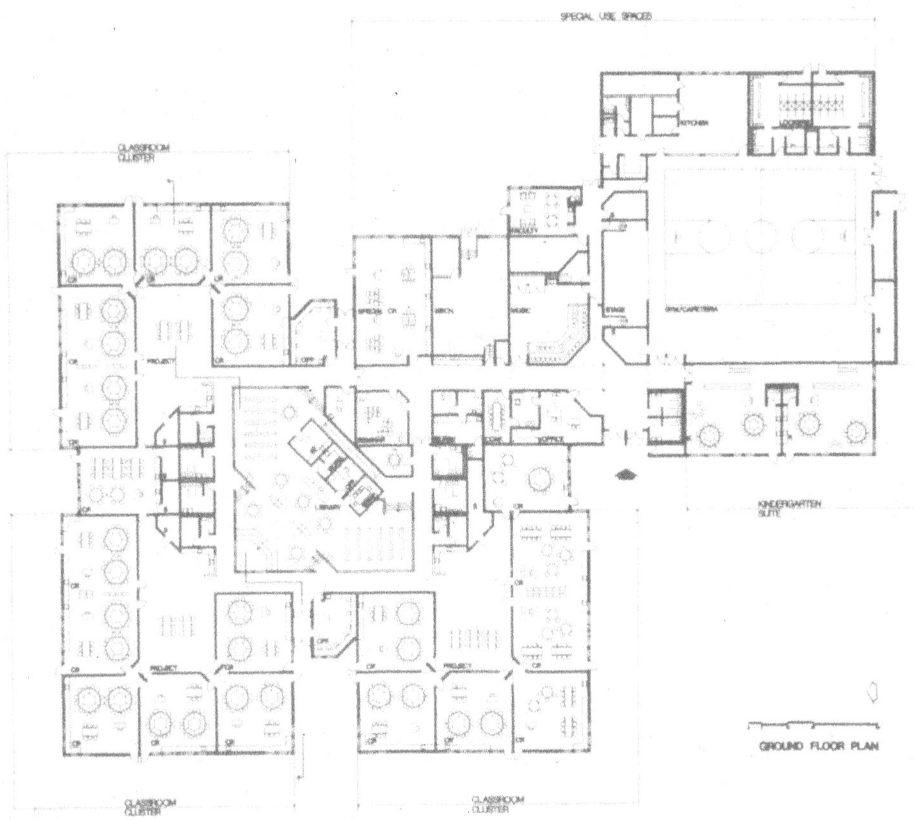

FIGURE 2-38. Plan of Nantucket Elementary School (Earl R. Flansburgh & Associates).

The educational program for this 600-pupil school called for the development of a 20-classroom facility, six of which are oversized to facilitate team teaching, an art room, two kindergartens, and a multipurpose activity area. The design solution consisted of three clusters, each consisting of six classrooms with its own project area, and each having its own identity characterized by the use of different colors. The clusters are grouped around three sides of a central sunken library which is open to classroom activity areas (Figure 2-39). The bright colors, graphics, and large areas of natural light, which contribute to the building's character, also provide for scenic views of the site and adjacent moors (Figure 2-40).

FIGURE 2-39. Central sunken library (Photo: Peter Vanderwarker).

Because of the historic significance of a new building in Nantucket, the Historic District Commission reviewed the progress of the design. Several architectural aspects were reviewed in detail, such as the size and character of the windows, and the character and height of the steeple on the roof (Figure 2-41). The steeple was eventually incorporated into the roof of the entrance. The sloped-roof classrooms were considered very important to the faculty. Both the School Building Committee and the Historic District Commission were interested in the scale, details, and proportion of the new school and how it would relate to the character of the existing town architecture.

The final design solution resulted in the largest building on Nantucket Island. Variations in roof planes, and window heights and configurations typical of buildings on the Island, resulted in a building character sympathetic to the site and to the quiet residential context of the Island (Figure 2-42). The building was completed in 1978, and was awarded design citations both by the American Association of School Administrators, and by the Boston Society of Architects, for the manner in which it reflects the unique character of the small island.

FIGURE 2-40. Building interior (Photo: Peter Vanderwarker).

FIGURE 2-41. Building exterior (Photo: Peter Vanderwarker).

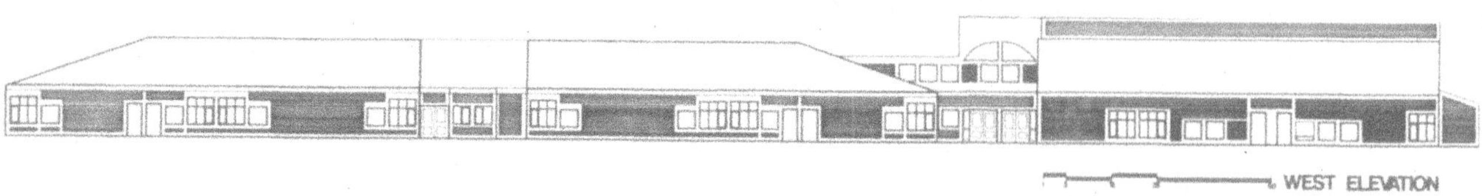

FIGURE 2-42. West elevation of school (Drawing: Earl R. Flansburgh & Associates).

Needham Broughton High School Addition

Attitude Survey	
Charette Process	
Community Meetings	
Design-In	
Focused Interviews	✓
Fishbowl Planning	✓
Game Simulation	
Group Dynamics	✓
Public Forum	
Task Force	
Training	
Workshop	✓

SUMMARY

The haphazard development of an old neighborhood high school, faced with continued random growth, precipitated the need for a feasibility study to explore expansion options. As a result, a design team from North Carolina State University's Community Development Group was requested to develop a needs assessment by the Wake County Public School administration. It was the administration's intention to pursue a consensus approach for identifying needs and priorities for the school community.

Discussion sessions were conducted with students and staff to develop each department's space requirements and to create a profile of student needs for additional support services. Daily patterns of people's movement throughout the campus were mapped to provide site behavior information necessary for site design and planning recommendations. Site-development recommendations were complemented by student assessments of their daily work environment, and of preferences for desired conditions. Alternative site plans provided the school administration with a direction for future action by suggesting advantages and disadvantages of each option. Construction was actually completed ten years later.

CLIENT

Wake County, North Carolina, school officials have presented the school system's long-range construction needs to the community, which required a vote to issue bonds to pay for building projects. A bond issue was needed to finance the $100 million for renovation and new construction to accommodate the present and predicted enrollment surge.

Broughton High School, located in Wake County, has held national distinction as an educational institution for many years, yet its facilities do not reflect that quality, since expansion in the past 30 years has occurred in a haphazard manner. While the county school officials were prepared to evaluate the physical conditions of the present facilities in order to establish budgetary requirements, the high-school staff was concerned that future modifications reflect congruence between student needs and physical changes.

PROJECT

Needham Broughton High School, in Raleigh, North Carolina, was originally built at the turn of the century. It was Wake County's oldest and best high school, and has undergone numerous additions and alterations since then, yet maintained its historic significance throughout the years. Like many inner-city high schools across the country, Broughton was threatened by numerous social forces, such as student rebellion and uneasy integration, which would compel it to change or close. As influential leader and school principal for 21 years, Dr. Richard Jewel has been an instrumental force in helping the school earn national accolades for academic achievement and racial diversity. Faced with a rapid increase in student enrollment, the county school board prepared a renovation budget, without any consideration of the functional or aesthetic implications of additions to a historic building. Because the school administrators and staff were fearful that plans for renovation would exclude their recommendations, they sought design assistance from the Community Development Group. This decision was prompted by the need for involving students, teachers, and administrators in a collaborative process aimed at distilling the expertise from all users of the building into the development of appropriate design recommendations. At Broughton, teacher and student committees were normally set up to have a say on changes.

The Broughton High School campus is located on an inner city, 15-acre site, cornering on two adjacent heavily travelled streets. The school is easily accessible by foot, bus, or automobile, and experiences heavy use by students and community members in the evening hours.

PROCESS

Participation by the school community in establishing user requirements was seen as a strategy that could be managed by the school to provide design guidelines to the county school administration and the future architect. In addition to a program of needs and requirements, alternative schematic plans were developed to demonstrate how verbal statements of requirements are transformed into spatial and formal solutions. To establish a program of future needs, it was necessary to collect two types of information: space requirements to accommodate future enrollment, and satisfaction and dissatisfaction with the present school environment.

An understanding of the academic program, of its organizational structure and of its objectives, was gained through a self-evaluation report conducted by the staff and a visiting team. To further supplement the information base, an inventory was conducted of the basic components of the school, which in this case was the department. A survey data form was prepared to enable administrators and staff to record information related to their objectives, activities, participants, and spatial requirements (Figure 2-43).

Interdepartmental and intradepartmental interactions were described by participants in this process, using a network diagram, where interactions were graphically plotted according to traffic and communications frequency. The process of examining departmental connections, through this diagrammatic technique of user movement or flow patterns, was a revelation to the participants, who were not aware that space planning, as a predictive procedure, could minimize many existing conflicts. In addition to information about user flow patterns of the facility, a series of "real-time" studies were conducted to disclose how students, teachers, and staff use the campus environment, and how they feel about their place in this environment.

Techniques such as cognitive maps provide useful insights into how the campus is understood by it users. These maps are individual drawings that show which street and building features are recalled about the campus (Kaplan 1973). The value of using such a map is

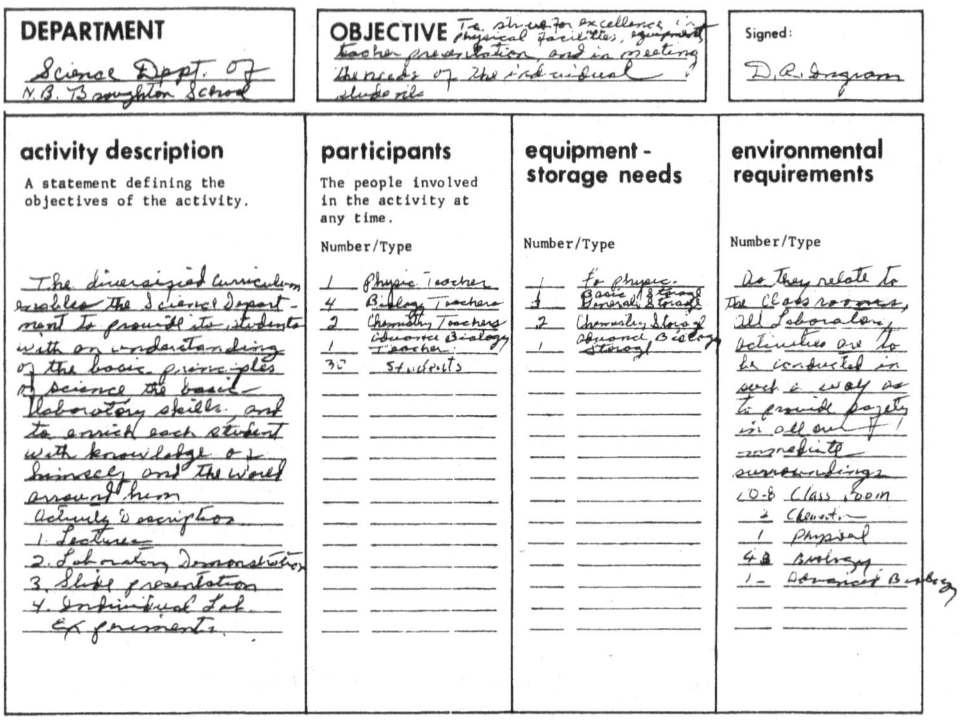

FIGURE 2-43. Typical department data sheet describing general requirements.

FIGURE 2-44. Front facade of existing school (Photo: Henry Sanoff).

based both on the belief that people store information about their environment in simplified form, and in relation to other information they already have, and on the assumption that this information is coded in a structure that people carry around in their head, and that this structure corresponds to the environment it represents. Maps are an indicator of important environmental features that require consideration when modifications are proposed to existing conditions.

Several classes representing different grades were requested to draw maps of their campus. These studies were conducted while students were in their classroom. Since the Broughton campus represents a collection of buildings, it was also necessary to understand the nature of the students' mental picture of the campus, or if they could depict the "main" building. While there is no commonly agreed-upon reference to a main building on the Broughton campus, this perceptual information complements the students' cognitive mapping studies. The results of the image study were very revealing, since all students made drawings of the original historic building, which is listed in the National Register of Historic Buildings (Figure 2-44). For them, the school derived its meaning from the tower. The students' drawings accurately located the entrance and tower of the main building, and carefully located the clock in the tower considerably larger than their representation of the windows (Figure 2-45). Few students, however, indicated building materials in their drawings. The mapping exercise yielded equally interesting results, especially when the students' drawings were compared to the actual environment the drawings represented. The plan drawings of the original or main building accurately depicted its basic form which was articulated by the auditorium, the girls' gym, and the interior courtyard. Very few students were able to represent the limits of the building or its proportions.

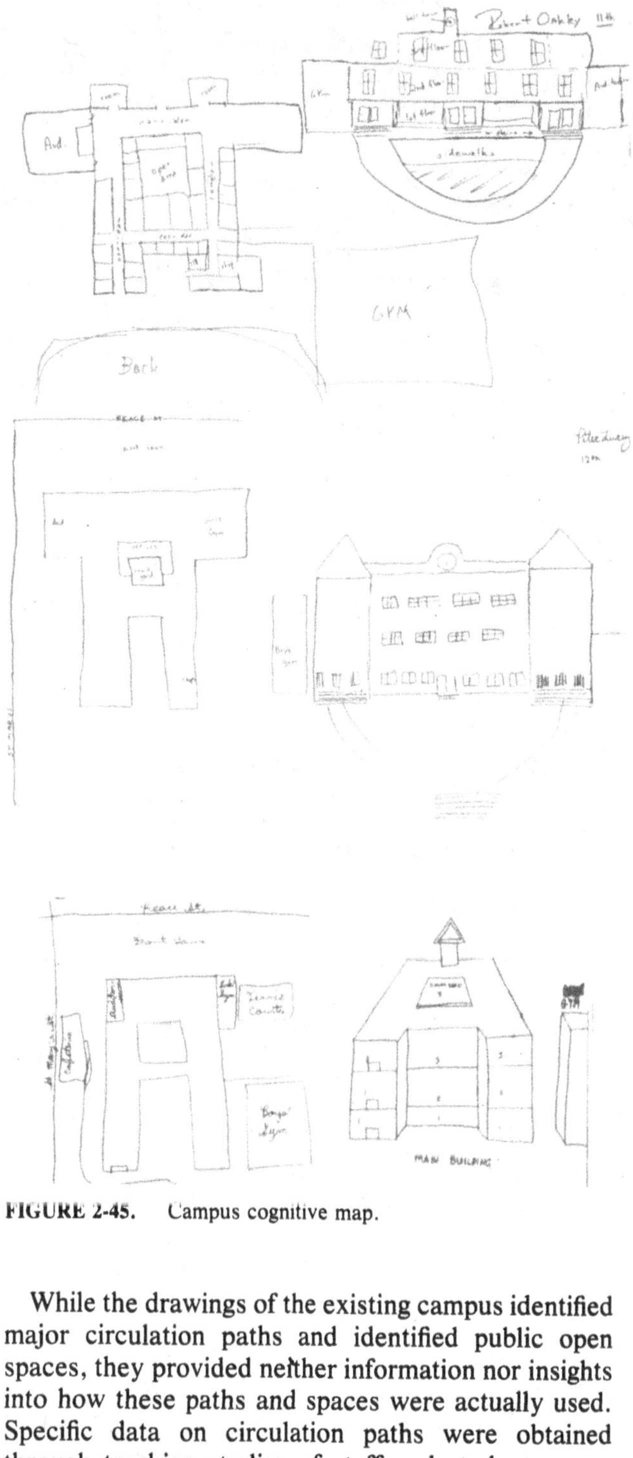

FIGURE 2-45. Campus cognitive map.

While the drawings of the existing campus identified major circulation paths and identified public open spaces, they provided neither information nor insights into how these paths and spaces were actually used. Specific data on circulation paths were obtained through tracking studies of staff and student movement during key hours of the day. By stationing observers at various locations on campus, people's movements were recorded at specific time intervals and subsequently transcribed onto a series of composite maps that described traffic patterns and their frequency (Figure 2-46). The unobtrusive tracking of people's movement revealed daily use patterns, congestion peaks and lows, and points of conflict.

Other information was compiled through student diaries or activity logs, which are a self-reporting of

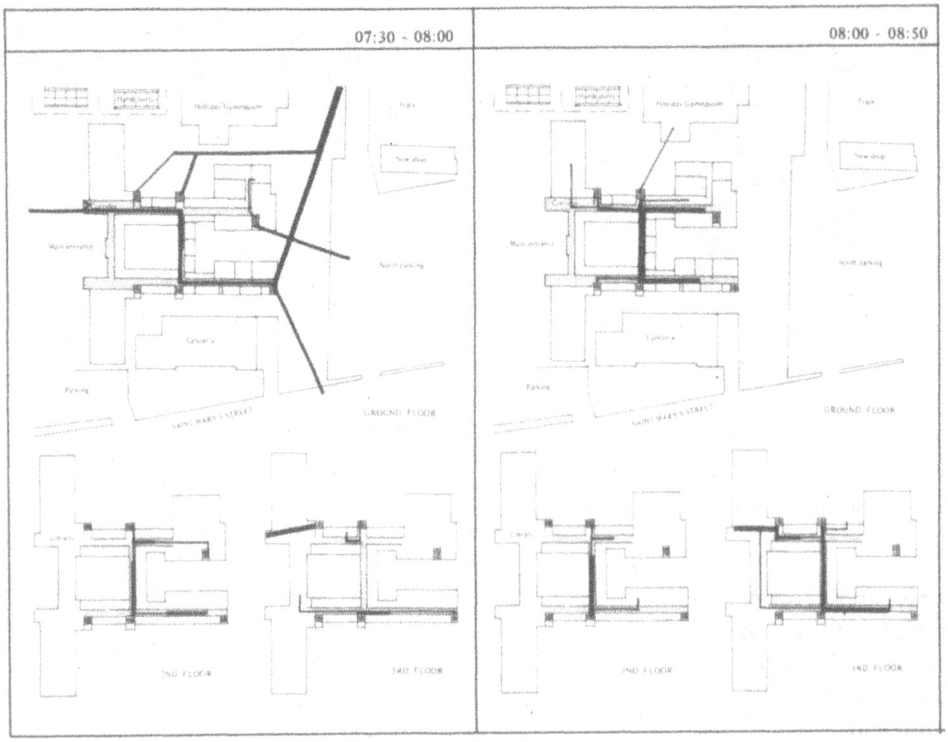

FIGURE 2-46. Tracking study of internal and external movement patterns.

QUESTIONNAIRE

Signed: Amy Wilkinson

EXAMPLE :

Locate on plan	Time table	Describe your activities of each time interval.
00	-07:30	Arriving at school
01	07:30-08:00	Coming from parking to English class with my classmate (3 students)
02	08:00-08:50	English reading, one teacher and 30 students.
03	08:50-08:55	Going to locker and talk with 3 friends, then to science class
04	08:55-09:10	Biological lab, working with 3 classmates as a group, 21 students in class and one teacher.

Locate on plan	Time table	Describe your activities of each time interval.
1	07:30-08:00	Leave my house - arrive at school - go to my locker and talk with 3 friends then go to English class.
2	08:00-08:50	English - watch film and take notes One teacher and 19 students
3	08:50-08:55	Leave English - go to my locker and then to homeroom, stop at water fountain and talk to a friend.
4	08:55-09:10	Homeroom two teachers - 17 students Talk to two friends
5	09:10-09:15	Leave Homeroom and go to the bathroom, leave and talk to 5 friends, then go to 2nd pd - French
6	09:15-10:05	2nd pd. - French - go over worksheets One teacher - 21 students
7	10:05-10:10	Leave 2nd period and walk to 3rd period - Photography w/ 2 friends.
8	10:10-10:55	3rd pd - Photography develop pictures, make prints One teacher and 20 students
9	10:55-11:00	Leave Photography - walk to 4th period, talk to 2 friends
10	11:00-11:50	4th period - Attendance Office Assistant - run errands and call homes. Work w/ 2 other assistants.
11	11:50-12:40	5th period - Data Processing - work w/ computers One teacher and 18 students
12	12:40-12:45	Leave 5th period - go to my locker and leave campus for lunch with 2 friends.
13	12:50- 1:35	Off Campus Lunch - usually to my house
14	01:35-01:40	Return to school - go to 7th period - Anatomy
15	01:40-02:30	7th period - Anatomy - listen to Oral Reports One teacher + 30 students
16	02:30-02:50	Leave Anatomy and go to Park Dr. and see what everyone is doing. Walk w/ 3-4 friends.

FIGURE 2-47. Typical daily log of student activities.

activities recorded at specific time intervals (Figure 2-47). This technique combines the features of observations and questionnaires, though it relies on the accurate logging of events by students. Self-observation has the additional advantage of clarifying information obtained from more conventional observation methods. As a result, it is possible to obtain a clearer picture of user activity and the corresponding campus locations of that activity. The activity log provides answers to the questions of who, where, and when of building use.

Student reactions to their existing environment provides yet another level of information that has a direct bearing on design proposals. By comparing existing settings with proposed school settings, it is possible to assess the relative satisfaction with a wide range of different types of learning environments. By presenting photographs of classrooms, work areas (Figure 2-48), study areas, and corridors, students were able to compare their environmental situation with three additional alternatives. Their preferences for the best settings were not surprising, since they were all characterized by informal, relaxed, daylight-filled settings containing learning areas that were highly concentrated. None of the existing school settings was included in any of the choices made by students. The exercises identified those elements that were most important, which portions of the existing building should be preserved, and what would constitute a satisfactory image.

1. Please select in order of preference where you would like to WORK.

   A__ B__ C__ D__

2. Your 1st choice is selected because :

3. Your last choice is due to :

FIGURE 2-48. Photo comparison of existing space to alternatives.

IMPLEMENTATION

The insights developed by the design team from results of the questionnaires, maps, and tracking studies provided a basis for generating alternative design concepts. Discussions with teachers and administrators also contributed to an understanding of the impact of the building design on student learning. This was particularly significant at Broughton High School, since the high enrollment required double-shift scheduling, which precluded the use of student free time, a source of considerable dissatisfaction. Discussions about alternative design concepts with faculty, students, and administrators, helped to evaluate each proposal according to its fulfillment of the school community's needs. These discussions involved having small work groups carefully consider four concepts: three proposals considered a new campus, while the fourth proposed an addition to the existing building (Figure 2-49).

While the proposals advocating a new campus were not considered feasible alternatives, they did offer amenities that could conceivably be integrated within the existing campus. The most important feature voiced by a majority of the participants was the need for an outdoor meeting place, or grand court, achieved by using the new addition to terminate at the north end of the campus and to create an internal connection from the gymnasium to the main building. The spatial requirements for the new addition that resulted from an analysis of existing facilities consisted of predominantly science classrooms.

The results of the investigation were submitted to the Wake County Public School System as a recommended procedure and solution for the school expansion. While there were several minor renovations to the school during the next several years, it was not until a decade later, in 1990, that the architectural firm of Milton Small was commissioned to prepare a design solution for the school's needed expansion to accommodate 1,900 students. A program for a new science addition was given to the architects by the Wake County Public School System. Since the elapsed time from the previous study was ten years, the project team headed by Associate Kerry Kane analyzed the existing use of space and possible locations for the new addition. Meetings were held with the principal, science teaching staff, and special consultants, to establish current science education spatial requirements. The procedure followed by the architect varied from the new approach used by the County School System, where specialists and staff consultants provide architects with a completed program, eliminating the need for direct contact with members of the local school community.

The solution proposed by the architect located the new science addition in the same position as it was initially proposed (Figure 2-50), in order to establish a grand court and serve as a secondary entrance to the school. The new addition was designed to respect

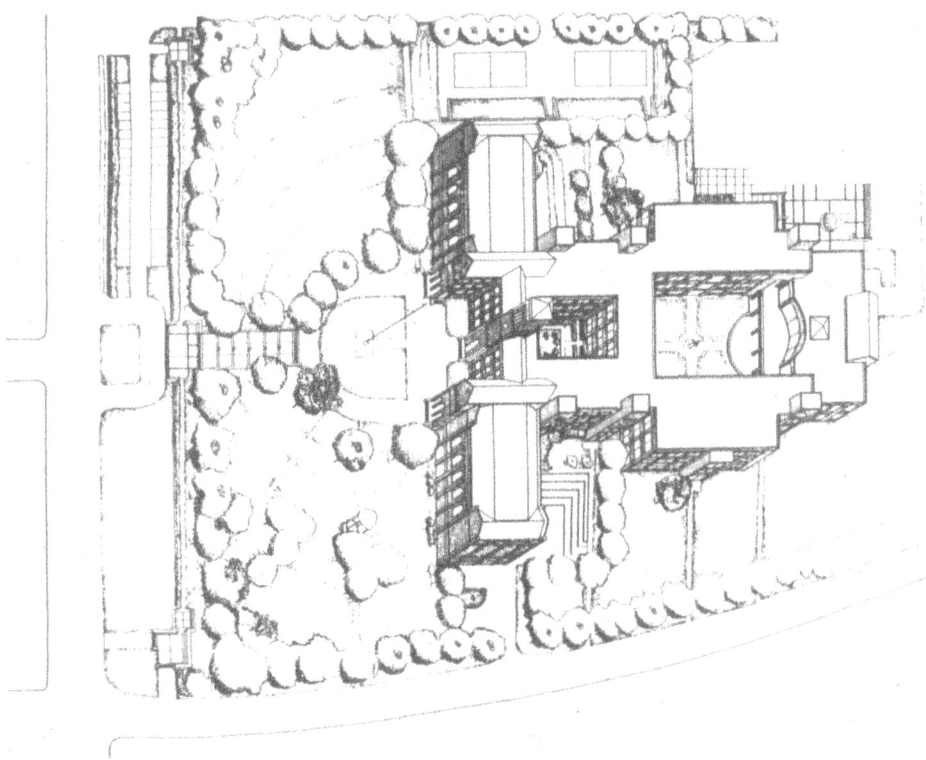

FIGURE 2-49. Proposed addition to existing school (Drawing: Tun Sing Chen).

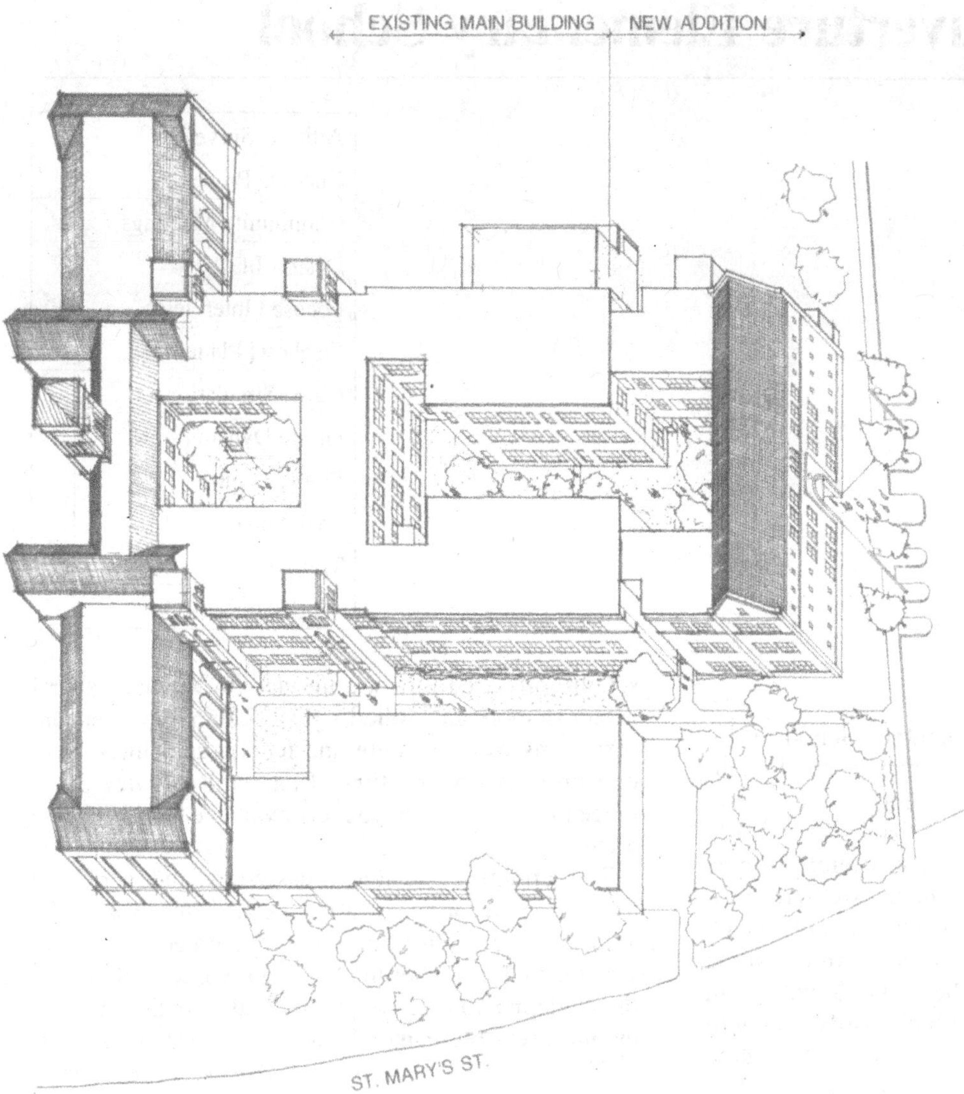

FIGURE 2-50. Plan of addition as built (Drawing: Kerry Kane).

the overall image of the existing building complex, in spite of the fact that it had undergone several additions since the original building was constructed (Figure 2-51).

FIGURE 2-51. Addition to existing school (Photo: Henry Sanoff).

ACKNOWLEDGMENT

A note of thanks to Kerry Kane, Associate of Milton Small, Architects, Raleigh, North Carolina, and Project Coordinator, who provided important insights about decisions related to the building process.

Toussaint Louverture Elementary School

Attitude Survey	
Charette Process	
Community Meetings	✓
Design-In	
Focused Interviews	✓
Fishbowl Planning	
Game Simulation	
Group Dynamics	
Public Forum	
Task Force	
Training	
Workshop	

SUMMARY

The Toussaint Louverture Elementary School is located in a North Central Miami neighborhood occupied by Haitian immigrants. This forgotten, inner-city neighborhood had grown so rapidly that by 1985, Little Haiti needed a school. The Dade County Public School administration hired Architect Bernard Zyscovich to design this "special needs" school, which serves a community where poverty and overcrowding are the norm. After visiting other schools with both crowded classrooms divided by chalkboards, and with strict programs without provisions to accommodate the entire student body, Zyscovich created a building with several courtyards, open corridors, and classrooms designed with movable soundproof partitions. Frequent community visits also helped to create a building to reflect the strong cultural identity and intense community ties.

CLIENT

The client for this school was Dade County Public Schools in conjunction with the State of Florida. Schools in Florida are built according to a code described as Chapter 6A-2, which consists of a set of formulas based on the student population, which determines the number of classrooms. The general guidelines, then, are elaborated by county school boards into education specifications. The local school board invited several architects to submit proposals for the design of the new school located in an urban, low-income Haitian neighborhood. The firm of Zyscovich, one of the architects short-listed for the new school, prepared for the interview by visiting several urban schools and soliciting and comparing their observations with the state and federal guidelines. Federal programs at the time, Chapter 1, provide assistance in making extra teachers available in low-income areas.

The architects visited classrooms and spoke to teachers and administrators, especially principals, who are often well informed. They noted several recurring conflicts resulting from faulty interpretation of the guidelines. For example, federal guidelines in low-income areas recommend student–teacher ratios of 15-to-1, instead of the traditional 30-to-1. To accommodate this requirement, Zyscovich noted that movable chalk boards were being used to divide the larger classrooms, thereby satisfying federal guidelines. Zyscovich also observed high noise levels between classes that were often disruptive, causing unnecessary discipline problems in the classroom. The perceptiveness of the preliminary investigation presented in its oral presentation persuaded the local school administration to award the project to the Zyscovich organization.

PROJECT

The Toussaint Louverture Elementary School was the first urban school constructed in the county in many years. The school was named after an eighteenth-century Haitian leader who led the slaves in a revolt against French plantation owners in 1791. Located in a low-income Haitian neighborhood, the school population was set by the Dade County School Board at 900 students, and would include kindergarten through fifth grade. In 1992, the reported school population was 1,200 students. The site, too, was selected by the local school administration. The building review process for a public-school building is complex and usually overseen by a district project manager representing the County. Specialists are assigned by the school district to consult with the architect and are required to approve the design proposal. Also included in the review process are the members of the Haitian community.

Initially, the building design was influenced by problems observed by the architects during their visits to other urban schools serving the target population. They also observed a standard pattern of modern school buildings that were built in the district, described as *pod schools*. The pod schools are a series of four classroom units, either one- or two-story, that also include a media and food-service pod, arranged on a grid. The pods are easily recognizable because they are repetitive units. Departure from this norm was an important aspect for Zyscovich because the new school needed to have a special presence, since it had to relate to a Haitian community and reflect a more personal and sympathetic image.

New classrooms were designed with an acoustic seal, yet maintaining the 15-to-1 student ratio in semi-classrooms that share a common space, storage, toilet, and vestibule. It was also apparent from Dade County Public School's strict program that the traditional auditorium had been removed and replaced by a cafeteria-auditorium combination called a cafetorium, which often required repeat assemblies. The architect's solution was to provide an outdoor area or academic courtyard, where the entire student body could come together (Figure 2-52).

Another fact learned from the architect's visits was to learn that students were dropped off as early as 6 A.M., while classes normally start at 8 A.M. By combining the teachers' planning rooms to form towers, the architects enabled teacher surveillance of children's activities prior to the beginning of classes. This interpretation of the location of teachers' rooms also represented a departure from the traditional approach of scattering them throughout the building. Other factors influencing design decisions included the location of the kindergarten as a separate entity, allowing for a separate drop-off area where parents can bring their children directly into the classroom. The kindergarten also had its own courtyard for outdoor play.

The preliminary design solution, which was based on input from the consultants and the architect's observations, was then presented to the Haitian community in the form of models and color renderings. Almost 500 community residents attended a regular meeting where the Toussaint School was only one of the agenda items. While the community members were excited about this building as an important cultural symbol, they noted that the yellow color scheme proposed by the architect was typical of what was used on jails in Haiti. The connotation, therefore, was not appropriate for their new school, though they favored a building that stressed light, color, and access to the outdoors. This large community meeting generated

FIGURE 2-52. Largest courtyard with concrete stage (Photo: Steven Brooke).

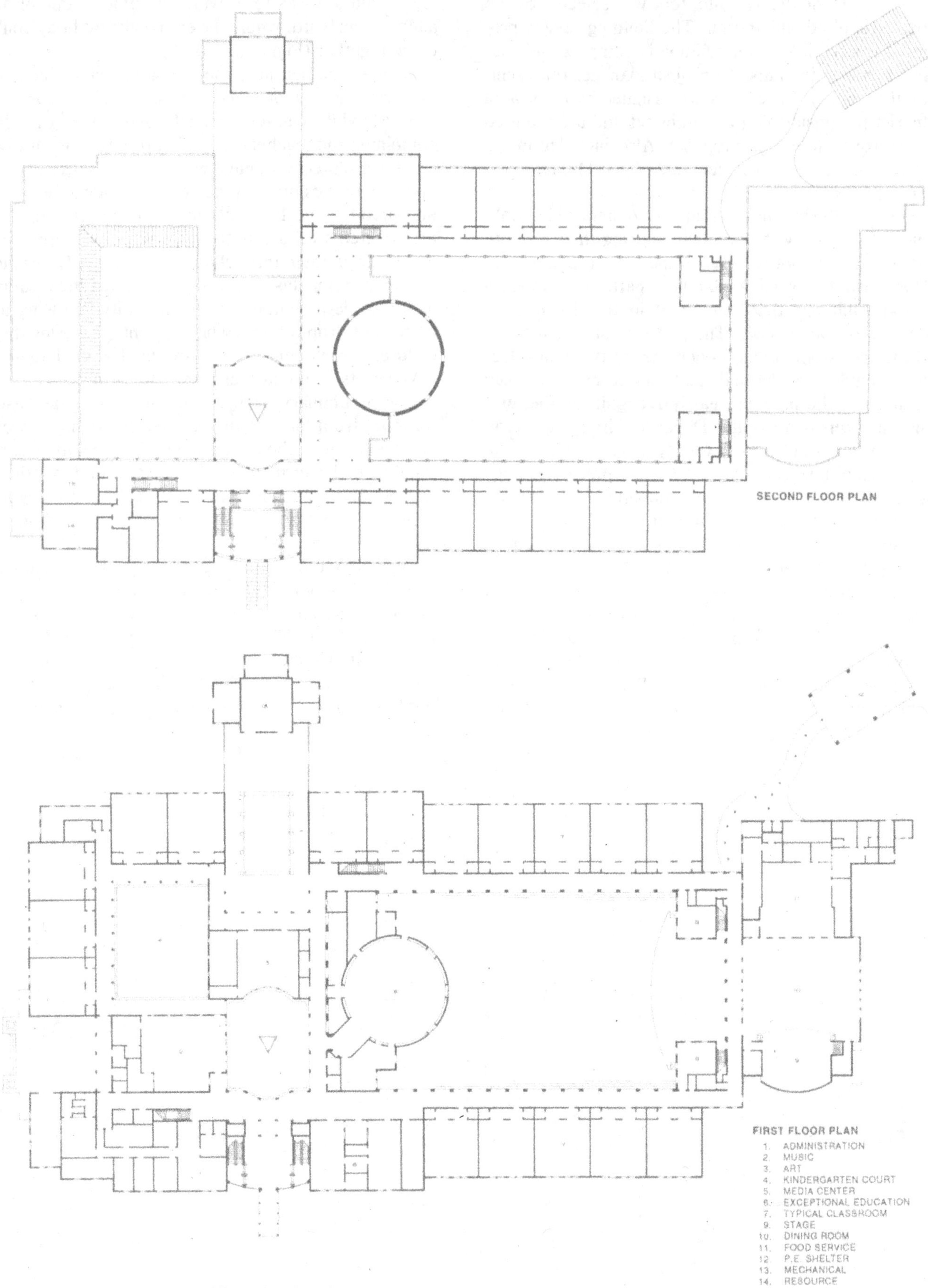

FIGURE 2-53. First- and second-floor plan (Drawing: Zyscovich).

FIGURE 2-54. Balcony looking on to courtyard (Photo: Steven Brooke).

smaller meetings with businessmen as well as with other organizations, for example, who desired to have the school be a source of festivals to introduce the south Florida population to the Haitian culture.

The Toussaint Louverture School has four courtyards (Figure 2-53), and all classrooms open onto them, linked by open-air corridors (Figure 2-54). The building forms are accented by colors reflecting a Caribbean palette. The original student population has doubled in the five years since its construction. Part of this rapid and unpredictable increase in population is that single-family houses are often occupied by more than one family.

AFTER-OCCUPANCY RESPONSES

Several years after occupancy, teachers from the Toussaint Louverture School responded to a questionnaire, asking them to list the three best and least-liked features of the building. Not surprisingly, the teachers commented on the attractiveness of the building, its lively colors, both interior and exterior, and the open design concept. The courtyards and patios, especially the outdoor stage, appeared to generate many outdoor activities. The abundant use of windows, especially in the art room, was also mentioned as a desirable feature.

Many of the features least liked about the building resulted from the increased student population — such as the lack of adequate toilet facilities and an overcrowded, noisy cafeteria. The covered, but open, corridors and stairs elicited a negative response from teachers who reported getting wet during a downpour. Acoustics, too, in other large-group areas, such as the media center, was reported as a disturbance. Combining a cafeteria with an auditorium, or cafetorium, while often seen as a space-saver, is another source of continual controversy. Often the auditorium stage is not adequately planned for entering and exiting actors without being seen by the audience.

Generally, there is a sense of pride associated with the Toussaint Louverture School as a carefully designed building, and as a community focal point. Recently, the cafetorium was filled with young Haitian-American school children, listening to a talk given by the first Haitian Miss America, crowned in 1990.

3
Alternative Schools

Alternative Schools

Alternatives have always existed in American education. The availability of alternatives has varied with the social and economic conditions of the times, but from colonial times to the present, educational alternatives have diminished. Educational opportunities in the colonial period constituted "a fascinating kaleidoscope of endless variety and change," reported Cremin (1970) in *American Education: The Colonial Experience*. There were enormous opportunities and countless types and modes of instruction during that period. Schooling went on everywhere, not only in schoolrooms, but also in kitchens, churches, meeting houses, sheds erected in fields, and shops erected in towns. The proliferation of types of schools was linked to the rapid increase in printed material for instruction and self-instruction which enabled people to consider a vast range of possible life-styles. In spite of the diversity of schools, they had a minor role in colonial America. The concern for literacy stimulated the development of laws making parents responsible for their children's education. By the mid-nineteenth century, the concept of universal elementary education was accepted. By 1900, compulsory education was assured. In America's 200-year history, what was originally a wide range of educational alternatives has been reduced to one monolithic public school system without choice for the individual family (Smith, Barr, and Burke 1976).

In a democratic society people should have choices in all aspects of their lives. The present monolithic structure for public education in which many students are assigned without choice is what Postman and Weingartner (1971) describe as "a fraudulent pluralism." In the present system people have no choice but to accept the approach offered by the schools. There is a view that people closest to the action should have the opportunity to decide what goes on in a school. The local community, the students, their parents, and the professional staff should share in the decisions that affect their own lives.

"In a society as diverse and complex as ours, no institution can effectively serve all people," says Owen Kiernan, executive secretary of the National Association of Secondary School Principals. While many students respond well to what educators describe as the traditional approach, others require alternatives in non-traditional categories. The very high rate of high school dropouts each year supports the assertion that standard offerings do not meet the needs of all students.

Many developments, such as consolidation of school districts, construction of larger school buildings, governmental intervention, and nationalized curricula, have operated to standardize schools. The creation of alternative schools is in part a reaction against standardization, because alternative schools would diversify educational opportunities within a community (Smith et al. 1976). The general revolt of the 1960s in education was against the assumption that learning must be imposed on children by adults, that learning is not something that one does by and for oneself. The activities of the traditional school were seen as institutional rather than personal and human. While there is no single goal that characterizes all alternative schools, the concept of freedom is central to the thinking of people involved in non-public "free schools."

There has, however, been some resistance to free or alternative schools and programs. Much of this reaction stems from the stigma of non-public alternative schools that opened in the late 1960s, and became associated with alternative life-styles and alternative communities. Many of the alternative schools of that period were influenced by A.S. Neill, the founder of a private school in England, whose *Summerhill* (1960) philosophy stated that letting children do what they want will eventually result in effective learning. This view of education has not had wide acceptance in the United States.

Another barrier to the acceptance of the alternative school concept is the pervasive view held by administrators, policymakers, and citizens that one school can be developed to satisfy the needs of all students. Historically, more experimental schools have developed in the non-public sector, and many educational researchers credit recent development of non-public alternative schools for stimulating public alternatives. The most noteworthy are the Montessori and Waldorf schools. Montessori schools are founded on the principles of Maria Montessori, who believed that children should learn by doing, and that a school should develop responsibility, self-discipline, and good work habits. The Waldorf School, which originated in Germany based on the pedagogy of Rudolf Steiner, believes in the art of awakening children to themselves in order to integrate the development of intellectual, artistic, and moral faculties, or the whole being, in all areas of learning.

Considerable pressure, however, allowed "alternative schools" to emerge as part of the public system, many of which were similar to the Summerhill type of "free school." The most dramatic was the "school without walls" as illustrated by the Parkway School in Philadelphia, which began in 1969. The school is structured around tutorial groups of 15 students, a faculty member, and a college intern, and provides traditional courses of study as well as relationships with over 200 local institutions. Art is studied in the museum, economics and math in the bank, mechanics at local garages, and child development at child care centers (Bremer and von Moschzisker 1971).

There is much confusion about what constitutes an alternative school. While no definition can be applied to all alternative schools, there are certain characteristics that can distinguish them from the standard school. Alternative schools must involve choice and they must be different from the standard school in the community.

Alternative public schools traditionally have had several different roles. These purposes have been characterized in John Fritz's *My Encounter With Alternatives* (1975) as:

- Providing educational opportunities for dropouts or disruptive students
- Providing opportunities for students to explore which are not available in regular schools
- Serving as experimental laboratories for developing ideas for subsequent wider application
- Developing alternative programs to satisfy the diverse needs of students and parents

One characteristic of alternative schools that distinguishes them from standard schools is that they are more responsive to a perceived educational need in the community. The alternative school usually has a comprehensive statement of goals and objectives since such programs usually go through a planning and development process that evokes clearly stated purposes. The school also provides opportunities for students, teachers, and parents to participate in the decision making on the school's program and on their individual roles within the school.

Bruce Cooper (1971) identifies six alternative school models:

1. Parent-teacher cooperative school
2. Community freedom school
3. Therapeutic school
4. Free high school
5. Public alternative school
6. Residential free school

Each model demonstrates different purposes; however, there are several representative goals that were identified in a systematic study of contemporary alternatives (Duke 1978). The most characteristic goals were related to exploration (freedom to pursue personal interests) and participation (in which students, parents, and teachers participate in the governance and administration of the school while demonstrating a particular approach to education). While participatory goals focus on the group and the community, therapeutic goals center on the individual student and effective growth. Finally, academic goals expose students to a broad variety of learning experiences. Many alternative schools exhibit a blatant rejection of the pedagogical traits widely perceived to exist in conventional schools.

The emergence of contemporary alternative schools constitutes a challenge to the bureaucratic structure of public institutions as regards their goals and methods. Although alternative schools have been present before, they have never existed in such abundance as they do currently.

Restructuring Schools

At an educational summit meeting President Bush and the nation's governors agreed to engineer a radical restructuring of America's educational system (Miller

1989, Oct. 4, p.1). The impetus for reform was primarily economic, since the United States was on the verge of being displaced as a major force in the world economy. The nation's sinking economic productivity identified schooling as part of the problem and part of the solution (Guthrie and Kirst 1988). This recognition, which began in the early 1980s, sparked a plethora of national and state reform reports. There was a growing belief that the current system was beyond repair and that a complete overhaul of the educational system was needed. As a result many school districts and states have explored new patterns of management, organization, and delivery of educational services. Many of the restructuring efforts tend to focus on decentralization and argue that the individual school community must become the focus of attention, and that the resources and authority to change must reside with those teachers, parents, and administrators who are closest to the learners. Proponents of this viewpoint believe that school-based management (SBM) allows principals, staff, parents, and students to be in control of their own destiny. With greater authority and responsibility comes greater accountability. Therefore, greater authority will increase the involvement and interest of all with a stake in a school. Such involvement will benefit the students. Allowing decisions on finance, staffing, attendance, content, and organization to be made by individual schools may result in more attention directed to teaching and learning, rather than to the implementation of plans formulated elsewhere (Elmore 1988).

Participation in management leads to a sense of ownership, which is linked to greater acceptance of and cooperation with the implementation of decisions, and ultimately greater satisfaction for all involved. The major rationale behind SBM is the belief that the closer a decision is made to a student affected by the decision, the more likely it is to benefit the student. Under a system of school-based management, accountability for student achievement rests with the individual school. People most aware of the diverse problems and needs in a particular school are those working at that level.

The Hartsbrook Waldorf School

Attitude Survey	
Charette Process	
Community Meetings	✓
Design-In	
Focused Interviews	✓
Fishbowl Planning	
Game Simulation	
Group Dynamics	✓
Public Forum	
Task Force	
Training	
Workshop	

SUMMARY

The Hartsbrook Waldorf School in Hadley, Massachusetts, began in 1981 as a result of the initiative and vision of a small group of people. The rapid growth and interest in the school enabled their move from the basement of a house on a small biodynamic farm in Amherst to a larger building, the Ben Smith Tavern, an 18th-century inn in Hadley. The success of that move stimulated the next challenge: the need for new buildings on a new site. The school purchased 19 acres of land close to their previous location, land surrounded by farms and a view of the Holyoke Range. After acquiring the site which sits in a meadow with a brook running through it, the school hired the architecture firm of Thompson and Rose of Cambridge, Massachusetts. Through intensive conversations with parents, teachers, and trustees, Thompson and Rose arrived at a design that reflects the intentions, needs, and ideals of those living in the school community.

CLIENT

An important feature of the Hartsbrook School is that the faculty is responsible for managing the school. They believe that this form of administration allows those most closely connected with teaching to make decisions regarding curriculum, school policy, and long-term objectives. The faculty receives support in its work from the Board of Trustees, who are active in capital development, building projects, and fiscal management. Parents are involved in all aspects of the children's education and in the life of the school. A Parent Council provides a forum where parent interest in educational and administrative issues may be discussed with teachers and trustees. The faculty have all undergone graduate training in the principles and methods of Waldorf education, which assert that children are at the center of the school. The class teacher meets the class at grade one, and continues with these children through eight grades. This provides a continuity of human understanding and a constancy balanced with a multi-faceted curriculum, one that exposes the student to many subjects and specialty teachers.

A small group of supporters founded the Hartsbrook School in 1981. Its continued growth led to the need for additional space, and the purchase in 1987 of ten acres of land through which the stream "Hartsbrook" runs.

PROJECT

Hartsbrook is a Waldorf School based on the work of Austrian philosopher Rudolf Steiner, who sought to develop free and self-directed human beings. Waldorf schools now represent the largest independent school movement in the world, with a total enrollment of over 500,000 students. Waldorf education is founded on respect for the child as a developing human being, and their teaching seeks to *prepare the mind, enrich and ennoble the feelings, and bring forth the strength of commitment necessary to meet the self-chosen aims of life*. Learning is conceived as an *enlivening* process. Learning is achieved through the integration of intellectual, artistic, and moral capacities. An important feature of the school is that the faculty assumes the

FIGURE 3-1. Long-range development plan (Drawing: Thompson & Rose).

responsibility for administration, supported by the Board of Trustees who are active in capital development and building projects. The teachers, trustees, and parents were interested in a new building that responded to the Waldorf ideals, as well as to the surrounding community of Hadley and the Pioneer valley. The school community sought "an architectural design which, while innovative, is also attentive to the particular vernacular of the New England farming landscape. We have aimed for buildings which in their forms and placement suggest the scale and simplicity of farm buildings while also expressing the very contemporary nature of the school." The 20-acre master plan proposes a hillside clustering of buildings for classrooms, music, arts, crafts, gymnasium, and dining hall, connected by gardens, walkways, and play areas (Figure 3-1). The positions of the buildings were established by placing wood poles, string, and flags to orient the buildings and the spaces between them to the topography, and to selected views of the landscape. These buildings will constitute the entire middle, elementary, and pre-school.

The first phase of the project involved the construction of a building containing space for four classrooms, and a room for assemblies and performances. This building, Piening Hall, named after a former teacher, is proposed to be the most prominent structure of the hillside cluster. It includes a bell tower, and a two-story lobby to exhibit children's work. At the center of the lobby floor, an inlaid geometric pattern reflects the position of the foundation stone in the earth below and marks the compass points. From the lobby is a staircase to the second floor assembly room with an exposed vaulted ceiling, to be used for activities such as eurythmy, movement and dance gymnastics, chamber music, and festive gatherings (Figure 3-2).

The ground floor of the building contains two classrooms and a solar gallery, and an interior arcade with a stone floor designed to absorb solar energy by day and radiate heat into the building at night. As funds become available for further construction, this building will be converted to its original intended use of offices and faculty rooms.

Piening Hall is a passive solar building, using the winter sun as a source of heating. The building is made from regionally quarried stone, and other "nontoxic" materials, and avoids the use of synthetic materials.

PROCESS

The architects set up an office in a farmhouse in the town of Hadley to understand fully the community's goals and aspirations. They attended many community functions and festivals, and participated in informal discussions in their office. In addition, there were a number of formal parent meetings, generally attended by about 20 people. The parents, however, were most comfortable when they reacted to propositions offered by the architects, leaving the educational issues to the teachers. Their primary concerns were related to materials, construction, and an image that was in character with the farmyard setting. The parents' roles were most active in the construction stages through painting, carpentry, and landscaping.

The architects initiated correspondence with parents, community members, and financial supporters

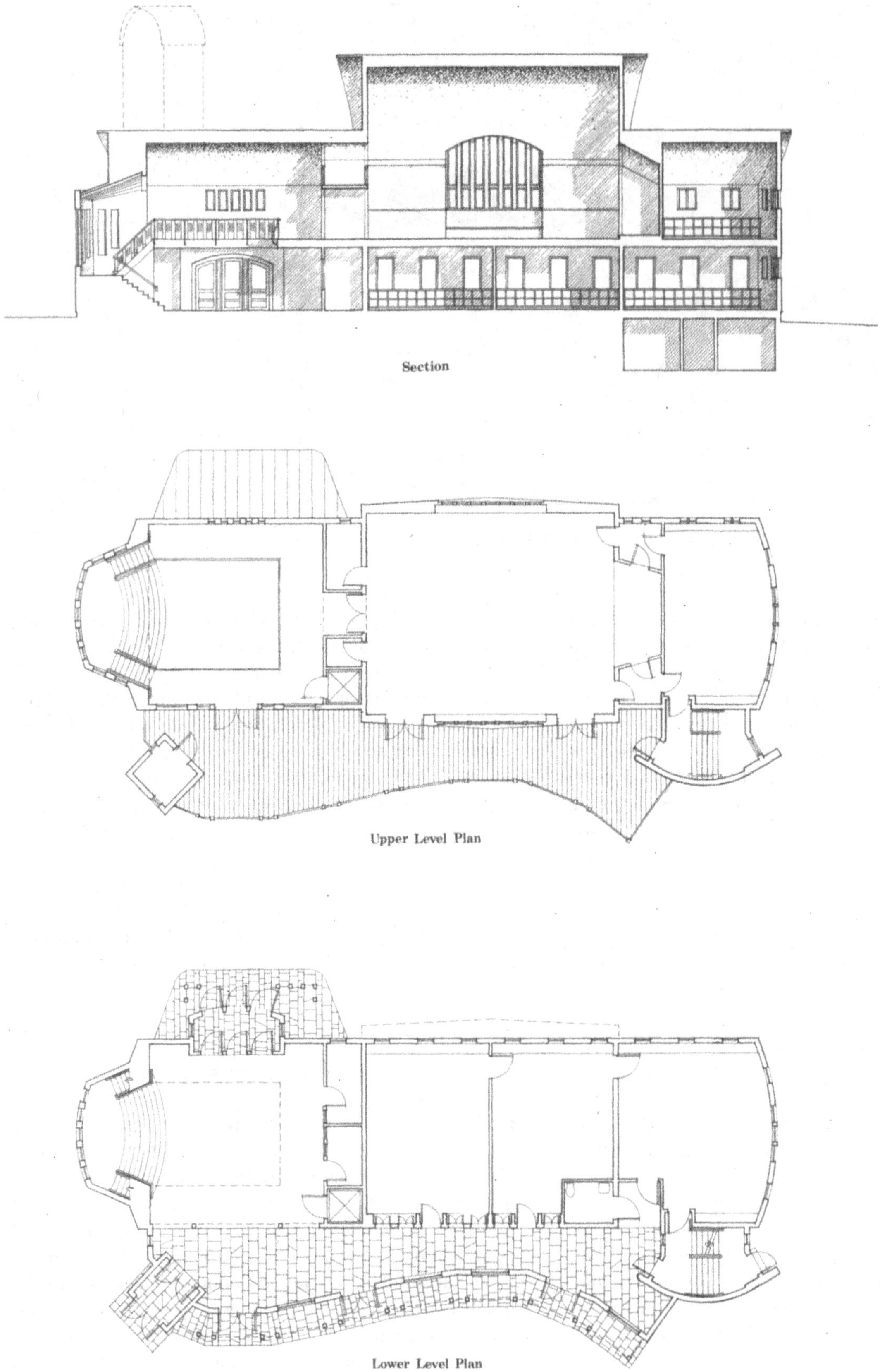

FIGURE 3-2. Floor plan of school (Drawing: Thompson & Rose).

by asking them for their ideas about the new school. The faculty, too, were contacted, and asked to furnish wish lists of their desires. The following comments were extracted from the architects' notes with faculty and parents:

Take forms of the building from the landscape.
Make a friendly gesture with the forms and the roof.
Buildings should talk to one another.
Children need a sense of orientation.
Beautiful, but not flamboyant, not pretentious, not monumental
People need places that are unique, that they can identify with.
Sense of change connected to corridors
Corridors should become a landscape in the building.
Follow the sun-morning work academic (Main lesson in the morning: The sun with loving light makes bright for me the day).

The primary design process of the new Hartsbrook School began with weekly meetings, lasting approximately two and one-half hours, of the coordinating committee that provided the philosophical foundation of Waldorf education. The membership included a trustee and founder, a parent-artist, and two faculty members, all of whom reported back to their individual groups. They were described as "imagination meetings" because they stimulated discussions about the spatial and experiential qualities of the master plan, the buildings, and their special places. Committee members, seated around a circular table, expressed the hopes and desires for the school through "chain stories," as they described aspects of a space or program. Participants worked with paper, pencil, and clay to give shape to their ideas.

Maryann Thompson and Charles Rose state that:

> The meetings focused on the curriculum and its appropriate enhancement through architecture and landscape. Our discussion considered such topics as the spiritual and philosophical foundation of the Waldorf education, the learning path of the child, the characteristic qualities of each class year, and how these qualities may be embodied architecturally. We also explored the vernacular architectural impulse, the land, and its history. The relationships of classroom spaces to the immediate site and distant views were carefully considered as were the spaces themselves, in terms of form, color, proportion, and detail.

The weekly discussions often focused on the relationship between the space to the activities it enclosed. One of the chain stories revolved around entering the lobby space, its view to the mountains, and the stair sequence leading up to the eurythmy or assembly room, the largest volume in the building. Using crayons on newsprint paper, people began sketching the form of movement from the lobby to the assembly room. One of the committee members generated the original form which was elaborated upon by the architects. This form represented one of the major decisions that grew out of the meetings, as did the building and its relationship to the hills beyond.

During the weekly meetings participants devoted a considerable amount of time to developing the program, reflecting the Waldorf educational philosophy. Fruitful outcomes from these meetings included the organization of the program on the 19-acre site in relationship to soil conditions, agrarian vs. wilderness views, relationships to the high and lowlands, the wetlands on the site, as well as to site specific issues.

Most of the decisions made at community meetings relied primarily upon site and building models, rather than drawings. Participation was most effective in discussions about the image and character of the building. The final design solution, the architects suggest, was primarily a response to community aspirations for a building that would embody the dynamic aspects of the educational program. As a result the building took on a more sculptural quality than their earlier designs had suggested.

Due to the large physical distances separating the surrounding parent community of 27 towns, the architects also conducted formal meetings with parents in their own houses. The architects and the coordinating committee visited 12 different "neighborhood groups" to discuss the project in small gatherings of ten people each, in order for all people to have a voice. Children, too, participated in the design process by sketching their ideas about the school.

Another strategy employed by the architects, characteristic of Waldorf communities, is the staging of seasonal festivals, which they developed around the building of the new school. The entire parent community participated in the celebration of the building, more so than in the planning meetings. The first was an equinox festival which consisted of driving a four-inch-by-four-inch column into the ground on the site at the center of the lobby. To the east a long, eight-foot-high white banner was hung across the site. As the sun set, the shadow of the column moved across the banner from north to south. Issues related to the sky and to astronomy are part of the curriculum, thus the marking of the orientation was an important factor for the community, raising their awareness of the features of the site. The festival also included story telling and kite flying. Another festival, in which 300 people participated, occurred prior to pouring the foundation. It was a Foundation Stone Laying ceremony, in which a copper vessel dodecahedron was placed at the location of the wood column; there, students and faculty made wishes for the building, along with a Foundation

FIGURE 3-3. Volunteers working the site (Photo: Maryann Thompson).

FIGURE 3-4. Community encircling Piening Hall on its Dedication Day Festival (Photo: Charles Rose).

Verse containing the former chair Ekkehard Piening's aspirations for the school (Figure 3-3). The building opening was the occasion for another festival in which people held hands and circled around the building, marking its circumference (Figure 3-4). These festivals were considered to be a source of inspiration about the building. The architects described their intent as creating a process and a ritual about the building.

Thompson and Rose also seek to educate the child through their architecture. This is consistent with the Waldorf philosophy of enlivening, which integrates the analytical and experiential aspects of learning. Through its design, the building will convey *the basics of passive solar architecture, and will present each day an example of a responsive and appropriate technology.* The solar gallery informs young people about passive solar energy, and how the building is being heated. They experience the movement of the sun by changing light qualities in different spaces. The exposed mechanical system and flue describe the heating system. Also, the use of different types of wood in their natural finish reflects the variety of tree species in the area, each used in special ways and for different purposes. Generally, the architects were sensitive to all aspects of the environment that would sensitize the children to these natural phenomena. This direct experience would then lead to a more analytical understanding, which is the basis of science education in the Waldorf tradition. The choice of building color, too, reflected an important element in the education process. Education in the arts begins with an understanding of the emotional qualities of color. Since

FIGURE 3-5. School building in its natural setting (Photo: Steve Rosenthal).

color conveys meaning, the decision of the building color took on special significance and consequently involved many community members. The choice of color for the first building was a controversial community decision. Faculty, parents, and trustees gathered to review a wide range of color options provided by the architects. They arrived at the choice of blue because they believed it was an intellectual color representing the essence of the Waldorf philosophy, as well as the character of the surrounding community.

Incorporating non-toxic materials into the making of the building was an integral aspect of the teaching philosophy, which embodies a strong sense of ecology. Concepts of organic farming are linked to homeopathic medicine, appropriate technology, and the use of natural materials. This integrative or holistic sensibility is pervasive in all aspects of teaching in the school.

AFTER-OCCUPANCY RESPONSES

An evaluation questionnaire was distributed to the teaching staff of the Hartsbrook School. In it they were asked to respond to the three features they liked best and least about the building. Commenting about the building features liked best, the majority of teachers believed that "the innovative design gives Piening Hall its landmark appearance. It is a distinct building that invites comment and puts our school on the map in our area." The form of the building is described as a striking sight in the natural landscape (Figure 3-5). Equally noteworthy is the lobby, cited as a positive feature because of its two-story height, and its evocation of a grand feeling in a relatively small building. The gentle curve of the corridor or arcade is inviting, and helps to create a sense of school community in the building. In general, the soft curves, the use of materials, and the way light moves through the building were features unanimously appreciated by the teachers.

The most common concern voiced by the teachers in responding to the building evaluation was the noise generated by the building's mechanical system, and the general problem of noise transmission throughout the ground floor. While some areas are reported as noisier than others, the "live" sound of the building drew the most comments. Other concerns tended to be rather small, idiosyncratic details, except for storage, which always seems to be inadequate.

Apparently the positive feeling of spaciousness the building evokes has some negative side effects, namely noise transmission. One teacher responded that the present use of the lobby area, for example, is not the way it was originally intended to be used. The enthusiasm displayed in the descriptions of the most-liked features of the building, however, appear to outweigh the features liked least. As one teacher states,

"I find it (furnace noise) annoying in an otherwise serene and inspirational building."

ACKNOWLEDGMENT

Many of the details surrounding the participatory design process were thoughtfully narrated on a micro-cassette tape by Maryann Thompson and Charles Rose. The teachers, too, of the Hartsbrook School were helpful in completing an evaluation questionnaire of the building.

Hokio Beach School

Technique	
Attitude Survey	
Charette Process	
Community Meetings	✓
Design-In	✓
Focused Interviews	
Fishbowl Planning	✓
Game Simulation	✓
Group Dynamics	
Public Forum	
Task Force	
Training	
Workshop	✓

SUMMARY

This project was conducted by a New Zealand team consisting of Chris Watson, Ministry of Works and Development (now called Works and Development Services Corp.), John Gray, David Kernohan, and John Daish, School of Architecture, Victoria University of Wellington. An evaluation of the process was conducted by Michael Edge. This paper describes the use of a process designed to establish requirements for change to a New Zealand residential school for boys. The Department of Social Welfare (DSW) operates the school as a correctional environment for about 60 boys. The case described here is from a Ministry of Works and Development (MWD) project. Thirty-two participants representing six "interest groups" took part in a two-day event. Day one was devoted to a series of Post Occupancy Evaluations (POE) using a "touring interview" method. The briefing workshop on day two was designed as "games" which utilized the results of the POE: an *Ideas* game involving each group in making decisions about what to keep, and a *Planning* game involving each group in mapping the location, extent, and urgency of changes. Plenary sessions compared results of group work, identified issues, and worked towards consensus. MWD and DSW executives rated the process successful and an improvement on the usual procedures in briefing and early design.

CLIENT

Hokio Beach School is the only extended stay residential school in New Zealand for boys of 11 to 14 years who are "disturbed, difficult, or delinquent." The Department of Social Welfare (DSW) sends boys to Hokio for periods of time ranging from a few months up to two years. The school provides for the educational, recreational, and social needs of about 60 boys in an attempt to rehabilitate them into society. The DSW had become concerned about the physical condition of the school and in May 1984, they asked the MWD to look specifically at substantially upgrading the kitchen to comply with Department of Health standards. After inspecting the school, the MWD concluded that major alterations would be needed to the kitchen and to other buildings as well. The DSW agreed to an MWD proposal to conduct a feasibility study with the intention of developing a strategy to improve the whole school.

PROJECT

This project was developed in several phases in order to consider the type of physical improvements to an existing school that would have long- and short-range effects on the entire school. Surveys of the site, buildings, and the mechanical services were carried out by the appropriate experts. From these surveys it was possible to suggest action for maintenance and general upkeep of the facility, but not to suggest changes which the DSW would know to be valid for the users of the facility. The problem facing the MWD and DSW was that the requirements for Hokio Beach School were uncertain, yet they had to make decisions about changes to the facility.

The MWD invited the Architecture Research Group

at Victoria University of Wellington (VUW) to monitor the assessment process at Hokio and extend the process so that the recommendations would directly inform designers and managers of the necessary changes.

The MWD and DSW questions were: How can we know what is required at Hokio, taking account of the range of interests and *needs* of the different people involved? How do we establish what should be kept, what should be changed, and the *priorities* for change? And given the diversity of interests, how can we work to reach *agreement,* within weeks, rather than months, on what should be done?

Planning and operation of the study was a joint effort among DSW, MWD, and VUW personnel. Overall coordination and project management was provided by MWD. Two members of the Architectural Research Group at VUW were project consultants, and later worked as Facilitation Group leaders in the field work. A Task Group was established to manage the POE. The four members of the POE Task Group included two from DSW, and two from MWD, and also included two females, two males, two Maoris, and two Pakehas (Europeans). The Task Group planned and trained together, but in the field, members worked in pairs. Each pair facilitated and recorded concurrent touring interviews to ensure that the POE events could be completed in one day.

A Facilitation Group was formed to run the briefing (programming) workshop which followed the POE. The seven members of the Facilitation Group included all four POE Task Group members and assistants. The POE used a series of touring interviews, in which each interest group toured the facility with a Task Group who asked open-ended questions to encourage participants to talk about important aspects of the facility. Each interview concluded with a meeting to review and record the main observations of each group.

The workshop was in two parts: the *Ideas* game and the *Planning* game. In the Ideas game, each group clarified their objectives vis-à-vis the school, and matched the most important of these with their key observations from the POE. In the Planning game, each group decided what features of Hokio should be changed, and arranged their priorities for change. Participants presented the results of each game in plenary sessions to identify areas of agreement and disagreement between groups.

The same participants were involved in all stages of the study. The Task Group selected them after discussion with the school principal, DSW executives, and VUW consultants. Six distinctly different interests were organized into the following seven participant groups:

- Maintenance
- Staff
- Residents (boys), group 1
- Residents (boys), group 2
- Management
- Casual Visitors

A total of 32 people, consisting of all groups, participated in the POE on day one, and in the workshop on day two.

DATA ANALYSIS

The POE's (seven touring interviews) and the workshop games (Ideas and Planning) resulted in four categories of data for analysis:

1. Observations and recommendations by each group about the existing facility
2. Objectives of each group with respect to the school
3. Priorities of each group expressed as an ordering of their main recommendations
4. Annotated maps showing each group's decisions about what should be retained, and what should be changed

In addition, flip charts and graphics from plenary sessions served to confirm agreements, disputes, and results of negotiations between groups. Keywords were assigned to code each topic raised by the participants, and then values were established for each entry to enable the topics to be ranked. Numerical values for the "recommendation" and "map" sets were devised by counting the number of mentions. Values were given to the "objectives" set of topics by counting the frequency by which topics were satisfied by an objective. Weighted values given to the participant indicated "priorities." All topics were then listed in average weighted rank values. Fifty-two separate topics were identified.

POE Touring Interviews

Each touring interview consisted of three parts: a briefing session, a walk-through session, and a recommendation review session (Figure 3-6). In the briefing session, the facilitators introduced themselves and outlined the procedure for the POE.

Participants were asked to describe their interest in the facility (i.e., "Please tell us what you do here."). A walk-through route was then planned with each group (see Figure 3-6, panel 2). The participants were asked to suggest any places they particularly wished to visit or talk about. The facilitators indicated that they were interested in being told about "what works" and "what doesn't work." They suggested the POE need not be confined to physical things but may include comments on non-physical features of the facility such as operational or management matters. The

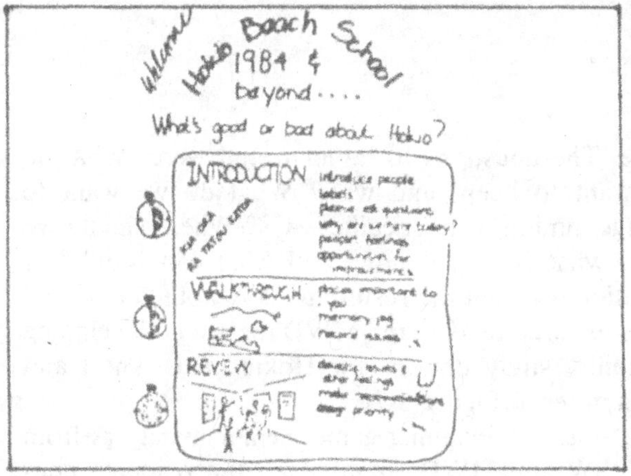

Introductory Flipchart

A Walkthrough

A Review Session

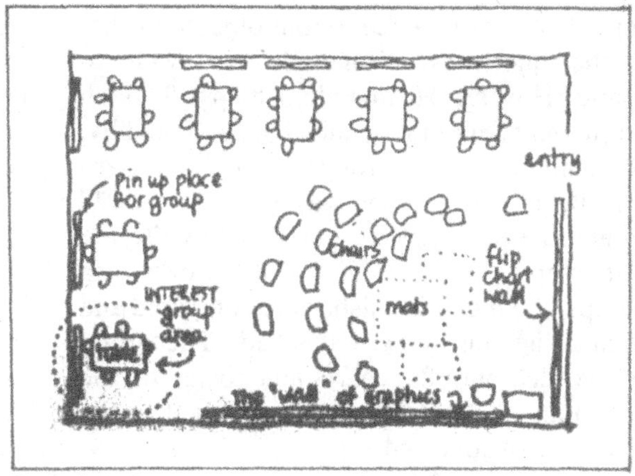

Room Layout

Interest Group at Work

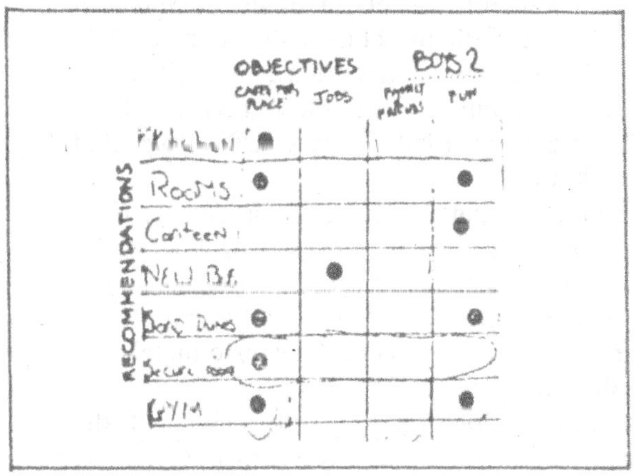

"Boys 2" Ideas Game Chart

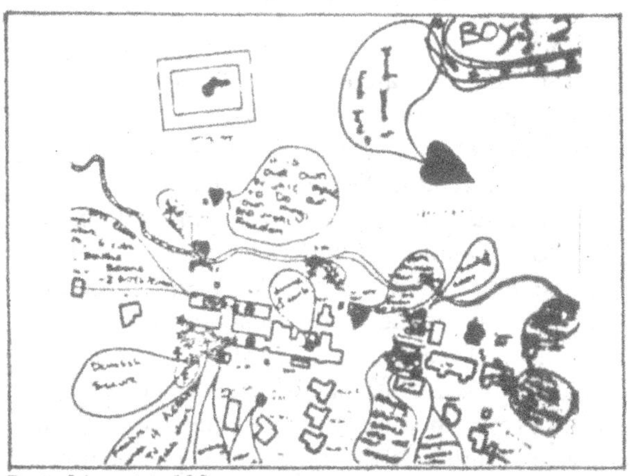

Part of Annotated Map

FIGURE 3-6. Project flow process.

walk-throughs were group interviews done "on the move." Participants were encouraged to talk about whatever they found important while the facilitators prompted with nonleading, open-ended questions.

In the recommendation review session, general discussion led to group observations and recommendations which were recorded in their agreed wording onto flip charts.

Workshop: The Ideas Game

Each group's task was to agree to four objectives that answered the questions, "What do we want to achieve?" and "How can Hokio School help us?" Each participant thought about these questions individually, discussed them in interest groups, then in plenary sessions. To begin, each person was given a list of 20 objectives and asked to select, adapt, or rewrite the seven most important statements. Then, working in interest groups, the individual lists were compared and discussed until agreement was reached. The group lists were recorded onto flip charts and posted on the wall. Discussions about differences continued in the plenary session that followed.

In round two of the Ideas game, participants were asked to compare or "match" a limited number of recommendations with the objectives established in round one. The starting point for this activity was each interest group's recommendations and comments from the POE, already recorded on flip charts and posted in each work area.

After reviewing and discussing their charts, each group selected seven of the most important recommendations, which could have been modified or expanded. The summary statements were posted in order of importance to permit the groups to match and compare their results.

To conclude the Ideas game, each group, with the help of the facilitator, self-reported their findings and identified observable patterns in their relationships. For example, "cared for place" was stated by Boys group two, and was strongly supported by five of the seven recommendations, whereas there was no support for the objective, "to develop settings for contact with family and friends." The facilitators closed the session by drawing attention to similarities and differences between the findings of each group, while encouraging future discussion of their differences. One difference concerned the "secure" (two cell-like rooms used as a lock-up). This emerged later as a major issue.

Workshop: The Planning Game

The purpose of the Planning game was to obtain an annotated map from each interest group which synthesized the work of the groups in the POE and Ideas game. The questions to be answered were: What do we want to keep, and why? What do we want to change, and in what specific ways? Where should we start, what is urgent now, and what can wait? The intention was that the resulting maps would be passed on to the architects in the MWD for use in developing feasibility study options for Hokio in the short and medium term (Figure 3-7).

To start the Planning game, senior managers from the DSW and MWD summarized the resource constraints for the project and outlined their work programs and the mandates of DSW, MWD, and the workshop. Participants sought and received assurances that their POE and workshop findings would be acted on, with the understanding that the final decisions rested with the DSW executive.

Each group then worked to decide what should be kept, and what should be changed in relation to the school, both physically (environmentally) and organizationally (behaviorally). To do this they used different shapes of self-adhesive labels to indicate on the map *keep* items and *change* items. Non-physical or non-locational items were noted on a blank part of the same sheets. In round three, groups discussed their options, and annotated the maps with their conclusions.

All participants came together in a final plenary session to compare annotated maps, to note the degree of consensus achieved, to note or resolve any further issues raised, and to discuss future action. One of the facilitators summarized each of the seven maps, indicating points of substantial agreement, and minority views.

The facilitators then brought the workshop back to reviewing the agreements which had been reached. To end the business of the workshop, some DSW and MWD participants outlined their answers to the question, "What happens now?"

POE and Workshop Recommendations

During the POE, the seven participant groups generated a total of 79 statements covering 41 separate features or aspects of the Hokio Beach School. Two features, "kitchen" and "secure," were mentioned by six of the seven groups. Several of the most frequently mentioned features, "kitchen, bedrooms, administration, A and B rooms, and boilers," account for almost half of the recommendations. Participants observed that the majority of the recommendations referred to specific physical features of the environment, such as particular rooms, or building elements, while four of the features (10 percent), "community interaction, family visit, atmosphere, and cultural perspectives," pertained to non-physical or behavioral aspects of the facility. The remaining features (about 20 percent)

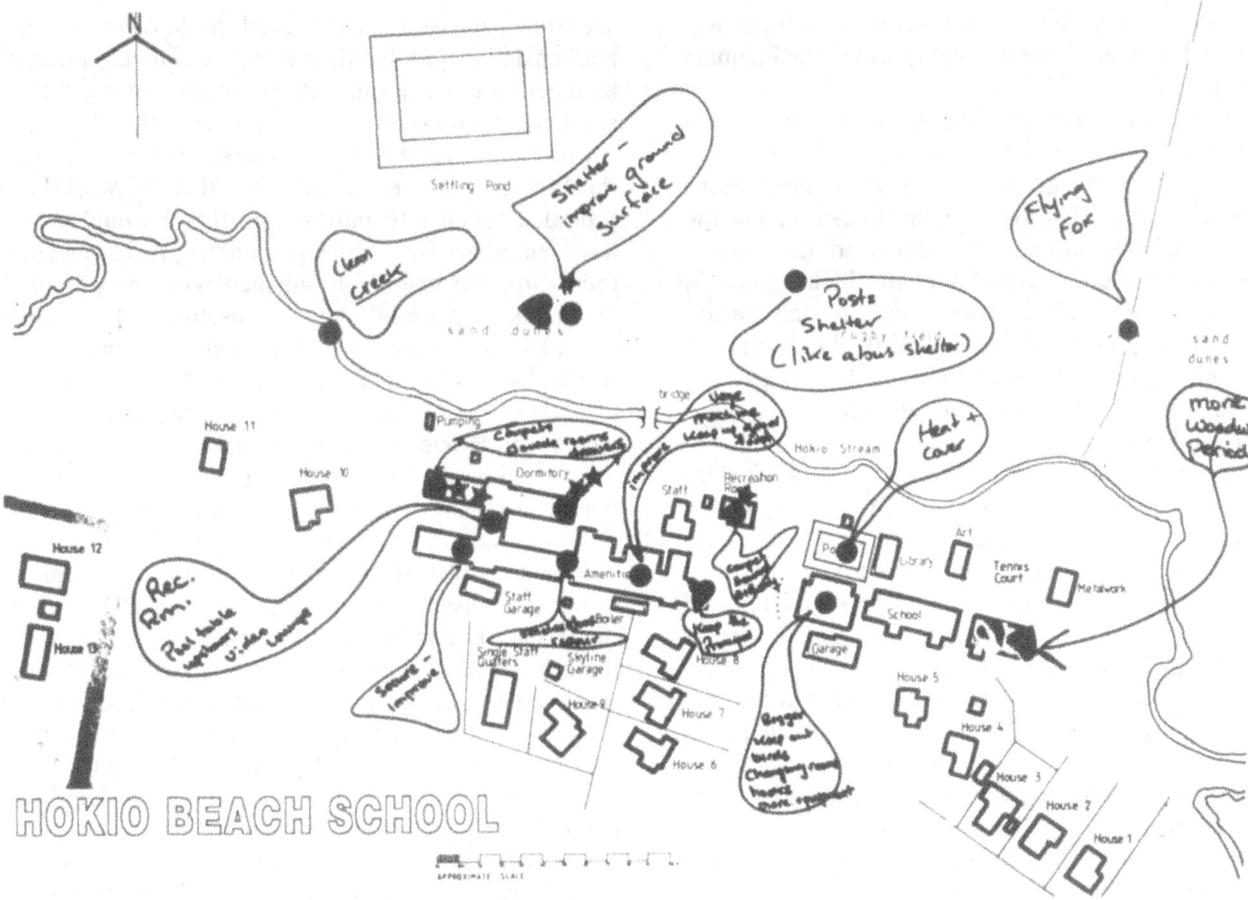

FIGURE 3-7(a). Annotated site plan by boys.

FIGURE 3-7(b). Walk-through.

FIGURE 3-7(c). Boys' planning group.

were less specifically tied to a nameable part of the environment. These included, "general upgrade, sports, sand dunes, and outside."

During the workshop, participants were given opportunities to change, add, or revoke recommendations made during the POE. Thirteen new features were documented during the workshop, for a total of 54 features of Hokio about which the participants wished to make comments. The new items appeared at different stages in the workshop; six during the Ideas game, and seven during the Planning game. From the 18 features addressed by two or more groups in the POE, only "community access, video, dining room, and repaint" were not mentioned in the Planning game maps.

Kitchen improvements, the most frequently discussed issue, had the highest priority. In the POE, six of the participant groups made recommendations about the kitchen. During the Objectives round of the Ideas game, the kitchen also received the highest score. In the matching round of the Ideas game, in which recommendations were ranked by the participants, the weighted rankings placed the kitchen at the top, well ahead of "bedrooms." In the Maps, the kitchen was identified by six of the groups, as were "pool" and "secure."

The secure was notable because it was rated as satisfying only one objective, but appeared high in all other recommendation counts, and as a priority. This finding suggests that there were hidden objectives associated with this feature. This view was supported by the fact that it was equal with the kitchen in number of mentions in the POE and Maps.

The "outside" feature was of special interest because, unlike the secure, it was rated very high because of the number of objectives satisfied, though it was not given very much attention in terms of recommendations.

"Outside" is one of the small number of features that are essentially good. This feature also received top billing from the participants when they were asked to nominate "things you like and want to keep about Hokio." All groups except Official Visitors, identified "outside" as special and valuable. Some groups wished to do things to enhance the outside, such as make a flying fox in the sand dune area, or clean up the polluted stream, but no one wanted to make substantial changes to the outside.

Assessment

Although both the MWD and DSW shared the basic operational question, "What is required at Hokio?" the MWD and the designers' focus was on the needs of the different people involved, especially as they related to the built environment. The POE and workshop provided a "shopping list" of needs expressed as recommendations, but the MWD did not have the mandate to undertake further design without formal instructions from the client. To facilitate client decision making, MWD and DSW prepared a report describing the POE-workshop events and outcomes.

A client assessment of the study was provided by the Director of Residential Services, Department of Social Welfare, Head Office, Wellington, who had attended both the POE and the workshop as a member of the "Management" interest group. He reported having some misgivings prior to the POE and workshop activities because he had "asked the MWD to fix the kitchen and feared that they were about to use a sledge hammer to crack a nut." Although he did not feel a sense of personal involvement during the POE, he contributed several positive suggestions for improving the POE process. He commented that the workshop provided "access to information that I would never have got otherwise." Reflecting on the process and the follow-up, the client felt satisfied with the progress made and remarked, "a very useful, sensible and down-to-earth report, which helped in setting priorities and providing a sense of support." In a letter to the MWD, the Department stated its requirements for change at Hokio, in terms of immediate work (11 items) and longer term work (ten items). The client's overall assessment of the study, in comparison with other decision-making experiences, was that this process had enabled them to move from a statement of needs to decisions and instructions to MWD quicker than usual. In addition to the efficacy of participation, the client was also aware of a more positive attitude from all participants than in his previous experiences.

With the expectation of appreciable benefits for Hokio's users, building controllers, and designers, the participatory nature of the POE and workshop was extended into the design approval phase.

Normally, design approval in government is a protracted process, involving the exchange of documents by mail with little opportunity for face-to-face discussion of any aspect of the project. Communication is distorted by the compounding of inadequate summaries, contextual information being lost, and a bureaucratic communication style that suppresses emotions and imagination. What was needed was a way to circumvent this ineffective, unwieldy, and time-consuming communication process. The client agreed that personal contact would be a more effective approach for continuing the process. As a result, design development meetings were proposed to evaluate proposals, to explore opportunities for design improvements, and to negotiate modifications as conditions for design approval.

Two months after the POE, four design development meetings focused on projects for bedroom modification, alterations to the gymnasium, improvements to the living room, and a conceptual plan for the school. There were four parts to each meeting: a verification of design objectives, a description of the proposal, a review of participants' strengths and weaknesses statements, and a discussion to agree to changes necessary to satisfy reservations about the design proposals. The meeting invitation included a statement of aims, an agenda, and sketch designs for each of the projects to be discussed. Attending the design development meetings were representatives of the Department of Social Welfare head office, the principal, other users of the Hokio Beach School, and the architects.

In order to be prepared for the meeting, participants were asked to consult with their peers to decide on the strengths and weaknesses of each project. Peer consultation was important to ensure that all ideas were adequately represented. Participants also received POE recommendations, qualitative design objectives (from the workshop), MWD comments, and DSW instructions for each project, all of which were used to generate design ideas. The purpose for the distribution of this information was to develop criteria with which to evaluate design proposals.

In the POE and workshop, interest groups identified particular objectives such as "make our place more cared for and attractive" and developed design solutions with the aim of satisfying these objectives. This meeting provided an opportunity for participants to assess the success of this process. Each project *was described* with the aid of the sketch designs in order to allow participants to consider strengths and weaknesses of the proposals. Modifications *were then proposed* to satisfy the weaknesses that the participants identified.

CONCLUSION

Senior managers from DSW and MWD assessed the process and judged it a success in terms of:

- Setting priorities, which helped decision making about the changes needed
- Establishing an agreement that decisions would be supported by staff and others involved in the school
- Gaining "better" information in the programming process
- Accurate and rapidly produced documentation usable by the client and architect
- And helping people gain an understanding and empathy for others, as well as building organizational support

The Hokio Beach School project lends support to the belief that the participatory process is efficient, cost effective, and produces better results than more traditional methods. Information was well documented, organized, and easily accessible by all participants. Facilitation graphics enabled all participants to see how their statements influenced the design modifications, while notations on the drawings became a permanent record of all transactions.

POST MORTEM: EVALUATION OF THE PROCESS

Several months after the design development and evaluation meetings, a perception study gauged the ways in which participants believed the process was significant to them as individuals, to their job, to their department, to other participants, and to future design and evaluation processes. A summary of responses to tangible short-term results indicated the implementation of many minor physical improvements. Intangible short-term results consisted of improved communications among kids, teachers, and managers; awareness of problems and needs of each other; and general improvement of morale of people working at Hokio.

Participants generally regarded the process as personally rewarding, challenging, educational, and enjoyable. For administrators and managers, the process developed a better understanding of people, clarified many issues, and reinforced the belief that involving users is a much better way of doing things. Generally, participants felt it was significant that all interest groups had gathered together, especially since this was the first time it had occurred. From the client's point of view, the process was valuable since it met their objective of obtaining information that would facilitate informed and confident decision making.

ACKNOWLEDGMENTS

The participatory briefing workshop was designed and facilitated using methods adapted from the work of Henry Sanoff, Gerald Davis, Robert Shibley, and Linda Schneekloth. Robert Morans assisted in designing the study while visiting New Zealand.

The workshop "facilitation graphics" were done by Peter Beaumont using methods developed by Daniel Iacofano.

Task group members in the POE and assistant facilitators in the workshop were Neal Cleaver, Raima Haronga, Tere Insley, and Tony Nixon.

Mowbray College

Attitude Survey	
Charette Process	
Community Meetings	
Design-In	
Focused Interviews	✓
Fishbowl Planning	
Game Simulation	
Group Dynamics	✓
Public Forum	
Task Force	
Training	
Workshop	

SUMMARY

Mowbray College is a new school near Melbourne, Australia, in the satellite town of Melton. What began in 1983 as a vision of a community school to supplement local education has developed with an annual building program to render a school valued at $15 million in 1996. There are 1000 students at present, from kindergarten to twelfth grade sited on a 40-acre campus. Architects designed the campus through a process of discussion, invention, and feedback. The participants in the process included the teachers, students, and parents, led by the principal, Alan Patterson, and the architect, Norman Day. Developments in curriculum and educational philosophy influenced the design, and the extensive landscape has been entirely carried out by the school. Parents are involved as teachers' aides, contribute to the gardening and maintenance of the school, and together with the students are responsible for all the catering.

CLIENT

Mowbray College is a private school begun in the 1980s when the State Education Department of Victoria (Australia) failed to respond to pressure to build additional schools in the rapidly expanding satellite town of Melton. A group of parents set up a cooperative and eventually obtained grants sufficient to start a private school of their own. Mowbray College first established itself in a refurbished factory on 12 acres of land.

The continuing challenge was to keep income at an appropriate level to ensure the maximum government contribution towards salaries, so that the fees were affordable by local residents with average incomes. The school design developed with extensive participation from the parents and students, under the leadership of principal Alan Patterson, appointed at the start of the project. Parents are involved as teachers' aides, as well as with maintenance and gardening, which helps to create a strong bond between family and school. The school is developed as an educational village and community for the children.

PROJECT

The principal perceives the school as an intermediate stage between home and the larger community; the architecture reflects this idea. In selecting the architect, the principal sought a long-term association of ten to 15 years with a person who would be willing to shape his architectural statements to the educational program. The original primary and middle school classrooms constructed in 1985 related in scale and form to the surrounding suburban housing. Each classroom has its own bay window and backyard. The intention was to create a school which resembled the students' home environment. The model for the development of the school described by the architect, Norman Day, is as follows:

1. A whole vision (not a plan) for the campus as an organic village (Figure 3-8)
2. A process for developing each part so it becomes the total development (Figure 3-9(a))

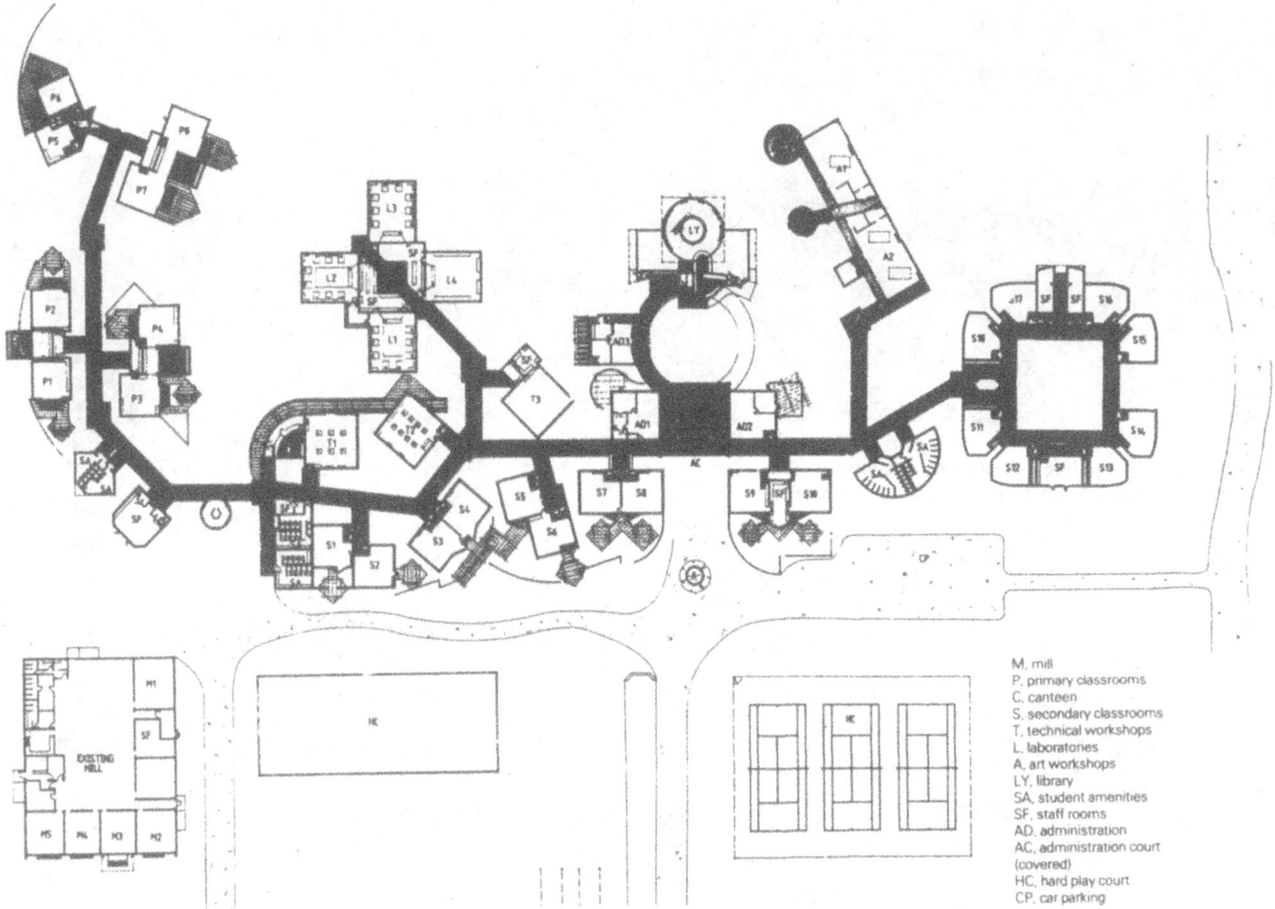

FIGURE 3-8. Plan of campus (Drawing: Norman Day).

3. A community of people and their interests which initiates the creative process
4. Equal importance of large and small elements

The school is a small city with side streets, lanes, and arcades; individual classrooms are arranged as "houses" and larger facilities as community foci.

Each classroom is a development of the two-room rural school; the library came from the idea that the Baptistry in Florence represented the center of growth; the toilets took up the slang term for ladies' toilets — the fort — and its round windowless walls are intensely protective. The Art buildings took process and fabrication as a theme. The Science center is cruciform and represents life discovery. The siting of each building considers the landscaping possibilities. A combination of long narrow vistas and secretive gardens combines to give the whole structure a feeling of twisting through an ever-changing landscape (Alan Patterson).

Alan Patterson's philosophical position was "that the school environment should heighten the student's curiosity and reduce anxiety. . . . The scale was to be fragile and kid-size . . . (Figure 3-9(b)). To build for children and not for systems. . . . To create spaces for human activity rather than to satisfy existing architectural dogma" (Figure 3-9(c)). In addition to his views about what school ought to be, he posed several questions and reponds to them by citing references to Mowbray. They are:

Why not remove the surveillance humbug — children do not respond to surveillance. They like to know where help and succor can be found but they value their independence and they thrive on trust. Mowbray gives them many nooks and niches to pass their secrets [Figure 3-9(d)].

Is hyperactive behavior needful? Most children go through the chasey stage. Their formal sport satisfies this need. The rest of the spare time is spent sitting and chatting. Mowbray has spaces to sit.

Where do students meet? The walkway is the spot where everyone smiles and says hello. I can meet nearly everybody in a day by strolling on the walkway. To esplanade is a sophisticated notion enjoyed by children.

Must libraries be silent? Libraries are not study halls, they are places of discovery and information exchange. The young need space and movement and excitement and a place to share their excitement. The library needs to be a happy productive human place where demands are

FIGURE 3-9(a). Building exterior showing integrated development with covered walkway (Photo: Mowbray College).

FIGURE 3-9(b). Child-size scale of buildings with lattice screen shading the walkway (Photo: Mowbray College).

FIGURE 3-9(c). Human scale space (Photo: Mowbray College).

FIGURE 3-9(d). Lattice screen with cutouts for views (Photo: Mowbray College).

quickly and efficiently met. Access should be easy and immediate. At Mowbray we have an open library where the drum is the meeting place. High technology provides networks and quick access and everyone is satisfied. There is no security book system and we lose no books to speak of. Innovative architecture can do a great deal to make the place happy [Figure 3-10].

Can room design reinforce education objectives? The art rooms are designed to reinforce the concept of manufacture and process. The clean geometric line with challenging textures and colors fails to mask the factory. It is a hands-on place, light, airy, and uplifting. Boys who love fabrication like doing art. It is not a girls' subject. I am quite certain that the design of the art building causes boys to feel at home and 'in the workshop.' Painting for them satisfies their 'fabrication' urge.

Can kids care for their buildings? Provided they perceive ownership and control they can. Small separate buildings enhance these perceptions.

Is landscaping open to question? The positioning of the small structures in an extensive garden network brings nature to the very edge of the school day. The Mowbray approach is to take each child along walkways through an array of plants, shady, leafy, showy, timid, and bold. Mowbray's landscaping is right for kids — there is a heap of gardening to do and horticulture holds a rightful position in the curriculum. The layout makes it abundantly obvious that this should be so.

Can schools be intimate? Schools are about intimacies. They are essentially human places and there is a great

FIGURE 3-10. Sitting area adjacent to library (Photo: Mowbray College).

need for contact and access. The spreading of staff offices throughout the teaching spaces flies in the face of most established practice. The monolithic staffroom, often remote from the center of things can hardly improve contact. In fact they are frequently designed to make it impossible for students to access staff on a 'demand' basis. Mowbray's little offices off a walkway, in a court and between rooms is an answer leading to greatly improved intimacy.

Should the toilets be on the official school tour? The washroom and toilet arrangements are most terribly important in the lives of students. Mowbray's toilet blocks are highly designed, light, airy, and interesting places. They are kept religiously clean and they are designed for easy cleaning. Too often the washroom facilities are less than well thought out and become a center of difficulty. At Mowbray they are given recognition and access is directly off a walkway.

AFTER-OCCUPANCY RESPONSES

While the teachers at Mowbray College responded to their best liked and least liked features of the building, each has also written an essay about the school. Excerpts from the essays are as follows:

Without doubt the effects of social contact on walkways, stimulating colors and student developed gardens has had a major impact on student behavior and attitudes. We forget, I think, the toughness outside our walls of many of our Mowbray families. We have created a haven of peace and tranquility — a safe harbor in a sometimes very stormy sea and the architectural design both building and landscape has contributed greatly to that (John O'Shea).

The design of the specialist classrooms reflects the type of activities that take place within — science rooms look like laboratories, the art rooms are like giant sculptures, and the technical studies building has the appearance of a workshop or factory.

The cluster of classrooms for non-specialist subjects provides the feeling of working within a small community. Each room has at least one outlook onto a garden space and is usually recessed from the main walkway giving it an air of privacy not often found in traditional classrooms. Within these workspaces furniture may be moved into any useful configuration to enable students to interact in small groups or to pursue individual study (Julie Thompson).

The use of small, self-sufficient stand-alone classrooms set down amongst semi-private play, relaxation, and study areas imports a special sense of 'belonging' to all students. This semi-isolated environment is truly conducive to academic pursuits and reflection. . . . Stand-alone classrooms are also free of the distractions and influences of neighboring classes and students activities and promote a relaxed focused learning environment (Robert C. Barnes).

Students find the walkways a pleasant place to be. They amble up and down the walkways for fun. Lunchtime and recesses see a parade of students up and down, unlike most schools where each student tends to gravitate to a favorite spot (Duane Wehrung).

The use of covered walkways throughout is of major importance to the concept of Mowbray College. These walkways are the lifeline or 'arteries' of the college as they provide the only physical means of movement and contact around the campus. By so doing, they ensure that the concept of total communication and involvement is maintained despite the relative 'isolation' of the individual classroom. It is not possible to function as a student at Mowbray without regularly interfacing with the greater college community via these walkways. Yet, these same walkways ensure that no classroom or quiet play area can be violated by unwanted noise or other interruption (Robert C. Barnes).

We are encouraged to get involved at every stage, as the school plans are an 'open book' inviting our comment and

> input. . . . Perhaps the pride that so many at Mowbray feel for their environment is there because the school is really a cohesive linking of all of the small parts — not small because they are insignificant, but rather that the parts are important to individual students, staff and parents of the school (Mark Valentine).

The positive features of the school stress the point that its design allows the teachers to change their environment, rather than regulating them to a certain order. The variety of shapes, too, gives teachers and children an opportunity to identify with a particular place. The walkways link the small clusters of buildings providing regular social interaction. Along the walkways are pockets of gardens that create venues for students, for large or small groups, active or passive.

Many problems identified by the teachers occurred as a result of the design or ideological intention. For example, the village-like atmosphere where decentralized offices were a goal did not provide opportunities for the entire staff to meet or even see each other. The orientation of some classrooms led to overheating in the summer, while others seemed to be too dark. Also, the irregular shape of classrooms creates some wasted space. The walkways and gardens, reported to be a major amenity, were sometimes unpleasant due to raging northerly winds.

The major consequences of a dispersed layout are clearly the cost of services, which increases substantially with campus growth, and the problems associated with disorientation especially for visitors and newly arriving students. In the balance, staff suggest, the strengths engendered in the novel concept that is Mowbray College today far outweigh the penalties.

The most unique aspect of Mowbray College is that its design is by intention; a collaboration between the architect and the educator. There appears to be an inextricable connection between the educational philosophy and the design of the building complex. Judging by the responses of the teaching staff, this connection is not only experienced in their daily activities, but also constitutes a welcome change to their previous experiences in more institutionalized educational settings.

New Futures School

Attitude Survey	
Charette Process	
Community Meetings	✓
Design-In	
Focused Interviews	✓
Fishbowl Planning	
Game Simulation	
Group Dynamics	
Public Forum	
Task Force	
Training	
Workshop	✓

SUMMARY

New Futures School (NFS) is an innovative facility for adolescent parents in Albuquerque, New Mexico. The school has two major components. A Prenatal Program serves the teen who enters during her pregnancy and remains until the end of the semester in which her child is born. The Young Parents' Center serves the most high-risk group of teenage mothers and fathers — those who are determined unable to participate successfully in a regular school program after the birth of their child. Both provide comprehensive services. It is an alternative school of the Albuquerque Public Schools (APS) and is also supported by a nonprofit community-based organization, New Futures, Inc.

The architectural firm of Dekker and Associates was selected to design this new facility to provide an adequate learning environment for pregnant teens and young mothers, as well as child care facilities for their babies. One of the principle considerations was to design a place infused with hope for some of Albuquerque's greatest "at-risk" teenagers, many of whom are already school dropouts.

CLIENT

New Futures School was begun in 1970 by volunteers of the Albuquerque YWCA who were concerned with the expulsion from school of pregnant adolescents and the health problems associated with adolescent pregnancy. When the YWCA, in 1976, expressed its desire to cease sponsorship, the Albuquerque Public Schools assumed primary responsibility for the program. At the same time a new community-based organization dedicated to furthering the cause of services for adolescent parents was formed, so that community involvement and support could be maintained.

The program had moved to a surplus high school in the inner city, then on to an abandoned middle school in a suburban area, before providing permanent housing. The Albuquerque School Board decided to locate the New Futures School on a site that includes another alternative facility for other at-risk students. Planning for the new facility began in 1987 when the architect, Dale Dekker, along with APS, and New Futures principal, Caroline Gaston, created the Building Planning Committee (BPC), made up of New Futures staff specially selected by the teachers, counselors, and administrators, to inform Dekker and his project team about the philosophy, history, and future needs of the school.

PROJECT

Albuquerque Public Schools have been confronting the problems raised by teenage pregnancy for more than a decade. Only recently has the successful program evolved to find a permanent home for the New Futures School, the first building in the United States specifically serving the needs of pregnant teens and teen mothers. The overall goal of the New Futures School is to break the cycle of adolescent pregnancy, child abuse, neglect, illiteracy, and poverty. Specifically, the program seeks to motivate teenaged parents toward completion of their secondary education, to mature, to have healthy pregnancies and healthy families, and to become responsible parents.

NFS provides educational services that include a comprehensive high school program, a G.E.D. preparation program, as well as classes in maternal and child health, parenting, and child development. Other services include individual and group counseling, childbirth classes, day care, and vocational education. In effect, the NFS is a combination of educational facility, child care center, and physical and mental health clinic. Because there was no such facility available as a model, the architect had to develop a complete building program for the school.

Students, staff, and cooperating users participated actively in the design process. The Building Planning Committee, consisting of teachers, counselors, and administrators of the New Futures School served as the client group for the building. The architectural team devoted special attention to the special needs and daily routines of the facility's users. Interviews were conducted with all school staff to discuss what features of the old facility they wished to maintain in the new school, and what new features they would like to see incorporated. As a result, special consideration was given to the grouping of nurseries convenient to the front of the school, with outdoor access to play yards for each one.

Workshops were held with pregnant teenagers, young mothers with infants, and mothers with toddlers. "Essentially, we were trying to get a feeling for what these girls did during the day, to get a focus on how their day went," Dekker said.

The resulting floor plan attempts to integrate the way the school works for faculty, staff, students, and infants (Figure 3-11). The main entrance of the school was designed for pick-up and drop-off of students who were pregnant or who carried babies and diaper bags (Figure 3-12). The cafeteria, also located in the front of the school, allows students and their babies to wait for rides after school. Directly behind the open cafeteria is the check-in area for all students and visitors, providing a panoramic view of the Sandia Mountains.

Since the old school had a central hallway where mothers and their babies often congregated between classes, Dekker designed a similar hallway "spine" in response to the students' desires. This spine contains classrooms grouped for high school-age students, and a smaller area for middle school. Nurseries are branched off the spine where there are separate areas for infants age two weeks to four months, five through ten months, and babies age 11 through 15 months. Students are required to work in the nurseries, changing diapers, feeding and tending children. The idea is to give the students the skills they will need as parents as well as to give staff the opportunity to observe how the young women react to children (Natale 1992).

The University of New Mexico runs a weekly maternal and infant care clinic at the school. Also included is an office for a social services representative, who screens students and babies for public assistance eligibility. A job-training program helps the neediest girls find work. Counseling sessions help students work through substance abuse or relationship problems, as well as through decisions about whether to give their babies up for adoption. There is also a store run by volunteers, where students can buy donated baby and maternity clothes at ten cents an item.

With a population of 230 students and 90 infants, the school is overcrowded but does not give that appearance due to its open design and cheerful feeling. Interior and exterior colors used for the building are shades of rose pink and turquoise. "The girls wanted pinks and bright colors. They said they wanted it to look like a pleasant place to be, not like an institution," Dekker said. For this particular student population, Gaston said, "color scheme and the overall feel of the school were highly crucial."

"You have to remember that this group of students has already given up and the regular school system has given up on them," Gaston said. "Many of the students come from troubled backgrounds. The emphasis of New Futures is to raise their self-esteem, teach them how to be good parents, while providing traditional secondary education, thus making them productive members of society. Each student is respected as an individual. The design of the school had to reflect this, which the new school does beautifully."

The students are proud to have been included in the design process, and to see some of their suggestions reflected in the new building. As a result, they have a marked pride in the school. Gaston related a story of how one student accidentally squirted ketchup on the cafeteria wall. The girl immediately got a cleaning rag from the cafeteria staff and cleaned the wall without any prompting. "You would be hard pressed to see that occur at any school, anywhere," reported Gaston, smiling proudly.

AFTER-OCCUPANCY RESPONSES

There appears to be unanimous agreement between the 24 staff members and four students who responded to an evaluation survey about the attractive appearance of the building, the use of bright and cheery colors, and the feeling of openness as one moves through the building (Figure 3-13). The use of skylights in the corridor also contributes to the overall positive atmosphere of the building. The organization of the classrooms at the perimeter of the building makes access efficient and rooms easy to find, while good lighting provides a cheerful atmosphere. The location of the classrooms in relation to the nurseries was reported to be convenient, though respondents ex-

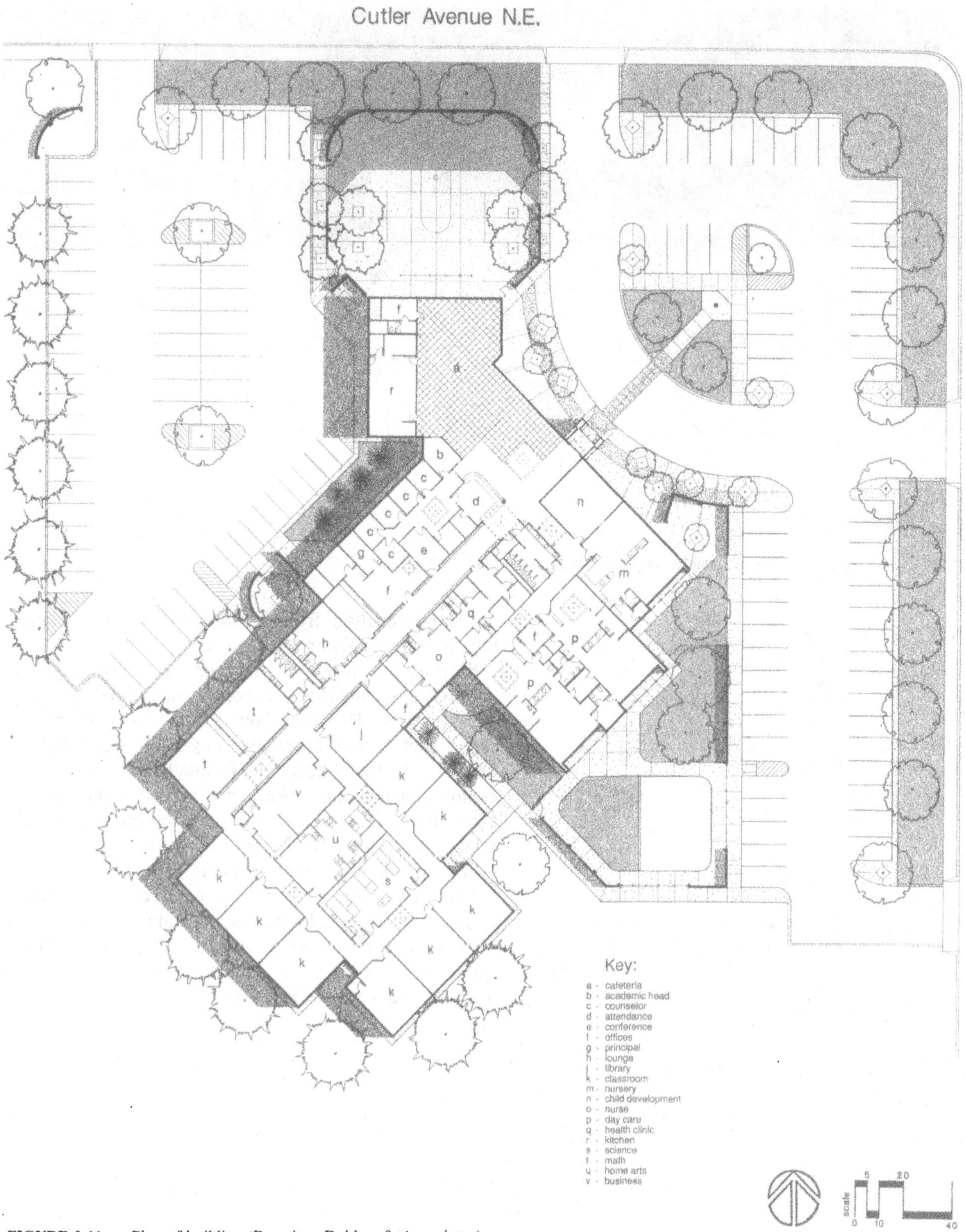

FIGURE 3-11. Plan of building (Drawing: Dekker & Associates).

pressed concern about the inconvenient location of offices with respect to the nurseries, and their relatively small size. Generally, most staff seem to be pleased with the organization of the building into areas of concentrations or suites, each with their own internal circulation. Staff located in interior spaces, however, such as home arts, library, and offices complained about poor ventilation and general lack of comfort control. Equal concern was voiced by many teachers and students about the unequal distribution

FIGURE 3-12. Building facade showing main entrance (Photo: Kirk Gittings, Syntax).

FIGURE 3-13. Interior view of building (Photo: Kirk Gittings, Syntax).

of heating resulting from the inability to control comfort in each classroom.

Surprisingly, there was no gymnasium included in the program. This lack was consistently noted by staff and students. This omission, as well as other measures, such as overcrowding, may have been a function of a limited budget, and initially an inadequate estimate of the population being served. Other comments about least-liked features of the building were related to relatively minor inconveniences experienced by individual staff members.

The New Futures School not only serves an innovative role as an alternative program for pregnant teens and teen mothers, but also, according to the people who use the building, conveys a positive meaning about educational facilities.

Saturn School

Attitude Survey	✓
Charette Process	
Community Meetings	✓
Design-In	
Focused Interviews	✓
Fishbowl Planning	
Game Simulation	
Group Dynamics	
Public Forum	✓
Task Force	
Training	
Workshop	

SUMMARY

The creation of the new Saturn School, a restructured middle school in St. Paul, Minnesota, demonstrates how the concerns of contemporary education can be fostered through collaboration. Saturn School grew out of the Secretary of Education's challenge to educators to do for education what General Motors did for automobile manufacturing by the creation of the Saturn plant. Initiated by the school board, parents, and staff, Saturn was shaped out of the desire for a school where students would be active learners, and where individual attention to their needs could be accommodated through intensive use of technology.

Saturn began in two rooms of an old building, and gradually with the help of parents, a new downtown location was chosen: a vacant YWCA building. The architectural firm of Rafferty, Rafferty, Tollefson was hired to create "workrooms" and "learning spaces" and remodel five of the existing eight stories of the facility to match the philosophy of the new school.

CLIENT

Many efforts supported the creation of the school including those of the St. Paul Federation of Teachers, the University of St. Thomas, the Minnesota Educational Computing Corporation (MECC), and a Saturn Council, consisting of parents, students, and staff, and the community at large. The council has had input on all aspects of program design, including school calendar, curriculum development, staff selection and evaluation, and selection of a permanent downtown site. Saturn was planned from the very beginning as a program that would operate in the downtown area. The educators, businesspeople, and parents who developed the program felt that the downtown area provided a rich environment for learning.

The downtown location also served to nurture one of Saturn's central ideas, that youngsters learn important lessons by serving others. Community service is an important part of the curriculum. Saturn students tutored handicapped students, helped nursery school teachers, and helped to gather, tally, and analyze a survey conducted by the City Council. Saturn's parents and teachers believe that their school should be a contributing neighbor, not just a resident, of downtown St. Paul.

PROJECT

From its inception, Saturn has been envisioned as a downtown school that draws on many community resources. Currently, students and staff use the facilities of the YMCA, the Science Museum of Minnesota, the Minnesota Museum of Art, and the St. Paul Public Library as integral components of the learning environment. Saturn is a city-wide math and science magnet program which serves a diverse student body from all socio-economic levels and from across the city.

Saturn's mission statement is: "The Saturn School Community is an interpersonal, individualized environment in which students become empowered lifelong learners prepared for the 21st century." A core concept at Saturn is a Personalized Learning Plan for each student. "Saturn is designed as a school where all learners succeed. Each student has a Personal Growth Plan designed by students, parents, and teachers to fit the needs, strengths, and interests of the student. The Personal Growth Plan identifies goals for each student, maps each student's progress towards mastery, and serves as a learning compass for further learning activities."

Learning technologies play a significant role in student learning at Saturn. Microcomputers and video-based instruction replace most lecture and large-group activities, particularly in basic skills learning. Each student works daily on a computer-based Integrated Learning System (ILS) which contains several hundred reading and math lessons. The ILS manages information on student achievement and provides the teacher, student, and parent with a daily record of performance.

Saturn School of Tomorrow is a unique and innovative response to the national call for school restructuring and reform and provides a working model for effective school change. Cramped initially in two rooms of a building designed for handicapped children, Saturn's early life was constrained by the limitations of traditional school space. Gradually, a new image was formed where classrooms would be replaced with "workrooms" and "learning spaces." Parents, too, were involved. They were part of a task force encouraged to find a new location for their school.

Saturn is now located in downtown St. Paul, and occupies five floors of an eight-story, unused YWCA building. Currently there are 290 students in grades four through eight. The building has a large auditorium, pool, and gymnasium. Students, parents, and staff participated in the selection and design of the new school space. The architectural firm of Rafferty, Rafferty, Tollefson was hired to work with the teachers and the students as they redesigned their roles as well as their workspaces.

Saturn School Parents Association, teachers, school board architects, and students met with the design team several times each week during the programming process to shape the educational program as well as the building. Large-group meetings were held with parents and students in the discourse room of their temporary facilities to allow for a broad base of participation. Issues brought forth by children for the architect's consideration included the exploration of an imaginative use of color, the creation of a variety of spaces, and the design of a building that was as unique as the educational program. After the first year of the program in their temporary facilities, children realized that they could affect their education; consequently they were eager to discuss future learning areas, unusual shapes of rooms, places to climb, and places for students to work together. Rafferty suggests that this participation was fruitful since all the students' wishes were incorporated into the design of the building.

According to the architect, the discussion of places where children learn (such as an independent learning center, discourse room, and other learning centers) was based on the activities that might occur in each of those areas, thereby freeing the teachers, students, and architect from thinking about classroom stereotypes. What emerged was a five-level building, three levels of which were designed to shape an educational idea, where each level conveyed its own theme (Figure 3-14).

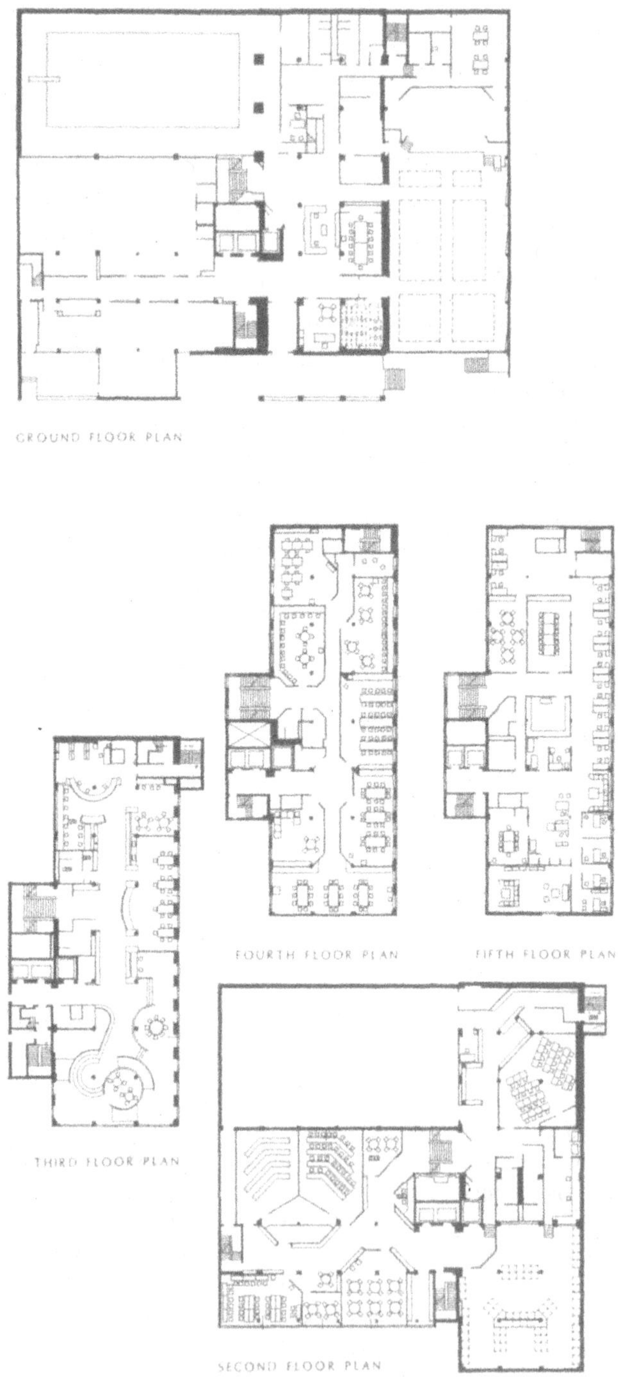

FIGURE 3-14. Floor plans of instructional levels (Drawing: Rafferty, Rafferty, Tollefson).

FIGURE 3-15. Cooperative learning level with active and passive zones (Photo: Philip MacMillan James).

FIGURE 3-16(a). Exposed columns prior to renovation (Photo: Rafferty, Rafferty, Tollefson).

FIGURE 3-16(b). Colonnade through which students circulate (Photo: Philip MacMillan James).

FIGURE 3-17. Specialized classroom (Photo: Philip MacMillan James).

The ground floor contained the reception lobby, auditorium, pool, and sufficient space for the future first and second grade. The second floor, designated as the technology level, contained a number of places incorporating the computer as a teaching tool. In this level different activity areas were represented by different colors. Color coding was created in response to the variety children were seeking. The level above was the cooperative learning level, an area in which there would be an active and passive zone for projects, meetings, and individual work (Figure 3-15). This area contained multiple levels for children to climb, explore, read on steps, and observe the riverfront view. The existing columns (Figure 3-16(a)) were used to create the co-op collonade, or main street, through which all the students would circulate (Figure 3-16(b)). The student radio station, newspaper, and art and media center were also an integral part of this level. On the level above was the learning center area: a series of rooms dedicated to reading, music, science, writing and study centers, thematically representing a small village. To strengthen the village concept, each classroom or house was treated differently in terms of color, trim, and window shape (Figure 3-17).

One particular group of students was involved through Mark French's architecture class. Craig Rafferty came to the class to discuss ideas about the new building with those students who responded to issues related to circulation, the need for open and closed spaces, and color schemes. The students then visited the architect's office following the building development's progress and, finally, visited the building site during construction.

AFTER-OCCUPANCY RESPONSES

An evaluation was conducted by Dr. Hallie Preskill in 1990, after the first year of the school's operation. It is one part of a larger evaluation that will, in three years, describe the effects of a project to restructure education in the St. Paul School system. The evaluation process consisted of on-site observations of students, staff, and teachers; individual interviews with teachers, staff, and district administrators; focus group interviews with students as well as with parents; and a mailed survey to all parents.

A summary of the findings indicated that the teachers were able to enlist participation from nearly all of the parents, and the goals of the Personal Growth Plan appear to be linked to what students are learning in their courses (Preskill 1990). Parent support constitutes a major success in Saturn's first year, since it helped teachers and students accomplish many more of the objectives. They especially liked the fact that students were becoming part of the community through the off-site learning opportunities.

Unanimous agreement to the color scheme came from the students. Many also commented favorably to the *design* of the building. The gym, the pool, and the discourse room were consistently described as the students' favorite places. Equally consistent was their negative reaction towards windowless rooms, a condition inherent in the shape of the existing building. Thermal comfort in the winter and in the summer also seemed to be a constant source of complaints. Most surprisingly, the steps were pointed out as a least-liked feature, particularly when level changes were discussed early in the process as a method of achieving variety. Responses from the teachers were not dissimilar to those of the students. They did, however, have many positive comments about building features that encouraged their exploration and experimentation with new approaches to teaching. More cooperative learning techniques and more project-based learning appeared to reflect the thrust of teaching changes. The variety of different types of learning spaces contributed to an increase in student-directed learning projects.

In summary, Rafferty believes that the intensity of interaction between all participants contributed to the successful design of the school. Even more importantly, he suggests, all participants, including city architects and administrators felt a sense of ownership in the process and in the building, since they all take credit for the ideas.

ACKNOWLEDGMENT

This section was written from material generously provided by the Saturn School as well as extensive comments conveyed through a microcassette recorder by Craig Rafferty, recalling the design process.

Seven Hills School

Attitude Survey	
Charette Process	
Community Meetings	✓
Design-In	
Focused Interviews	
Fishbowl Planning	✓
Game Simulation	
Group Dynamics	
Public Forum	
Task Force	
Training	✓
Workshop	✓

SUMMARY

The main building of the Seven Hills School, housing grades three and six, computer and science labs, offices and the library, was destroyed by fire in July 1987. The kindergarten through second grade wing was only smoke- and water-damaged. The fourth grade classrooms were intact and subsequently moved to a new site on campus where they have become the new science center. Progress towards re-opening, however, moved rapidly with the acquisition of seven temporary structures to be used for the following academic year. The volunteer efforts of students, parents, teachers, and alumni also enabled a speedy school start. While temporary facilities were being prepared, Architect Otto Bauer-Nilsen was working with administrators and teachers on plans for a new building. Their vision was to build something that was aesthetically pleasing and would fit the spirit and tradition of their great school. Their new facility was dedicated in January 1989.

CLIENT

Seven Hills is an independent, nonsectarian, college preparatory day school which comprises elementary, middle, and upper schools and occupies two campuses in Cincinnati. The Lotspeich School comprises pre-kindergarten to fifth grade, and was founded by Helen Lotspeich in 1916 as a supportive place where the natural curiosity of children would provide the basis for their education. It is a school where education extends beyond the classroom to the laboratory, the library, out-of-doors, studio, and stage, as well as in service to the community. The faculty develop the curriculum for the needs of children at different age levels, with individualized groupings and instruction to meet the unique needs and abilities of students in all grades. In addition to their specialized work in the arts, their program in community service brings student art and performance to nursing homes and hospitals. Children also perform their music, drama, and studio work in various festivals and galleries.

Parent involvement occurs through a variety of activities. Parents have an active role in the direction of the school, as trustees, as well as through a parent association.

PROJECT

The Seven Hills Schools of Cincinnati serve the needs of their students with a program marked by academic rigor, a strong faculty, individual attention, and participation. For 70 years they linked the concept of learning to active exploration, interaction, and discovery in their child-centered program. In July 1987, the 57-year-old main building of the Lotspeich School was struck by lightning during a severe thunderstorm. Most of its frame portions, including the library, offices, science room, computer room and classrooms for grades 3 and 6, were destroyed. Classrooms 4 and 5, separated by a masonry addition, were badly damaged by water and smoke. Eventually part of this section was moved to a new site and restored. It now houses the science program. Classrooms for kindergartens and grades 1 and 2 were reusable after extensive smoke damage was cleaned.

The trustees met immediately and made two decisions: to begin school on time in September and to hold school on the campus, not in various other church-school facilities that had been offered by a generous community.

Many of the teachers had lost the accumulation of a lifetime of teaching in the fire. Children, too, stared in disbelief at what had been their classrooms only one month before. The two weeks after the fire were filled with images like the sight of the bulldozer at Lotspeich for the demolition and removal of what remained of the building. Under the direction of the Parent Association, hundreds of student, parent, and alumni volunteers did many necessary jobs to allow the school to reopen on time in September. Just before the start of school for the academic year, counseling was offered to assist teachers in dealing with their own feelings of grief and loss, as well as with possible post-traumatic stress in their students.

Several weeks after the fire, Seven Hills obtained several temporary buildings from different cities while plans were underway for a new building. Seven temporary structures located near the Fine Arts building supplemented the undamaged parts of the school. Housing the library, French and computer rooms, science lab, and 3rd through 6th grade classrooms, the structures were adequate, and in some cases larger than the rooms they were replacing. The new rooms had been decorated by teachers and volunteers to make them especially cheerful and home-like for the opening of the school year.

A new Middle School serving grades 6, 7, and 8 had been the goal for the Red Bank campus when the Lotspeich School was destroyed. As part of the initial planning, several teachers spent time exploring the question "What if 6th grade were added to the Middle School? What advantages would this have for 6th graders — educationally, socially, emotionally, and physically? What physical facility would we need to carry out this dream?" The teachers were attempting to merge the qualities of both campuses in a synergistic way that would create an exciting new school. The conclusion was a new Middle School serving 6th, 7th, and 8th graders. Adding the 6th grade to the Middle School would lower the age level of the entire school, lowering the average age, which would have the effect of preserving childhood a little longer for the older children. It was generally agreed that a three-year program would give identity to the Middle School experience. The move from a junior high school approach to a middle school program was a move from subject-oriented school work to child-centered schools and signified a recognition of a unique period of life with its own strength and needs.

Successful schools for young people ages 10 to 14 years are positive environments where there is "as much consideration for who the student is and becomes — his and her self-concept, self-responsibility, attitudes toward school, and personal happiness — as for how much and what he or she knows" (Elkind, *The Hurried Child*). The philosophy for the new Middle School would emphasize that true learning comes from active exploration, interaction, and discovery, not from passive transfer of knowledge. True teaching focuses on the needs of the learner; hence, a child-centered curriculum which addresses the physical, cognitive, psychological, and social development of children is highly valued. This view steered the faculty away from a departmental structure with English, math, or science teachers, which would stress content. Rather, they developed interdisciplinary faculty teams which would address the instructional and developmental needs of the students. The classroom experience could then be enhanced by more ways to involve the students actively in symposiums, panel discussions, simulation games, and role-playing experiences. These activities were not possible in their previous facility because of the lack of space to divide students into discussion groups, or for rehearsals for dramatizations.

A workshop involving teachers from the Seven Hills Schools and educators from different schools stressed that the focus of the Middle School should be the needs of the child, an assertion that reinforced the current thinking of the teachers.

In the meantime a Cincinnati architect, Otto Bauer-Nilsen, was working with administrators and teachers on plans for a new building. They were determined to build something that was aesthetically pleasing and that fit the spirit and tradition of the school. Lotspeich was founded in 1916 by Helen Gibbons Lotspeich, who held strong views about children and education. One of her views, shared by the people of the day, was that fresh air was good for children and learning. Her original school in her home was called the Clifton Open Air School, and it had no heat. The building built on Red Bank Road in 1930 also had no heat in its early days, so students sat in individual woolen bags and wore mittens. Many alumni trace their poor handwriting to the years of writing while wearing mittens. While the new building certainly has heat, the feeling of openness has been maintained through the use of doors from each classroom to the outside and an abundance of windows. This was one of the issues conveyed to the architect by the teachers. In addition to housing offices, classrooms, language and computer rooms, conference, tutoring and work rooms, their new library is one-third larger than the old library and complete with a fireplace. Each grade is marked by hand-carved ceramic tiles designed and created by an art teacher, Diane Kruer, and her student, Dede Gay.

The faculty met to review what they had learned

FIGURE 3-18. Outdoor access from classrooms (Photo: Kathy Deubell).

FIGURE 3-19. Interior view of kindergarten (Photo: Kathy Duebell).

from this experience. Eileen Driscoll, principal, stated that, "We have learned from each other, in a close-knit community, students watching their teachers respond with strength and ingenuity to loss and change, teachers absorbing their students' savoring of the present, of the what *is*, rather than the what *was* or may be." The director of operations, Ted Colebrook, facilitated the collaboration between the architect and the faculty. He initiated a brainstorming session, from which a list was generated, including the following considerations:

All on one floor
Air-light-space
Large library for holding school assemblies
Direct access to outdoors from each classroom (Figure 3-18)
Display areas for student work
Areas in classroom for quiet work and messy projects
Sinks and water fountain in every room

In addition, the teachers had pooled their past experiences with classroom size, and agreed to a square room for about 20 students with tiled and carpeted areas, and a counter for making and displaying projects. The meeting structure tended to be informal and consensual, and matters pertaining to the building were often folded into other agendas in faculty meetings, administrative council and board meetings, parents association meetings, and buildings and grounds committee meetings.

IMPLEMENTATION

The architect included all the teachers' requests into the building program. In addition, he provided a large oculus window in the kindergarten which permits sky-gazing and meditation on the change of seasons (Figure 3-19). Further, he set library and hall windows low, at child height, and created hallway jogs and alcoves so that halls would look less institutionally "tunnel and funnel." He also provided a fireplace in the library. "The architect's first design," reports Ms. Driscoll, "was already close to the mark, and he readily incorporated virtually all elements of the faculty 'laundry list' program."

Parents were consulted on the program, but their concern focused largely on the safety and non-toxicity of the building materials. Children's involvement was informal — teachers asked what they wanted and it generally reflected what the teachers had already requested. They did ask for loft spaces, but these were not incorporated for code and safety reasons.

"The result of a close and respectful collaboration," reports Ms. Driscoll, "has been a building that is both functional and unusually attractive. The atmosphere is warm, bright, energizing and welcoming. The spaces work for different teaching styles including contemporary hands-on and collaborative. There is virtually nothing we cannot do in this building from reading partners to cooking and serving dinner from Thomas Jefferson's cookbook." Ms. Driscoll concludes that "faculty involvement in school building design results in a finished product that really works and one that truly expresses the soul and spirit of the school" (Figure 3-20).

AFTER-OCCUPANCY ASSESSMENT

When commenting on the most-liked and disliked features of the new building, the teachers liked the large sunny classrooms and their access to the outdoors. They also commented on a planning feature which created the library as the "heart of the school," with

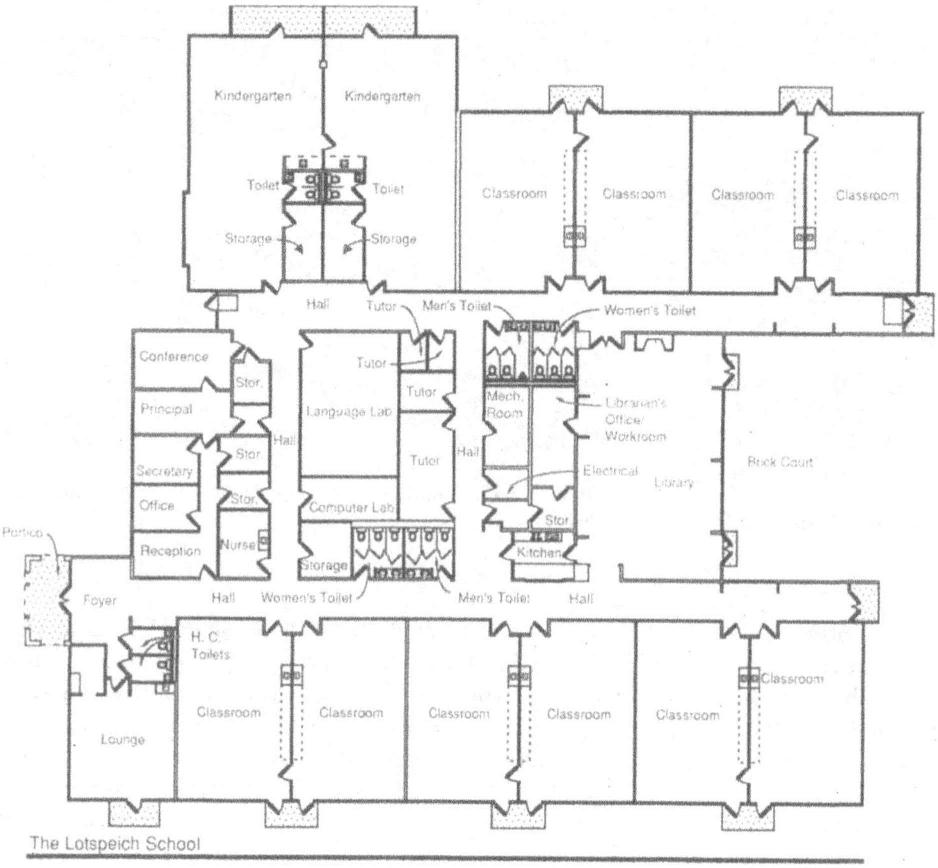

FIGURE 3-20. Floor plan (Drawing: Otto Bauer-Nilsen).

easy access from all classrooms. They disliked the results of their recommendation for square classrooms, reporting more wasted space than rectangular rooms. The location of the teacher's workroom not being central to all grades, and inadequacy in size and number of counseling rooms were also least liked features. They had not been discussed, however, by the teachers during the programming sessions.

Wallace O'Neal School

Attitude Survey	
Charette Process	✓
Community Meetings	
Design-In	
Focused Interviews	✓
Fishbowl Planning	✓
Game Simulation	✓
Group Dynamics	✓
Public Forum	
Task Force	
Training	
Workshop	✓

SUMMARY

A private elementary school in Pinehurst, North Carolina, chose a participatory planning process to develop a long-range building program. This was predicated on the need to develop better communications between the parents and the teaching staff about the future of the school. The school's building committee invited parents, teachers, and children to become involved in intensive work sessions to define collaboratively their educational goals.

The initial sessions began with the children, who were asked for their response to educational goals through various modes of expression. Through the use of poetry exercises, drawing, and role play, the children were able to voice their concerns in shaping their new school. The adult members of the school community, too, entered similar activities, and also participated in small-group discussions in which they were asked to consider appropriate educational goals, and how they could influence the type of spaces that would occur in a new school.

The final result of the process was a building program identifying the range of students' activities and how they should be spatially accommodated in their facility. A follow-up "walk-through" assessment, conducted ten years after construction of their new building, revealed that hasty building decisions had affected its proper functioning. Many of the teachers who had participated in the charette process ten years earlier had maintained their student-centered orientation, and attempted to humanize their classroom in contrast to the stark institutional setting.

CLIENT

The Moore County Public School System, which includes the Pinehurst-Southern Pines area, is in many ways one of the most progressive in North Carolina. Several of the schools in the area provide open classrooms, non-graded classes, team teaching, and other innovations that are still relatively rare in public education. Even so, the Wallace O'Neal School was created as an alternative to this public system, and the motives for this shift were fundamental to the emerging educational program. There was an expressed desire for "quality" education of a kind to be achieved through energetic, well-paid teachers, and relatively small classes. On a continuum between child-centered and teacher-centered approaches, the Wallace O'Neal program was best described as teacher-oriented, with emphasis on the teaching of subject matter, rather than on student learning. Equally significant was a determination to develop a school that would be responsive to both the needs of the children and the wishes of the parents. There was a feeling that the public schools were too large, too bureaucratic, and too inert to be affected by any individual, whether child or parent. The desire to participate and to have an effect is an important motive in the creation of any alternative school, and the charette process is an especially appropriate planning mode in such a situation.

PROJECT

The major objective of this project was the creation of a parent-child coalition to develop an educational program and to plan and implement physical spaces to complement that program. One approach for reaching this objective is referred to as a "charette," from the French term, which in architecture implies a period of brief but intensive planning. In its present adaptation, a charette is an activity that brings community members and experts together for a limited time period to study specific community problems. The essential ingredients are:

- A problem to be solved
- Community members willing to participate
- Experts in both substantive and process issues
- A commitment to implement the plans and recommendations of the charette

PROCESS

The planning team for the charette consisted of William Laslett, project architect; Henry Sanoff, charette planner; George Barbour, psychologist; and Joan Sanoff, child development consultant, who conducted the student session. This team was responsible for planning the charette process, which was conducted during three consecutive evenings and three full days bridging a weekend.

The process began when the board members of the Wallace O'Neal Day School, a newly formed private school in Pinehurst, North Carolina, developed a long-range building plan to include a new facility for a proposed kindergarten through ninth grade program. In the course of interviewing architects for the design of the new school, the building committee encountered one architect who proposed a participatory planning approach involving members of the school community as well as architects and consultants. In sharp contrast to other presentations based on the architect's experience in planning educational facilities, the building committee was invited to become involved with students, teachers, architects, and consultants in the creation of an educational program as well as a building. The Wallace O'Neal community's acceptance of this pluralistic approach was a measure of their commitment to their school.

The concept of community participation was fundamental to a charette, and set it apart from problem-solving methods which involve experts but exclude people. The school planning charette involved the consumers: the teachers, parents, and children who would have to use and "live with" the results. The most valuable by-product, one which in many ways gave life to the results, was the sense of commitment and cohesiveness which grew from the struggle of planning together.

These ideas were the beginnings of an educational program, but there had been little articulation of their relevance to the day-to-day workings of a school; in fact, there were, within the school community, some latent but very strongly felt disagreements about the best way to implement the program. The parents had discussed their objectives in general terms; the structure and techniques of the school were left to the headmaster, who was selected because he shared these objectives. The school's orientation had been relatively traditional in its distinction between "academics," which are emphasized, and "non-academics," which occur during semi-structured "activity periods." The probable traditionalism of the Wallace O'Neal community was recognized in the early team meetings, when the consultants stated their concern that the community may be apprehensive about their possible "hidden agenda" aimed at propagandizing for a "radical" school program. Since many of the team members were, in fact, interested in developing a non-traditional program and building, the problem was genuine, and carried the risk of disintegration of the working relationship.

Within the team, the issue was dealt with in terms of relative emphasis. Was the team composed of "experts" whose responsibility was to advocate their own opinions of the best educational direction for the school, or was it to be a group of "consultants" whose obligation was to help the Wallace O'Neal community articulate and implement its own ideas? Although the question could not be resolved completely, one decisive factor was that the original charette presentation had emphasized the "consultant" role and had been accepted on that basis. For this reason, it was generally agreed that the team would serve a facilitative role, and that the biases, though present, should not be allowed to interfere with the growth of consensus within the client group.

The charette began with a morning-long session attended by students from different classes. In the following week, charette sessions were scheduled for Tuesday, Wednesday, and Thursday evenings, as well as the following Saturday and Sunday. Invitations were extended to the entire Wallace O'Neal adult community: parents, members of the board of trustees, building committee, and faculty. The desirability of representation and continuity of participation was emphasized, but although this ideal was approached in the early sessions, the group was soon reduced to the faculty and those building committee members and trustees who would carry the greatest responsibility for implementing the decisions emerging from the charette.

STUDENTS' SESSION

The charette team felt that it was important to have the students of the school understand the events that

I Wish My School

I wish my school to be the neatest place in the world.
I wish my school to be very unusual.
I wish my school to be out-of-the-ordinary.
I wish my school to be a nice place to go instead
of a torture chamber.
I wish my school to have many different things
going on.
I wish my school would be pleasant to come to
and still be learning all the things
we need to know.
I wish my school to be
as free as it could be
unless we broke a rule
and destroyed the privilege.
I wish my school to be a place you
can go
anytime of the day.
I wish my school could be
as fun
as it is hard.
I wish my school to have freedom of choice.
I wish my school to be as long as I want it.
I wish my school to be without classes
and mostly recess.
I wish my school to be beautiful
with lots of trees
and not big brick buildings.
I wish my school to have bright colors.
I wish my school to be seen and be noticed
when someone is driving
on the road.
I wish my school to be nicely planted
with bushes and flowers.
I wish my school to have many things
you can play on,
inside and outside.
I wish my school to be a racetrack,
a baseball diamond,
a horse stable.
I wish my school to be with teachers
who don't boss you around.
I wish my school to have breaks
after every class.
I wish my school to have a
little store
where you can buy cokes,
candies,
sandwiches.
I wish my school room to have
an upstairs
and to have stairs that
go around and around.
I wish my school to have lots of room to run.

FIGURE 3-21. Children's wish poem.

would be taking place, and to give them an opportunity to generate ideas of their own about the kind of school they would like to have. Because their direct participation in the charette was not considered feasible, it was agreed to conduct a session at the school in which a representative group of 14 students could, through various exercises, be made part of the planning process.

The session opened with the construction of a collaborative poem, a group of statements composed of responses to the phrase, "*I wish my school . . .*" (Figure 3-21). This approach permitted the students to fantasize about their dream school through an open yet structured process. Wish poems were considerably more effective than stating objectives, particularly if the intention was to keep the thinking global and exploratory. The results of the wish poem indicated concerns about the administration, curriculum, and the physical environment.

A follow-up exercise required the children to rate their present school environment using a pre-selected list of adjectives. This technique, described as a polar-opposite adjective scale, provided students with a broad vocabulary for describing and evaluating their environment. It was particularly revealing when students were also asked to describe their "ideal" school using the same list of adjectives. Not only was it valuable to compare the results, but it was also a way of expanding the students' conceptions of the environment. The next exercise, from the progression of abstract to concrete experiences, was for the students to draw pictures of typical and ideal schools based on their mental images. Since people react to the built environment in terms of the meaning the environments have for them, the image of a school certainly is quite symbolically loaded. The drawings of the typical and ideal schools conveyed both positive and negative characteristics (Figure 3-22). For example, all drawings depicting a typical school revealed brick factory-like buildings, similar to their stereotypical image of school buildings constructed in America in the 1920s. Their drawings of the ideal school, on the other hand, were more complex, angular, cast in a wooded setting,

FIGURE 3-22. Children drawing the image of schools (Photo: William Laslett).

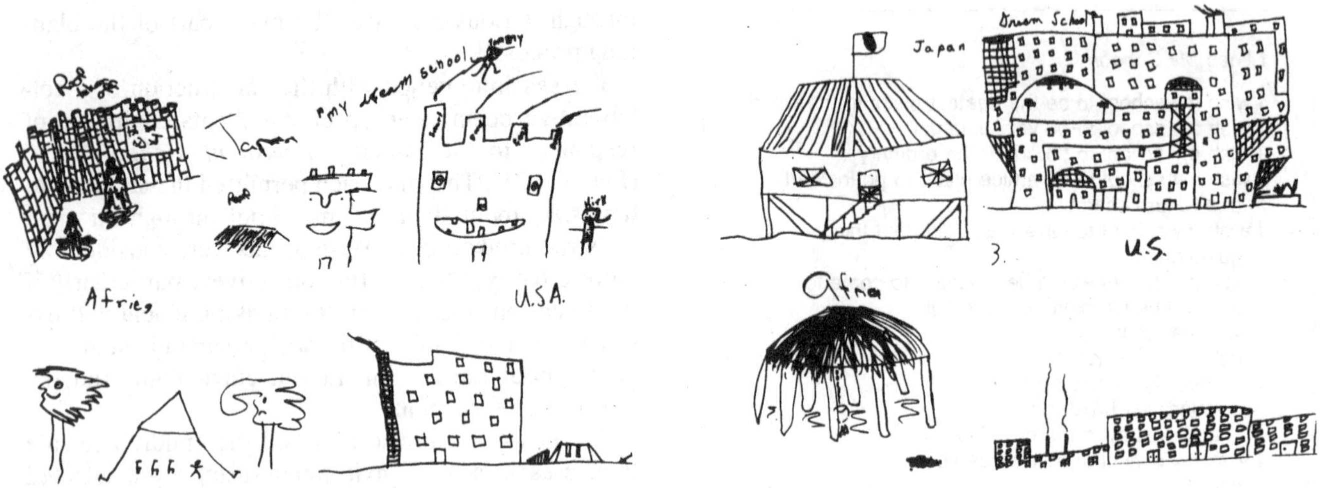

FIGURE 3-23. Children's drawings of schools.

and conveyed a different attitude about a building as well as its context (Figure 3-23).

The results of the exercise characterized the students' concern about their new school. Since their present school comprised six wood-constructed mobile units, they wanted to convey that their new building should not separate them as the present arrangement does. Follow-up discussions indicated their desire for more interaction that could be better enhanced in one building. Here, as in the wish poem and in verbal ratings, the desire for variety, spontaneity, daylight, and color were apparent.

The students' final experience was an introduction to the process of planning a school through a role play of the charette itself. This activity was developed with the belief that children are interested in playing with adult roles in order to try them on for size. Role play relies on the spontaneous performance of participants when placed in a hypothetical situation. In role play, the essential core of the activity was understanding the situation of another person. A student was placed in a position in which he or she was given the opportunity to "feel" what was at stake once given the basic information. Through such participation, students can gain a greater understanding of other roles and relationships, as well as a better awareness of what they themselves are doing.

The task was to develop a program for the school; however, the actors were characterized by hypothetical descriptions of school board members, teachers, and an architect. The session lasted well over two hours and into lunch period while students fought and argued and finally fired the minister from the building committee because they did not want to include a chapel in their new school.

Results from student involvement in the process were twofold. First, students' drawings of the ideal and typical school buildings sensitized the parents and teachers to the importance of the building's image, even to 11- and 12-year-olds. Students' drawings showed an awareness and concern for their new school beyond the expectations of the adult participants. Second, the summary of the results of the student exercises, which constituted the opening of the adult sessions, set a positive tone for the event. This was particularly important since the overall goal of the charette was to help the Wallace O'Neal community compile information about itself, information that could be used to create and evaluate a building design proposal.

During the course of the charette, the team used a number of techniques and strategies, each designed to generate, summarize, contrast, and translate into spatial terms the information and ideas of the client group. The planning team decided that a sound building program could be derived only from a clear and consensual educational program and, for this reason, the bulk of the charette time was scheduled for discussion of education issues. This choice was questioned from a number of viewpoints: some felt that the educational program was already clear, and that they should begin planning and building; others felt that they had nothing to contribute to a discussion of educational objectives; still others seemed to feel that the consultants were avoiding their responsibility by expecting the school community to produce its own plans and ideas.

With these issues partially resolved, the second and third evenings were used to formulate an educational program using a structured process. Participants were divided into small working groups in order to provide opportunities for each member to voice his or her opinion (Figure 3-24). Voting to reach decisions was discouraged in order to allow all ideas to be fully explored as well as to have participants resolve their

FIGURE 3-24. Parent-teacher workshop (Photo: William Laslett).

differences early in the process, so that their continued involvement would be productive.

Relating Objectives for Learning to Education (ROLE) was a group discussion process developed by Sanoff (1984) to familiarize lay people with a design procedure in which they could contribute their ideas, learn from each other, and learn about important design relationships established by the structure of the process. Similar to a parlor game such as "Monopoly," a set of rules was developed to ensure that each participant would make individual and group decisions. Beginning with educational goals, community members examined how goals generate different ways in which learning can occur, or learning methods; how teachers and students would collaborate (interactions); and, finally, the places where learning methods and interactions would occur, or settings.

For each goal that was agreed upon, the work groups had to identify four compatible learning methods (see Chapter 5, Participatory Theories and Methods for a listing of goal statements and learning methods). For most groups, this step in the process was the beginning of discussions about the relevance, desirability, and implications of unconventional methods such as non-gradedness and student decision making. The final step in the process consisted of matching each learning method with a photograph from a set of 36 possible choices. This process revealed to the members of the community a procedure for evaluating the appropriateness of spaces within a school building.

Over all, it was clear that each member of each group had been given an opportunity at some stage of the process to define and defend his or her own ideas, and to reach out for agreement and shared understanding within the group. The five groups participating in the gaming sessions selected a total of ten different goals, two of which were common to four of the groups.

The final session of the charette began with board members, teachers, and parents assembling to re-evaluate the findings of the previous game session, and to reword, clarify, and amend the material into a new set of goals that the entire group could support. The several new participants who joined the planning group were readily accepted, and were acquainted with previous processes and decisions.

The collaborative wish poem was reviewed, and from it a set of statements were distilled that included concerns about fostering social awareness, working with less fortunate children, challenging students, learning through direct experience, and identifying parent and community responsibilities. With these statements and the game objectives in mind, the group was asked to meet without the consultants to produce a set of goals, written in their own words, that would serve as the objectives for their school. The group returned after a long and often boisterous discussion with a list of thirteen statements that they felt satisfied their needs.

The procedure used to establish the schools' priorities within this list was a method in which each goal was compared with every other one, and to select from each pair the one that was most important. This technique is referred to as *paired comparisons*. Although this required 78 separate decisions from each participant, the procedure was carried out easily by participants, acknowledging their decisions by a show of hands, so that the results were immediately tabulated. Thirteen goal statements were ranked in order of importance, according to the paired comparison technique.

This product — the participants' goals ranked according to their own priorities — provided a great sense of satisfaction for the school community. They were especially pleased that their overall objectives emphasized personal growth rather than a concentration on academic achievement. From this consensual base, a model was proposed for translating the community's objectives into instructional procedures, and subsequently into educational settings. The first goal statement, *developing a sense of responsibility,* was used as an illustration by soliciting responses for instructional methods to implement this goal, using the alternatives already familiar from the previous discussion sessions. Some of the methods suggested were: *independent study, experimentation, small-group activity, problem solving, role playing, lecture-demonstration,* and *group discussion.*

Each proposed method was then coded according to student-teacher relationship, and evaluated against the 13 goal statements to determine the methods and relationships best suited to the program goals. This approach enabled the group to understand fully the means by which their goals could be realized. It also held in abeyance emotionally loaded discussions of "open" or "non-graded" classrooms until some general agreement of children's learning processes was shared by all participants. This helped prevent the "fixing" of concepts too early in the planning stages, by allowing solutions to evolve through goal-oriented discussion rather than through arguments based on prejudgment. In this way the architect (who participated in all sessions) was given a more complete view of the intention and direction of the school program and, as a result, was in a position to generate alternatives appropriate to this community's needs, rather than having to follow currently fashionable prototypes.

This session heightened the confrontation between faculty and parents. During the process of associating learning methods with objectives, it became clear that the student-teacher relationship should be a function of the goals intended, regardless of the popularity or convenience of any "teaching" model. The teachers were made aware of the fact that while they had a body of knowledge to convey through the academic curriculum, the school's objectives were to determine the way in which students were exposed to "content" areas.

All preceding discussions centered on the development of a consensual educational base from which a building program could generate. The following session attempted to synthesize previous discussions through the graphic representation of the newly formulated goal statements and learning methods. While the charette participants suggested learning methods, a team of architects responded with spontaneous sketches depicting the physical realization of the proposed ideas. This session had a twofold impact on the community group. First, it permitted the participants to view the architects' interpretations of verbal statements into physical form; second, the participants became more sensitive to the processes designers utilize in shaping space. While it was evident that the emerging forms were merely illustrative suggestions, the group's awareness of the links between learning methods and appropriate spaces was substantially sharpened.

Although this marked the end of the planned activities, the charette was extended at the request of the participants in order to provide more specific design directives to the architect. The intention was to describe all of the activities that the children would engage in (the activities that the facility would be designed to serve), and to select the learning methods appropriate to the objectives of the school. The primary activities of the school day were initially defined as:

Art
Construction
Drama
Independent study
Language arts
Music
Science
Social science
Sports

In order to facilitate a productive discussion, data sheets were prepared whereby each activity for each grade could be treated independently (Figure 3-25). The data sheet became a permanent record of the requirements of the facility as the development of each of the primary activities suggested its relative importance in terms of the allocation of spaces. This information provided the architect with a reasonable starting point for the development of a building design, as he assumed the role of translating objectives, methods, and activities into an accommodating spatial organization.

The charette had reached this point through a series of structured techniques which enabled the participants to define with increasing confidence and independence their educational objectives, and the type of environment they would need to implement those objectives.

AFTER-OCCUPANCY RESPONSES

Based on the program developed during the charette, the architect submitted four alternative proposals and accompanying cost estimates for construction. Figure 3-26 represents one plan alternative. An extremely limited budget, however, and an overconfident board of trustees, composed mostly of parents, caused them to dispense with the services of the architect in favor of visiting schools until they found a floor plan that could easily accommodate their perceived needs. A local builder constructed their new school based on a set of modified floor plans of a similar private school elsewhere in the state.

Follow-up interviews with the principal and teachers, as well as observations of the school building in use several years after construction, revealed numerous problems that resulted from the hasty actions of the trustees. The principal clearly stated that concerns for reducing the initial building cost and dispensing with the architect were unwise, since the utility and operating costs and the construction modifications have plagued the school for a decade. An indoor swimming pool, constructed to satisfy one of the earlier objectives of bringing the community to the school,

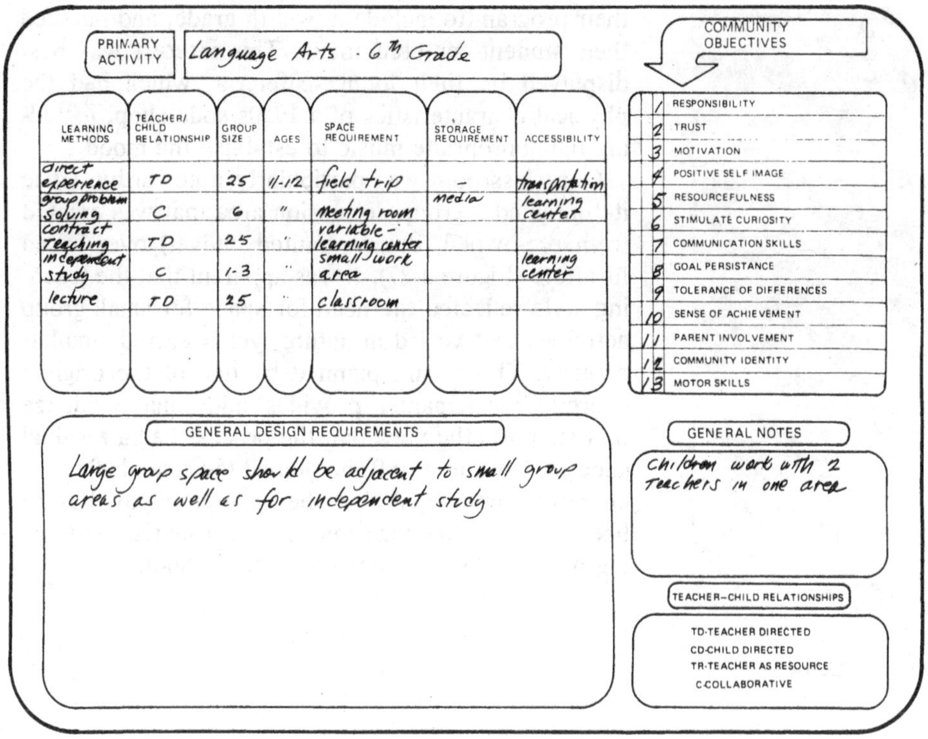

PRIMARY ACTIVITY: Language Arts · 6th Grade

COMMUNITY OBJECTIVES

LEARNING METHODS	TEACHER/CHILD RELATIONSHIP	GROUP SIZE	AGES	SPACE REQUIREMENT	STORAGE REQUIREMENT	ACCESSIBILITY
direct experience	TD	25	11-12	field trip	–	transportation
group problem solving	C	6	"	meeting room	media	learning center
contract Teaching	TD	25	"	variable - learning center		
independent study	C	1-3	"	small work area		learning center
lecture	TD	25	"	classroom		

1 RESPONSIBILITY
2 TRUST
3 MOTIVATION
4 POSITIVE SELF IMAGE
5 RESOURCEFULNESS
6 STIMULATE CURIOSITY
7 COMMUNICATION SKILLS
8 GOAL PERSISTANCE
9 TOLERANCE OF DIFFERENCES
10 SENSE OF ACHIEVEMENT
11 PARENT INVOLVEMENT
12 COMMUNITY IDENTITY
13 MOTOR SKILLS

GENERAL DESIGN REQUIREMENTS

Large group space should be adjacent to small group areas as well as for independent study

GENERAL NOTES

Children work with 2 Teachers in one area

TEACHER–CHILD RELATIONSHIPS

TD-TEACHER DIRECTED
CD-CHILD DIRECTED
TR-TEACHER AS RESOURCE
C-COLLABORATIVE

FIGURE 3-25. Typical activity worksheet identifying community objectives and learning methods.

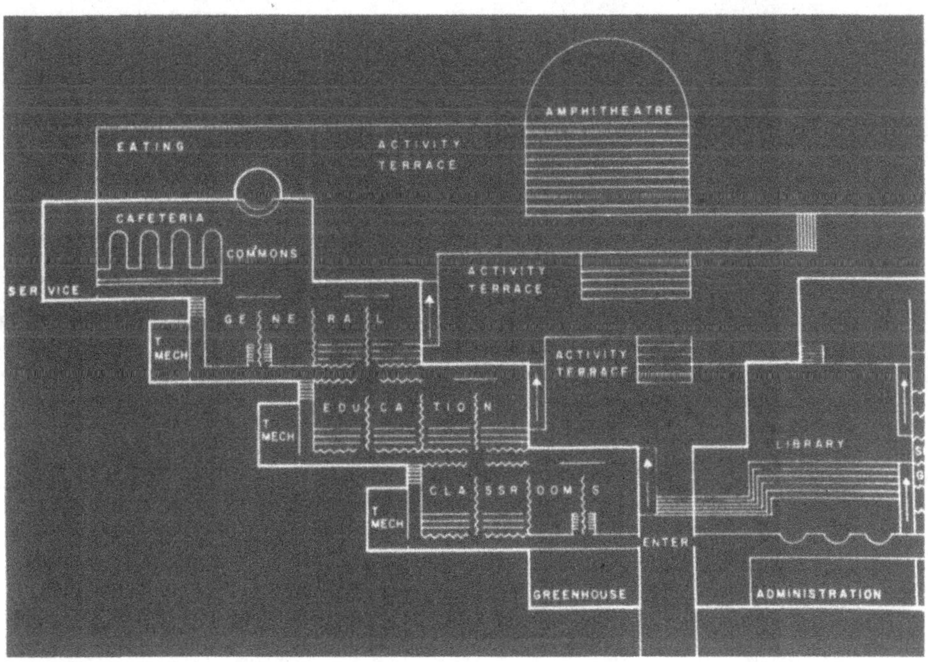

FIGURE 3-26. Proposed floor plan (Drawing: William Laslett).

had to be closed for four months during the year because of excessive heating and dehumidification costs.

Discussions with teachers who participated in the charette revealed a feeling of alienation by not being directly involved in the plan review process. This role was delegated to the overly zealous trustees and the principal. Even ten years after construction, the teachers believed that their involvement could have improved the building appearance as well as its proper functioning. On the positive side, the charette process increased the teachers' sensitivity to the emotional needs of the students, particularly as they expanded

FIGURE 3-27. Classroom in new building modified by the teacher (Photo: Henry Sanoff).

their program to include a twelfth grade, and pursued their student-centered focus. This interest was best displayed by their lounge-cafeteria, which had the physical characteristics of a 1950s soda shop, including the appropriate music to establish the mood.

One classroom was particularly noteworthy, since it contained a group discussion area that was created from pre-owned (due to limited budget) overstuffed furniture (Figure 3-27). It was apparent that the teaching style reflected the need for space for small-group activities that varied in nature, yet occurred simultaneously. This room, planned by one of the original charette participants, provides additional evidence that supports the view that the process had a residual success. Teaching staff that joined the school after the charette commented that they regretted not having been a part of the occasion that represented the turning point in the development of the school.

4
Higher Education Environments

Higher Education Environments

Campus design warrants attention because many older buildings can no longer serve their function, changing demographics will create competition for students through the turn of the century, and, finally, college and university campuses are in poor physical condition today. Rapid growth and inflation have caused deferred maintenance and constructed buildings of poor quality. In recognition of this factor, most American campuses propose to enhance their physical condition through restoration, renewal, or replacement in the coming decade. While campus planning methods are often used to guide physical development, it is useful to consider linking design, behavior, and participatory planning methods in establishing the campus plan agenda.

Current campus planning methods have evolved from the ideal rooted in English medieval universities, where students and teachers lived and studied together in tightly controlled colleges. In its most formative period, the early 19th century, American higher education experienced rapid growth but found itself in crisis. Traditional education, requiring mandatory chapel services, strict dormitory rules, and adherence to a prescribed curriculum, gave rise to student frustration. Vandalism and violence were not uncommon and concern for student order often affected architectural planning (Turner 1984). Much of the collegiate work of that period was thought to belong to the architectural category that included prisons and asylums. Classical curricula seemed to embody the classical style of architecture, and the Greek Revival which was popular for nearly all building types seemed particularly well suited for colleges. Symmetry and order were apparent in the planning of all schools, and grand physical plans were often considered more important than academic matters. By the mid-19th century, the traditional university was criticized for not meeting contemporary needs. An aspect of the new democratic reform of education included educational planning, and books on school design with plans showing classroom flexibility. The Land Grant College Act fostered the right of education to all social classes and the freedom of students to choose their courses of study. With this change of focus came a change in attitude about campus planning. Noted landscape architect Frederick Law Olmstead, who was involved in the design of about 20 schools during his career, proposed to adopt a picturesque, rather than a formal and perfectly symmetrical, campus arrangement. This approach, he argued, would harmonize with the character desired for the neighborhood as well as allow for modifications in the general plan of building. By the 20th century, architectural competitions became a common method for selecting designs for universities, though the Beaux-Arts movement advocating monumental organization and orderly planning at a grand scale influenced campus design many years following.

After World War II, rapid increase in enrollments and changing patterns of education dramatically affected campus planning, particularly traditional forms of design. Traditional design usually produced a unified design with a particular architectural character. Master plans were abandoned in favor of establishing principles for future growth, since many college administrators found such plans unrealistic and difficult to implement fully. By the mid-20th century, the view of the university was that it could never be complete. This gave rise to the individual campus building, with little regard for the whole. Campus open spaces were filled with large lecture halls, large dormitories, and student unions, without any attempt to conform to an existing campus style. Concern for unprecedented and unpredictable growth made institutions think about flexibility. Consequently, the location of new buildings was based on traffic patterns, densities, and other environmental conditions. Dober (1963) described each building on a campus as a planning unit, where the manipulation of each would have consequences for all. Therefore, he argues for constant testing, adjustment, and feedback to reach agreement on the location of roads, and connections between buildings.

Dober (1992) conceives of campus planning today as a product and a process, in which there is a well-defined sequence of activities, and an equitable division of labor and responsibility between constituency representatives and consultants. Campus-wide discussions to inform, to endorse, and to receive comments are integral to achieving an acceptable plan. General agreement is achieved when there is consensus about the meaning and consequences of the findings.

The campus environment consists of a number of interdependent relationships including physical structures, organization, and people (Evans 1983). An approach for understanding the effect of the environment on the well-being of students is described as the campus ecology model (Crookston 1975). The campus ecology movement (Banning 1978, 1980) emphasized the importance of considering the influence of the campus environment on the behavior and performance of students and of attempting to change conditions that were negatively affecting students' lives. Developed by a task force of the Western Interstate Commission for Higher Education (WICHE 1973), the establishment of campus design centers was advocated whose staff would devote full time to the assessment and redesign of campus environments. Environmental assessment and redesign projects in a variety of settings have been conducted. A few researchers have attempted to assess the total campus environment (Coyne 1975; Treadway 1979). Others have investigated the environment of a medical school (Huebner et al. 1979), an academic department (Huebner 1975), and residence hall systems (Daher, Corazzini, and McKinnon 1977; Schuh 1979).

The mainstream of research in post-secondary school environments is in the area of university residences. Moos (1979) developed a University Residence Environment Scale which investigates students' perceptions of their own interactions, the emphasis in the residence upon social versus intellectual activities, the extent of order and of innovativeness, and student influence in making decisions about house operations. Other researchers have also explored the influence of the college environment on students and developed theories to account for these influences (Astin 1968; Holland 1973; Moos 1979). In general these theories suggest that the degree to which student's characteristics and needs are congruent with various aspects of the environment influences their satisfaction, happiness, and achievement. A format that asks about perceived discrepancies between the ideal and real environment provides an estimate of the degree of their congruence.

Studies of the physical environment indicate that distance, spatial arrangements, and amenities have been found to influence behavior and attitudes of people working or living in various settings. Information concerning these environmental factors can be assessed using floor plans, lists of amenities in a particular location, or rating scales that assess the impressions people have of the physical characteristics of an environment (Evans 1983).

Research in the assessment and manipulation of college and university environments is even more fragmentary than research into elementary school environments. Much of this research is based on interaction patterns between individuals and different meanings associated with the use of *environment*. Gump (1987) suggests the ordering of findings into groups such as site, paths, enclosure, and seating, all of which are modified and shaped by interpersonal relationships. This ordering would provide a common framework and the development of cumulative findings.

Florida A&M University School of Architecture

Attitude Survey	✓
Charette Process	✓
Community Meetings	
Design-In	
Focused Interviews	✓
Fishbowl Planning	✓
Game Simulation	
Group Dynamics	
Public Forum	
Task Force	
Training	
Workshop	

SUMMARY

The Florida State Legislature was not only concerned about producing high quality, energy-conserving buildings; they also endorsed a number of innovations such as selecting an architect by competition, as well as modifying some steps in the normal building delivery system for the new architecture building at Florida A&M University. As part of this process a team was selected to conduct a Post-Occupancy Evaluation (POE) to examine the process of design and construction, and to evaluate the completed building. The data were collected in four phases including pre-move evaluation, construction monitoring, settling-in evaluation, and evaluation after one year of occupancy. The results are contained in a final report prepared by the College of Architecture, Georgia Institute of Technology, and Min Kantrowitz (1986) and Associates. This POE process was unique in that the responsibility for all phases of the project, from identification of issues, through data gathering and analysis, to implementation planning has been shared between the project team and students, faculty, and key decision makers from the university, and the state of Florida.

CLIENT

In 1980 the Florida State Legislature, concerned that state-owned buildings be of highest possible quality and be delivered quickly and efficiently, explored a number of innovations for the new School of Architecture building. They allowed the Board of Regents to select the architect by competition, hire a construction management firm, and track the planning, construction, and occupancy of the building. As part of this process, the School of Architecture and Board of Regents (BOR) selected a team to conduct a Post-Occupancy Evaluation to examine the design and construction process and to evaluate the completed building. The results are documented in a Final Report prepared by the project team which included Min Kantrowitz, Project Manager; Craig Zimring, Principal Investigator, Georgia Tech; and Edward T. White, Project Officer, Florida A&M University.

The Capital Improvements Office of the BOR served as the owner during design and construction. The university, through its Campus Planning Office, administered the contract. The owner also included the facility users, the School of Architecture, which played a more active role in design and construction because of their expertise.

The architect was the firm of Clements/Rumpel/Associates, winner of the design competition whose program was prepared by the School of Architecture. The program established the requirements for image, building function for occupants, and building performance.

PROJECT

The FAMU School of Architecture was perceived as a continuing experiment and teaching tool. Organizers intended for students to learn by studying how the building was designed and constructed and by observing what works and wears well over time and what does not. By using both the successes and shortcomings of the facility as teaching tools, the entire building becomes a valuable resource in the educational program. Several of the experimental aspects of the facility involve the passive heating and cooling system. Other features of the school included the use of small individual studios, the reduced size of faculty offices in favor of shared meeting space, and the open circulation system to facilitate human interaction.

The design competition for the new School of Architecture stressed a structure that "pushed the limits of current definitions of architecture, one that emphasized economical construction, programmatic flexibility, community accessibility, and energy conservation (Wineman and Zimring 1986)."

The building is located on a sloping site along a major campus road. The library, computer lab, and lecture hall are contained within a front block, partially buried to relate in scale and material to the facing houses. Perpendicular to the front block are four wings containing offices, labs, and studios (Figure 4-1). The wings are constructed with low-cost steel framing and corrugated steel and fiberglass cladding.

One of the objectives for the new architecture building was to avoid the large, barn-like rooms in favor of smaller, individual and separate studios which hold only one class of 16 students each. The intention was to create an atelier atmosphere in the design classes, a sense of ownership of the space, where students have their own work station and are encouraged to move in.

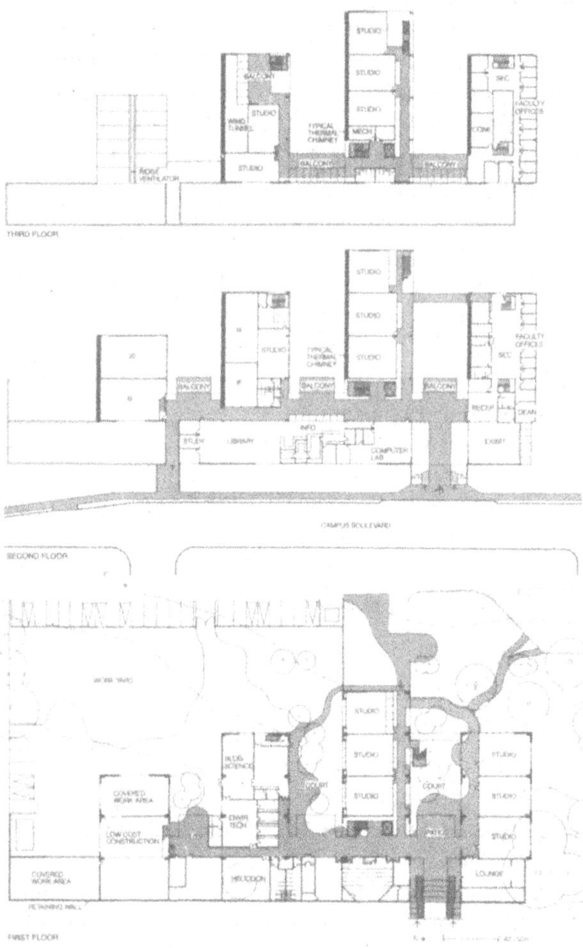

FIGURE 4-1. Building plans (Drawing: Clements/Rumple/Associates, Architects/Planners, Inc.).

PROCESS

The School of Architecture was established in 1975 as a result ot "Florida's Plan for Equalizing Educational Opportunities in Public Higher Education" in 1974 and the 1973 State University System's "A Study of Florida's Future Need for Architects." The goals set forth were to establish a quality professional degree program.

The school was housed in space designed for and occupied by other academic programs on the A&M campus. The rapid growth of the program and its space requirements were not met by the school facilities. As a result, a School of Architecture building project was proposed to be consistent with similar programs throughout the country that would satisfy professional accreditation requirements.

A facilities program was prepared by the school's faculty, establishing requirements for image, building function for occupants, and building performance. A faculty design charette was used to generate a building requirements list that was structured into the building program in four weeks. The architect was selected through a national two-stage competition held in 1980. Thirty-four entries were received from across the nation, of which six were selected for participation in phase two of the competition. After much deliberation, the jury settled on the Clements Rumpel submission as the first place scheme. In addition, a construction manager was used rather than a competitive-bidding process. A major program goal was to "demonstrate 'state-of-the art' techniques in passive heating, cooling, ventilation and lighting systems." Other related goals were to "utilize advantages in the area's climate," and to "present image of 'leading edge' quality of school." This was the basis for selection of the design from the competition. Promoting social interaction between students and faculty and effective workspace were equally valued goals. Using the concept of community as an organizing element, organizers hoped that a new building would support a sense of social community among the students: "a place where people would want to go, where they would want to spend time." Comfort was also seen as important: "Environmental factors have a significant impact on teaching and learning processes."

POST-OCCUPANCY EVALUATION PROCESS

The Post-Occupancy Evaluation (POE) of the Florida A&M University (FAMU) School of Architecture is one result of the Florida State Legislature's aim at testing a number of innovations in building design and delivery. The project team selected to conduct the study organized an Advisory Task Force composed of key decision makers from Florida state government, Florida A&M University, and the FAMU School of Architecture. Their evaluation addressed many issues related to building use, maintenance, and flexibility. Of particular concern was how the building met the program objectives concerning building image, energy conservation, social interaction, and security. The Task Force relied heavily on walk-through interviews. These interviews helped the faculty feel they were part of the process, and that their concerns were heard and understood. These participatory "self-report" measures were balanced by observation and physical monitoring which allowed more quantifiable information to be gathered.

The evaluation took place in four phases:

1. Pre-move evaluation
2. Construction monitoring
3. Settling-in evaluation
4. Evaluation one year after occupancy

Over a three-year period the project team examined the former building occupied by the School of Architecture, analyzed the new building construction process, studied the newly occupied School of Architecture as occupants settled into it, and assessed the building after more than a year of occupancy.

Pre-Move Evaluation. The evaluation team gathered information about the school's former quarters by conducting walk-throughs with staff, faculty, and students. The team studied building use patterns, physical conditions, and the users' assessments of their old building and expectations about the new one. Documentation consisted of questionnaires, individual interviews, walk-throughs, and observations of student, faculty, and staff activities.

Construction Monitoring. The construction process was monitored to see why changes were made and if they affected the design. The team analyzed the program, attended construction meetings, and analyzed changes to the construction documents. Interviews with the architect, construction manager, and client representatives also enabled the team to examine other issues related to the construction process.

Settling-In Evaluation. The team visited the school ten weeks after initial occupancy to compare issues identified during the walk-through with expectations and programmatic intent. Documentation consisted of faculty logs, individual interviews with administrators, and walk-throughs with staff, faculty, and students.

Evaluation One Year After Occupancy. A follow-up building use analysis and physical condition study was conducted by a walk-through with faculty, students, and staff, observations of student and faculty activity, and measurements of noise, light, and temperature levels.

A variety of data collection methods were used to reflect the client's desire to involve the school and important decision makers in the process.

Jean Wineman and Craig Zimring (1988) summarize the results of an evaluation of the school by stating, "Students and faculty are proud of their new building and bring visitors often. The school is a campus landmark." The building has become a major stop on tours of Tallahassee by students and faculty. In addition, newspapers and architectural magazines have praised the building's visual interest (Figure 4-2). In 1985, an international jury of the Florida American Institute of Architects gave the building an award for design excellence.

The consequences of programmatic decisions also clearly demonstrated conflicts between different "users" of the building. While the students and faculty wanted a building with a strong image, this emphasis has increased the expense of long-term maintenance and operations for the university. The client and architect were concerned with making a building that would be flexible and efficient for a school of architecture. Changing uses for the school, however, may present a serious future problem. While many of the spaces can accommodate a variety of uses, they are not able to change their size easily. The relatively small studios make it difficult to schedule small or larger classes. As a result some studios are overcrowded and are required to utilize space originally designated for group discussions. In addition, the small dark studios create a feeling of isolation between studios and between levels of students. Students feel there is insufficient interaction as a result of the design of the individual studios.

While the finger plan and building organization are clear and facilitate easy movement between inside and outside, segregating faculty into an administrative wing received mixed reactions from faculty and was generally disliked by students. Although most students and faculty feel social interaction is enhanced by the ability to see each other on the open walkways, there appears to be greater isolation of faculty from students because of the "wing" organization of the building.

FIGURE 4-2. Exterior of building (Photo: Florida A&M School of Architecture).

The faculty-administration wing offers few opportunities for casual faculty interaction which is felt to exacerbate the feeling of isolation in the school. The exterior spaces intended for socializing, circulating, and teaching are heavily used for all of these purposes. Students and faculty are enthusiastic about the openness of the plan. They enjoy the convenient relationship between interior and exterior spaces and often take advantage of good weather to hold classes and meetings outside. The stairs to the street from the first courtyard come from a natural amphitheater, and sessions with the entire school are frequently held there.

One of the original competition goals was that the building would serve as a continuing experiment and teaching resource. The building was to demonstrate steel-frame construction and leading edge design. To accomplish this aim, the architect felt that exposing the mechanical system and joints between materials would allow students to visually trace the working of the heating and ventilating system and details of construction (Figure 4-3). This has occurred, and the building is frequently used as an example in technical classes. Faculty from the department of education expressed the desire to develop and formalize ways in which the building is and can be used as a teaching tool.

In an effort to achieve a state-of-the-art energy conservation system, some of the elements appear to be overly experimental. Thermal comfort is reportedly difficult to control, and while the faculty have taken responsibility for running the complex computer-controlled system, there are substantial complaints about excessive humidity. It was proposed by the architect

FIGURE 4-3. Interior view showing the building's structure (Photo: Florida A&M School of Architecture).

as a "hands-on laboratory," yet little can be done to alter uncomfortable conditions.

Benefits of the POE Process

A variety of benefits resulted from the POE process. Not only did the findings help fine-tune the building, but the evaluation provided feedback to [illegible] state about the building process. The evaluation increased awareness of POE within the FAMU School of Architecture and provided an ongoing case study for classes in the school. The POE also enhanced communication among the organizations involved in the state building delivery process.

Kellog Community College, Science Laboratories

Attitude Survey	
Charette Process	
Community Meetings	
Design-In	
Focused Interviews	✓
Fishbowl Planning	
Game Simulation	
Group Dynamics	
Public Forum	
Task Force	✓
Training	
Workshop	

SUMMARY

In the belief that the design and management of a college building could affect the quality of the education given inside it, Kellog Community College (KCC) commissioned Facility Management Institute (FMI), a division of Herman Miller Research Corporation (HMRC), to design interiors for a 60,000 ft four-story science-health building.

The building, designed by Sarvis Associates, was evaluated after its completion using objectives established in the original program. Using interviews with the occupants of the building, as well as observations of lab activities, the evaluation team monitored the spatial behavior of administrators, instructors, and students (Zimring and Reizenstein 1981).

The objectives of having a building that could adjust to curricula and enrollment changes were approached by the use of a modular laboratory and office furnishings, mixing all functions in the same open interior space. So far, there have been many environmental changes including the enlargement of faculty offices and classrooms at costs lower than for a conventional facility as well as increased faculty-student contact. Findings of the post-occupancy evaluation support the notion that the environment's performance can be measured in both facility and human terms. Student interest in science increased and faculty-student contact doubled in the new building. Operating costs for inventory storage, materials handling personnel, and space rearrangement were all lower than for a conventional facility. The college also plans to continue the evaluation process by examining in-lab activity patterns and guiding plans for reorganization of the environment and the management system.

PROJECT

The project was innovative in that HMRC and KCC established performance objectives and evaluation techniques before the building was built. HMRC then designed the interior space, implemented a materials handling system, and performed a post-occupancy evaluation.

Working together on performance criteria, HMRC and KCC agreed that the Roll Building should contribute measurably to the quality of education at KCC and be a cost-effective facility. The college was committed to a building which would have low maintenance and change costs over the coming years, and which necessitated the use of versatile subsystems to provide an adaptable space configuration.

An 18-month performance evaluation was conducted by FMI using objectives established in the building's original concept documents.

CLIENT

Kellog Community College, Battle Creek, Michigan, had experienced all the facility problems associated with changing curricula and migrations of students from one program to another. Its existing building, only ten years old, had been unable to adapt. A new autotutorial program needed storage space and a laboratory had been converted to a storeroom. Faculty and curricula growth resulted in instructors sharing offices. New science and health courses were being taught in the drama and engineering buildings.

The college trustees approved a new science-health program and the college was anxious that the new building would avoid the pitfalls of the old one. The college wanted spatial efficiency without compromising function. The college also intended to house its science and health courses in a facility which would have a positive effect on the quality of health-science education and on student interest in the sciences.

PROCESS

Changing demographic characteristics are substantially influencing higher education facilities. More older students are enrolling than ever before, which has influenced the shift in emphasis of many existing programs. The pressure for changing curricula, coupled with declining enrollments, has forced higher education to accommodate these changes in their existing facilities. While many college buildings are obsolete, rising operating costs and short supply of funds have created the dilemma of inappropriate surplus space (FMI 1983). There are, however, institutions with the resources to build or reuse buildings that regard facilities as assets to be managed rather than as liabilities to be maintained.

With the assistance of FMI, Kellog Community College (KCC) attempted to enlarge the realm of facility concerns to include work process and people issues, emphasizing facility performance and ways to measure it when building a new classroom-laboratory building.

Although KCC's main laboratory building was only ten years old, it could not accommodate the technical and material changes necessary in the science and health area. The college trustees therefore approved a new building whose program was to permit major modifications of space allocations, spatial efficiency without compromising function, to a facility that would have a positive effect on the quality of health-science education and on student interest in the sciences. For this goal, four different approaches were proposed:

First, to increase creative cross-fertilization of ideas by increasing contact between disciplines. This could be accomplished by consecutive use of the same space by different classes and by visibility of ongoing classes.

Second, to remove impediments to constructive student-faculty contact by spending less classroom time in noneducational activities, such as searching for equipment and supplies.

Third, to provide a responsive building which would allow or encourage faculty to propose new courses or teaching methods readily accommodated in the building.

Fourth, to create an attractive, modern building that would enhance the sciences' general attractiveness and modern image.

HMRC and KCC agreed that these concepts and goals would have top priority in design decisions about physical layout and interior design. Consequently, the building was designed with some unusual features intended to maximize flexibility. The building was designed with a minimum of permanent walls and columns in order to use demountable partitions varying from four feet to ceiling height. The exterior walls and the wall separating the corridor from the main area were the only major walls in the building. The only corridor in the building ran along the side, rather than the center, of the building. To facilitate removal or storage, all furniture including lab benches, work surfaces, book shelves, and work lights were modular and suspended from the demountable partitions (Figure 4-4). All functioning areas, whether classrooms, laboratories, reading areas, offices, project areas, or lounges were separated by demountable partitions. Services such as water, electricity, vacuum, and compressed air were surface mounted along the full length of the north and south exterior walls, as well as on the columns.

The final design for the laboratory areas in the building contained a mixture of classrooms, small study areas, reception, teaching laboratories, with offices and project work areas on one of the floors (Figure 4-5). Teaching laboratories were without doors and were buffered by reception or reading areas (Figure 4-6), though varied in their arrangement and services. While the physics area contained work benches without plumbing, the chemistry work areas contained a full range of services at the center of each bench with all utilities available for each pair of students (Figure 4-7). Each laboratory area contained storage shelves, space for lockers, and mobile carts which are the main vehicle for the materials management system.

FIGURE 4-4. Modular components (Photo: Herman Miller Research Corporation).

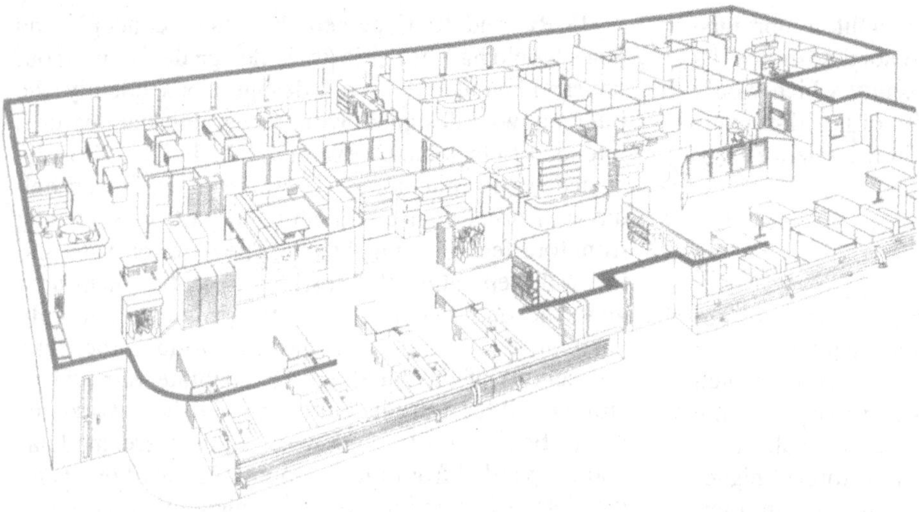

FIGURE 4-5. Layout of science floor (Drawing: Herman Miller Research Corporation).

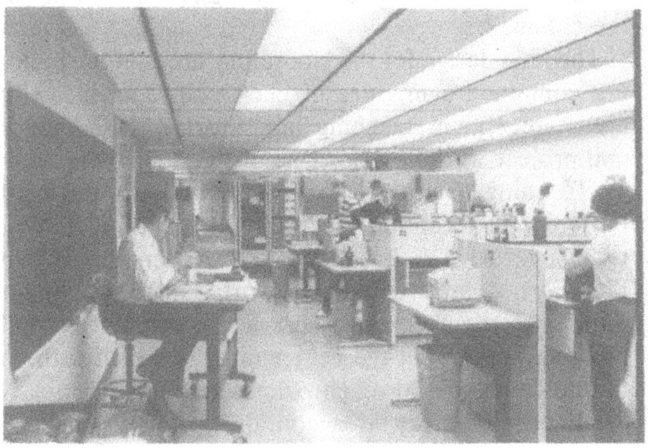

FIGURE 4-6. Instructional laboratory (Photo: Herman Miller Research Corporation).

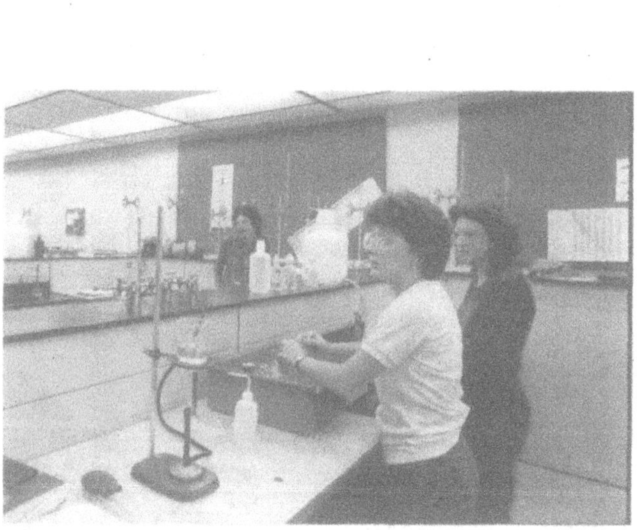

FIGURE 4-7. Laboratory work area (Photo: Herman Miller Research Corporation).

An important feature of this building was the development of a materials management system in which a fixed staff maintained a central inventory. This system eliminated most materials storage in the laboratories and relieved instructors and students of many non-learning tasks. Centralized storage permitted the total inventory to be reduced and minimized the time students and faculty devoted to searching for, preparing, and cleaning up materials (Figure 4-8). This approach to materials management is referred to as a "kit" system in educational institutions, a "case-cart" system in hospital surgery suites, and an "exchange" system in the military.

IMPLEMENTATION

There is little doubt that the Roll Building was different from all other college laboratories, and most industrial-clinical laboratories. Because the original goals of this building influenced its form, describing the Roll Building is difficult without considering whether or not it achieved its goals. Working together on the building performance, HMRC and KCC agreed that the Roll Building should be cost effective and improve the quality of education.

Plagued by science buildings that were overcrowded, obsolete, and full of huge quantities of uninventoried supplies, the college wanted a building that would be able to adjust to curricula and enrollment changes. The college was committed to a building that would have low maintenance, cleaning, and change costs. Cost effectiveness was translated into building objectives related to reduced maintenance, avoided high cost for renovation compared to conventionally designed facilities; reduced fixed storage; and

FIGURE 4-8. Central storage system (Photo: Herman Miller Research Corporation).

reduced labor costs to operate materials management systems.

The Roll Building cost $4.1 million, including furniture and equipment. Per-square-foot cost was about the median for college laboratory buildings. Fixed storage was reduced by 88 percent. Additional mobile storage made the total reduction in storage 66 percent. Less equipment is required and expensive laboratory space is no longer being used for storage due to the materials management center.

The cost effectiveness of the building was demonstrated by the renovation performed after the building was occupied. Thirteen offices were redesigned at a cost far below industry estimates of change costs.

QUALITY OF EDUCATION

Several quality education objectives were stated as specific hypotheses that were tested as part of the facility performance evaluation. These included faculty-student contact time, and reduction of student-faculty time in materials handling. Data on each of the measures were collected before and after the move to the new building. The type of data included grades, library records, enrollment records, and requests for transcripts, and were used from the three-year period prior to the move. In addition, interviews and subjective impressions were used. In all cases, data-gathering methods used can be repeated by the college in the future.

Objective. Both faculty and students should be freed from the necessity of materials handling and the free time should be used for educational activities.

Hypotheses:

1. Students will spend less laboratory time searching for, setting up, cleaning up, and putting away materials.
2. Students will spend more laboratory time performing experiments in contact with instructors.
3. Faculty will spend less laboratory time searching for, setting up, cleaning up, and putting away materials.
4. Faculty will spend more laboratory time in contact with students.
5. Faculty will spend less non-laboratory time preparing materials for class.

Time sampling was used in ten classes to monitor the amount of time spent on different activities by a sample of students and instructors. Observations were made over a four-week period during the term immediately before the move and one year later. Interviews with the faculty were used to determine how much time they spent preparing for a typical laboratory in each course. The results indicated that contact time between faculty and students doubled during a typical lab hour. This was partly because of the materials management system, but also because instructors became able to spend more time in the labs. A mobile office table in the lab area allowed them to do work and class preparation in the lab rather than elsewhere. This was a major aim of the faculty and was indicative of the building's success.

Objective. Student interest in science and health technology courses should increase, and result in increased enrollment in courses in the building, more science majors, and more outside projects and reading.

Hypotheses:

1. Science credit hours, as a percentage of total college credit hours, will increase.
2. Fewer students will withdraw from science courses after enrolling.
3. More students will choose science majors.
4. More students will transfer to science-related programs in four-year colleges.
5. More science-related books for outside reading will be checked out of the library.

College records were used to measure the increase in science credit hours. Total enrolled credit hours in science courses were calculated as a percentage of total credit hours for the college. Figures were obtained from six semesters prior to the opening of the new building, and three semesters after opening. College records were also consulted for course withdrawal information and transfer information.

College records indicated an increase in the percentage of science credit hours as a percentage of total college enrollment. Once enrolled, the number of students withdrawing from science courses decreased 25 percent. The number of science majors increased by

22 percent. Finally, science students withdrew 23 percent more science books from the college library after the new building opened.

The administrators also hoped that a modern elegant building for science courses replacing outdated buildings would improve student interest. Evaluators followed enrollment figures, numbers of science majors, science books withdrawn from the library, and numbers of students finishing science courses. All these indicators rose after occupancy. Interviews with the program chairman indicated that there was also an increase in new course proposals from instructors as well as the initiation of science clubs, and increased field trips and outreach programs.

A cost-effective building and improved quality of education were two specific outcomes of this study. In addition, this project showed that facility management had a positive influence on productivity. It was apparent from this project that ongoing responsiveness to organizational growth and change were critical factors in the management and renovation of existing facilities as well as in new building design. While there is a growing interest in increasing the range of future options, work environments have to respond effectively to immediate needs as well. There will be growing interest in determining the extent to which a facility supports or exhibits a greater number and variety of activities, user adjustment of interior systems, and more efficient, less costly organization, storage, and retrieval of materials and supplies. Those persons responsible for educational facilities will be increasingly preoccupied with this idea.

Lawrence University, Wriston Art Center

Attitude Survey	✓
Charette Process	✓
Community Meetings	
Design-In	
Focused Interviews	
Fishbowl Planning	✓
Game Simulation	
Group Dynamics	
Public Forum	
Task Force	
Training	
Workshop	✓

SUMMARY

The Wriston Art Center fulfills a long-standing university goal to make the fine arts an integral part of campus life. The building was designed as a landmark on the Lawrence University campus and named in honor of a former president, Henry Merritt Wriston. Henry Wriston believed that the fine arts should have a significant place in the liberal arts college. In an essay on the "Nature of a Liberal College," Wriston states that "students should be surrounded with works of artistic merit . . . , hear great music and see great art . . . , find plenty of examples of fine architecture . . . , and give expression to such artistic talents as they may have. . . . Beauty apprehended and responded to through the discipline of appreciation brings life aspects of fulfillment which no other experience can contribute." Located at the crossroads of the campus, the building embodies Wriston's belief that art should be a central part of the Lawrence experience.

The design process involved students, faculty, and administrators in a series of five workshops consisting of the site, building program, discussion of alternative schemes, scheme refinement, and final review of drawings and model.

CLIENT

The trustees of Lawrence College initially anticipated an addition and renovation of their existing art center built in 1949, the Worchester Art Center. This simple one-story building stood between the student center and a six-story library. The college administration also felt that the art center entrance should face the campus green and a small plaza located adjacent to a newly constructed recreation center. Prior to the design workshops, Jefferson B. Riley of Centerbrook Architects discussed the feasibility of renovation compared to an entirely new building. Many options were discussed, including saving the existing building and locating the new art center in a more remote location. The administration reviewed its original goals of the art center being an integral part of student daily life, and decided to demolish the existing building and locate the new building on the same site. Site selection was discussed prior to the workshops because the decision to demolish the old building and construct a new one involved major financial considerations.

PROJECT

A programming committee documented the spatial requirements for the new art facility, as well as interviewed and recommended Centerbrook Architects to the university administration. Prior to the beginning of the workshop process, the committee submitted to the architect the programming document, which contained very clear architectural implications. Contained in this document was the belief the building should integrate the study of art history and supporting spaces, and the study of studio art. As a result, the architect was well informed about the university's needs, as well as the underlying philosophy of the building prior to the planning stages.

A series of five consecutive workshops occurred within one week in January 1987. With the assistance of the building committee, a working group of 44 people was formed at the suggestion of the architect, including the town planner, all the art faculty, the gallery director, the directors of development, finance, and physical plant, other faculty members, trustees, parents, and students. In addition to the working group, there was an executive committee that made the final decisions and arbitrated any impasses between working group participants. Although it initially seemed like an unwieldy size to some committee members, it resulted in an effective and productive group.

From the university's perspective, reported by committee chairman Michael Hittle, the proposed workshop served two main purposes: "Principally, it gave the architect an opportunity to educate the community to the nature of architectural decisions. Secondly, it gave participants the opportunity to raise precise questions about the nature of the building as it took shape during the course of the week-long workshop. There are demonstrable instances where the design was altered in response to these kinds of interactions between the members of the Lawrence community and Jeff Riley and his team."

The first workshop was devoted to site considerations. It was held on a wintry Sunday afternoon. The architect conducted a site walk and distributed an accompanying questionnaire, which allowed participants to rediscover the area that was so familiar to them. Questions required participants to locate trees, landmarks, and major routes on a map of the immediate vicinity surrounding the site. Other questions required participants to estimate distances and heights of buildings, building materials, and their feelings and impressions about neighboring buildings, and the area in general. After the site walk, the architects and participants returned to a lounge in the student union where they set up an office for the duration of the workshops. The lounge was in a popular location and heavily used by students and faculty. It was also located adjacent to the site for the new art center.

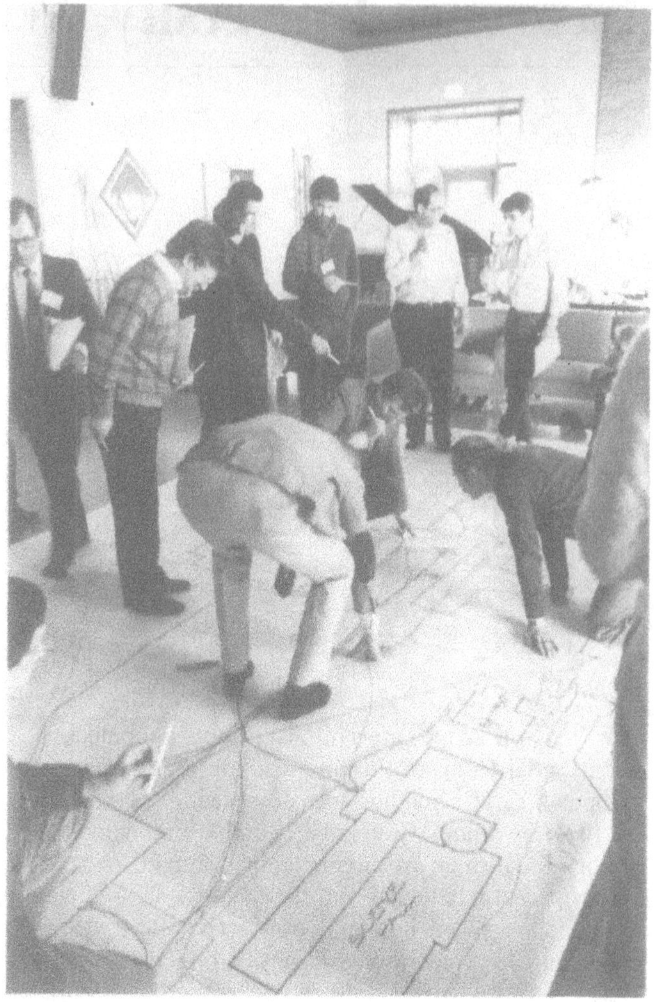

FIGURE 4-9. Community workshop (Photo: Centerbrook Architects).

Participants had written comments during their site walk, stimulating a discussion about important site features (Figure 4-9). The architect pointed out critical aspects of the site unnoticed by the community members, and how those characteristics might shape the design of the building. Comments were also freely voiced by the participants about features of the site they valued and wished to preserve. This generated a common understanding among all participants, provided clear insights to the architect about their desires, and allowed the discussion to proceed to the next stage. That same evening, a programming workshop explored community feelings about the building. Since the faculty of the art department had previously prepared the spatial requirements for the building, the architects tried to gain insights into the collective spirit of the campus, the nature of the building's users, the image, and character of the environment. This was achieved by asking the participants questions about "building philosophy." Should the center be a benign shelter for the works of art, or should it provide a context for works of art? The architects also questioned how the center could help the arts become a greater part of the lives of the Lawrence and Appleton communities.

Another workshop activity was described as a beauty contest, in which slides were shown of a wide variety of building images. Participants responded on a ballot sheet whether the images were either liked or disliked, and appropriate or inappropriate for the new art center.

The major results of the first two workshops were that the building should not face the green as had been assumed by the programming committee and college administration, but rather should be accessible from the major campus paths, as well as provide easier access to a variety of parking possibilities. This decision supported one of the major goals of the center, which was for it to be a town-wide asset and attraction. The other factor that surprised the architects was for the new building to provide some form of visual relief to the predominant use of brick and beige stone on most of the campus buildings.

Workshop three consisted of a discussion of two alternative schemes prepared in a period of 12 hours. The schemes dealt largely with site issues, and with the relationship between the new building to the student center to the south, the campus green to the west, the high rise library to the north, and Law Street to the east. One scheme was designed with an entrance onto the green, while the other faced the building toward the library, leaving an outdoor space between it and the student center. This scheme had the advantage of relating to the social center of the campus, and it was the scheme that was selected. This scheme prevailed, explains Riley, "without much controversy, and I believe this was due to the fact that everyone saw the same information, understood the reasons why one scheme was better than another, even though they had come with a preconceived notion of where the building should face."

Another issue considered in the development of the alternatives was circulation between the three major functional groups occupying the building. One group consisted of the faculty offices and the art history department with its slide room and lecture hall; the second was the art gallery group; and the third was the two- and three-dimensional studios. Circulation was necessary to allow all groups to meet yet remain separate. Public lectures and gallery openings, too, suggested the need for formal gathering of large groups.

On the following day, the office, which was located in the lounge, was open to the public for people to review the sketches displayed on the wall, and to write their comments on the plans or on index cards. The preferred scheme was further refined where the space between the Art Center and the student union was shaped, giving some form to the galleries, and how the three functions of history of art, gallery display of art, and the making of art would come together in one place.

At this scheme refinement workshop, disputes emerged over the galleries. One group envisioned a flexible, non-descriptive space in which anything could be done, while the other group voiced concern for permanent spaces with architectural character. This conflict was resolved by the design solution which featured a series of galleries, with greatest flexibility provided in the largest, and a progression of rooms allowing for architectural character and variety. The issue of natural light, too, aroused some controversy. Some feared that ultraviolet intrusion would damage the collection of paper and fabric works, while others favored natural light as a means to overcome "museum fatigue." This conflict was resolved by introducing natural light through light towers located at the transition spaces between the three galleries. Similarly, the conflict between those who felt that the creative purposes of the studio could diminish the reflective purpose of the classroom, lecture hall, and galleries, and those who wanted everyone to mix together, was resolved by the design solution. The studios were located below grade with daylight introduced through lightwells and large windows on the southside that were made possible by virtue of a sunken amphitheater. As a result, the studio noise is separated but visible from inside and outside, and people meet through a central stairwell. It is at this location in the building where the art office is located which monitors the access to any of the three major functions.

Another issue that required an innovative solution was the location of the loading docks where art work is brought in on semi-trailers, and trash is removed from the studios. This location, at the front door of the building, resulted from the conflict of having access to the building from all sides making it difficult to provide these services. The solution was to create two loading dock towers that could be accessed by large trucks. As Riley observes, "They became in effect the symbols of the building itself. The one loading dock tower being for the arrival of raw materials for the studios and symbolizing the making of art, and the other being the tall tower for the loading dock to the art galleries and symbolizing the study of art."

At this point, workshop four, the scheme was considerably refined and consequently more detailed comments were offered. By the end of the evening, most of the major issues were resolved. The following two days were devoted to preparation for the final presentation to the trustees. A mechanical engineer was brought in to make some preliminary determinations, and passers-by also stopped to make comments. While the design solution may not have answered everyone's concerns, everyone was given an opportunity to participate. The process was open and explanations were given to allow all participants the opportunity to understand why particular objections were not completely satisfied. The most outspoken opponents of the design solution became the strongest proponents after the building was constructed.

In retrospect, participants reported that the virtue in the design workshop was that they recognized the reasons that led to the different kinds of design solutions proposed by the architect. For the participants, the building design made a great deal of sense. They described the principal function of the workshop as

FIGURE 4-10. Building exterior (Photo: Paul Warchol).

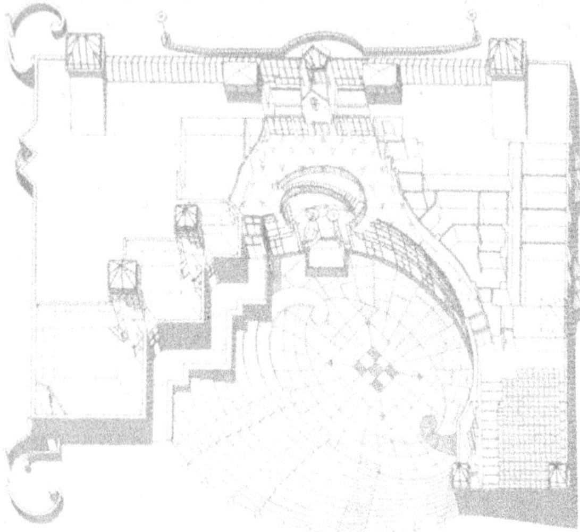

FIGURE 4-11. Axonometric of building (Drawing: Centerbrook Architects).

that of educating and preparing them for an intelligent continuing dialogue with the architect over the remaining months.

IMPLEMENTATION

The dark red brick and blue metal art center, set apart from the surrounding beige buildings, is located at the crossroads of three main pedestrian paths (Figure 4-10). To the north is a small garden plaza, and to the south, an elevation opens onto a recessed amphitheater and sunken plaza, providing an informal gatheringplace and a formal place for concerts and performances (Figure 4-11). Devoted to art history and exhibition, the upper level includes a serpentine galleria for the display of study reproductions and transitory exhibits (Figure 4-12); a 150-seat auditorium; a slide library; and faculty offices. The west side of the lobby features three galleries of ascending size. A curving staircase descends from the upper to the lower lobby, which opens into the center's studios and outdoor amphitheater. The studio complex includes a flexible area for painting, drawing, and print making; a multipurpose studio with facilities for computer art; a photography suite; and studios for ceramics, metal, and sculpture (Figure 4-13).

FIGURE 4-12. View from gallery (Photo: Paul Warchol).

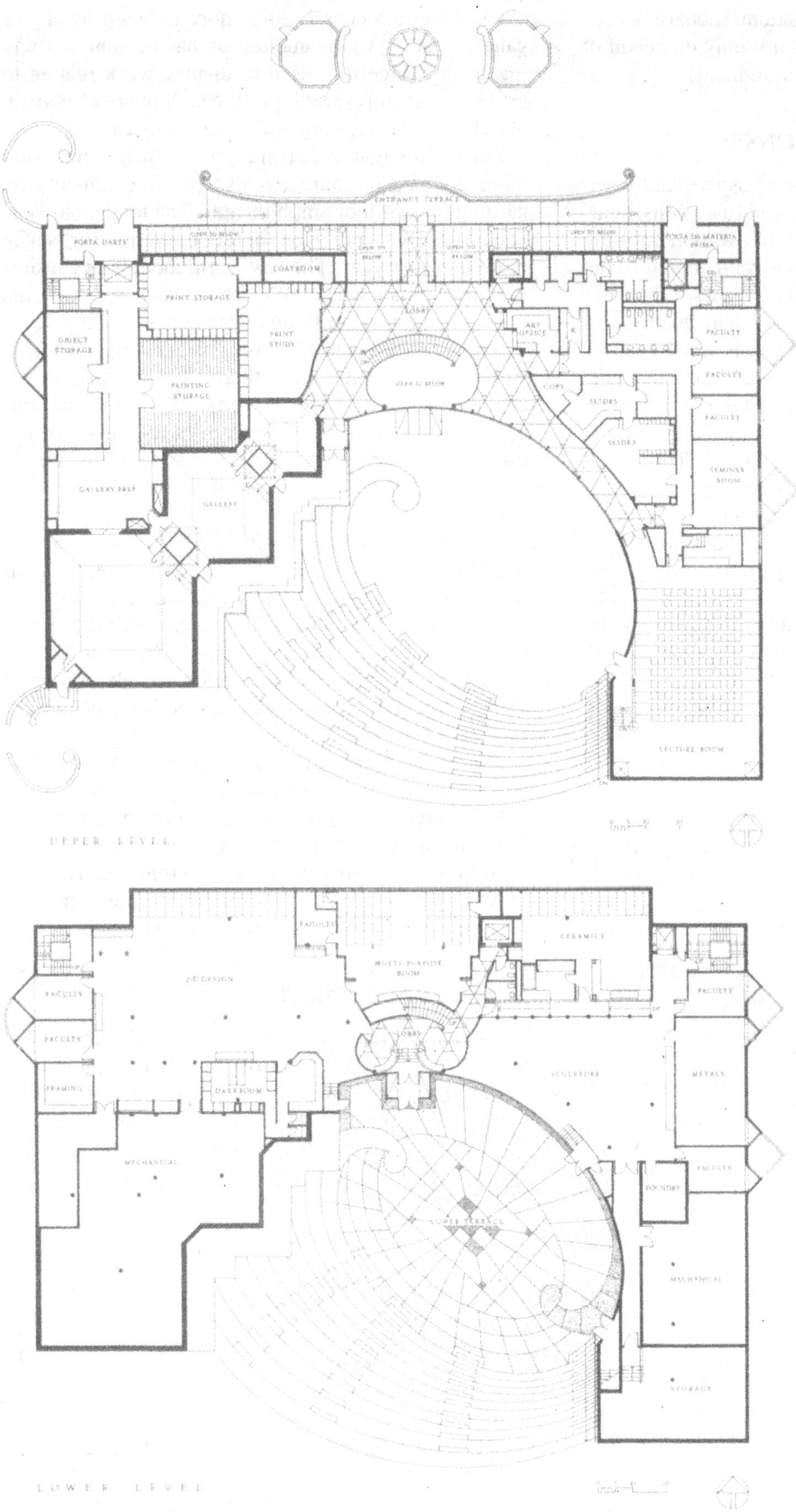

FIGURE 4-13. Floor plans of art center (Drawing: Centerbrook Architects).

As Lawrence University President Richard Warch states, "The building beckons us not only on behalf of itself, but on behalf of what goes on inside it."

AFTER-OCCUPANCY RESPONSES

Responses from the faculty to the positive and negative features of the building appeared to be consistent. Generally, there is a strong sense of awareness of the spaciousness of the building which is attributed to the planning. The spatial organization appears to be clear to occupants as well as to visitors. Light quality also contributes to the spaciousness, and is welcome during Wisconsin's long winter. Above all, the building is pleasing and inviting, and is a contrast to the surrounding buildings. One of the original objectives was to make the building visible on the campus. This effect has also been achieved by allowing students and faculty to take a path through the art center on route to the cafeteria from the student union or academic building. People passing through the art center also observe the activities of the lower-level studios (Figure 4-14). Consequently, the movement pattern on the campus has been altered by allowing people to penetrate the shell of the art center. At a more detailed level, the galleria leading to the auditorium has become a teaching space, since it is used to display work related to art history lectures. Slides of the lecture are also available for public viewing in the galleria area.

FIGURE 4-14. Outside view of the lower level studios (Photo: Paul Warchol).

Most of the features disliked about the building were more detailed in character, except for comments regarding the outdoor amphitheater. The long, cold Wisconsin winters preclude outdoor events for seven months of the year. The few warm months occur during the summer when there are no classes, and at the beginning and end of terms, which are difficult periods in which to stage a production. During the period from April to June, however, there are informal social events, and noon-hour concerts. While the outdoor area was a controversial issue from the outset of the project, it was generally agreed that this would be the only public gathering area on the campus and a valuable asset.

Daylight in buildings is often perceived as an amenity; for art galleries, though, it is sometimes difficult to control the lighting of art. The windows and skylights in the art center's gallery proposed those problems for some of the respondents. The storage and movement of art between galleries was also reported to be cumbersome and awkward because of narrow corridors and floor level differences.

Interestingly, the majority of people who responded to this survey are recent faculty and staff who were not involved in the design workshops conducted in 1987. While it was difficult to ascertain their working conditions prior to coming to Lawrence University, they all perceived the building as offering many opportunities to expand their teaching approach.

ACKNOWLEDGMENT

The author wishes to thank Jeff Riley of Centerbrook for his vivid recollection of the workshop process which he narrated into a microcassette recorder. Also, thanks to Michael Hittle, Building Committee chairman, for his comments about the workshop process. Finally to Christa Decker, who organized the faculty reactions about the building.

Michigan State University, Laboratory Classroom

Attitude Survey	
Charette Process	
Community Meetings	✓
Design-In	
Focused Interviews	✓
Fishbowl Planning	
Game Simulation	
Group Dynamics	
Public Forum	
Task Force	
Training	
Workshop	

SUMMARY

An examination of the influence of the physical environment on the satisfaction and proficiency of students and faculty was the subject of an experiment jointly sponsored by Michigan State University, Herman Miller Research Corporation (HMRC), and Herman Miller, Inc.

Two older conventional laboratory classrooms were converted to an experimental environment designed to support innovative programs. Organizers proposed that a more responsive environment supported by a facility management plan could improve educational proficiency and a more intense use of building space.

A year-long evaluation was conducted by The Herman Miller Research Corp. comparing the performance of the experimental workplace with that of the same environment prior to renovation. Using interviews, observation, and departmental records that measured formal and informal space use and personalization, the performance of the experimental workplace was judged to be better than the university averages for class-lab space in conventional new facilities.

CLIENT

At Michigan State, a group of educational administrators had been exploring the need for more effective and efficient educational programs and the type of services and facilities to support them. Within the Crop and Soil Science Department, an innovative educational program had been underway since 1965, utilizing learning objectives and an auto-tutorial format. The department converted a conventional teaching laboratory into a learning center with carrels, display tables, and a central "wet" lab bench. The results of the new program became the keystone of a proposed facility experiment in which HMRC would demonstrate that a more responsive facility management service could effect improved educational efficiency and a more intensive use of building space.

PROJECT

The project intended to conduct an experiment in which two older, conventional laboratory classrooms with fixed lab benches and casework would be converted to an experimental environment. The research team proposed the development of a Resource Service Store in the new facility which would provide raw materials, assistance, and service to students and faculty. Its staff would be responsible for the day-to-day operations and facility management of the experimental environment. The premise of the experiment argued that the satisfaction and proficiency of students and faculty would be significantly affected by the direct physical environment of the educational facility.

The first step in the program was to analyze and document the effects of the conventional setting on the functions and activities of the educational programs operating in that space. The second step was to develop and implement an experimental facility aimed at supporting an innovative educational program. The third step was to gather data on the performance of the new facility and to compare it to the effects of the conventional setting and the performance of university classroom-laboratory facilities in general.

The experimental test site consisted of rooms forming an L-shaped space connected by a door passageway between the two rooms. Rooms 219 and 220B, and 218 (an adjacent storage space) comprised 2600 square feet of space. The rooms were dominated by tall windows running along two sides of each room. Mounted side by side, the nine-foot-high windows created glazed areas 12 feet long. The original purpose of such extensive glazing was to maximize the amount of natural ventilation and lighting. But even with the addition of ceiling-hung fluorescent lights, the lighting quality in the rooms ranged from glare on bright days to mild gloom on overcast days or in the evenings. The smaller of the two rooms, 220B, was set up as a conventional laboratory with two fixed lab benches down the center of the room.

Originally a research laboratory, room 219 had been converted to a combination lecture-laboratory space. A portion of one of the lab benches had been removed to make room for a group of tablet armchairs. The rows of chairs were located near the entrance of the room facing a small chalkboard. In the center of the room were two rows of double laboratory benches like those in room 220B.

Located adjacent to room 219 was a storage area filled with forgotten, obsolete equipment and materials. As a result of extensive interviews, direct observations, and university and departmental records, organizers noted that a growing number of faculty chose not to teach there, increasing the load on other educational spaces in the college. This situation was due to the fact that teaching methods have changed, and laboratory courses have become less wet, while the original space was dominated by rigid furnishings designed for educational programs now outmoded. The limited vocabulary of functional settings, i.e., a formal lecture, or wet-lab activity, did not permit new educational activities, nor the use of new instruments as teaching aids. The limited storage facilities inhibited the development of a storage retrieval and dispensing service of materials and laboratory equipment. Materials, soil samples, and displays were frequently lost and wasted. There was no place for the preparation of display and laboratory exercises nor was there any way to provide individual students with auto-tutorial review materials.

Rooms 219 and 220B were examples of facilities whose furnishings were designed originally to be nearly indestructible. However, failure inevitably occurs, either in appearance or function, and a long period follows in which they are disliked by everyone before a decision can be made to dispose of them.

The dominant thrust of the experiment was that the new facility should support the daily program intention of the teachers, administrators, and students who proposed to use the place. Meetings with the users revealed the importance of the teaching mission and the ways it hindered or helped by features of the physical environment. The research team obtained abundant information and ideas on use and needs before it engaged in design activity. After several weeks of briefings, the group focused on the conceptual possibilities for the test setting. The tonality and expression of the place were discussed. What should the place tell students and professors when they enter? What capability for visual display and graphic communication should be provided?

As a result of the assessment of the existing laboratory and description of new users and needs, the research team explored the conceptual possibilities and arrived at a proposal for the new facility that would include a wet laboratory in close proximity to the auto-tutorial area. There would be a Resource Service Store that would serve the auto-tutorial program by checking out course materials and assigning carrels. There would be a place for reception and casual interaction as well as a sense of entrance. Architects presented the concept drawings to the user team in a series of meetings to insure that there was an operational understanding of the potential view of the new facility. In order to give the user group a highly tangible impression of the new facility, architects prepared a bird's eye perspective drawing (Figure 4-15). The experimental facility was installed and used for the test year almost exactly as presented in the conceptual sketches.

IMPLEMENTATION

The analysis of the experiment focused on the environment's ability to contribute to satisfaction and proficiency. A comparison of the conventional facility to the experimental setting was expressed by a series of ratios, derived from various measurement techniques.

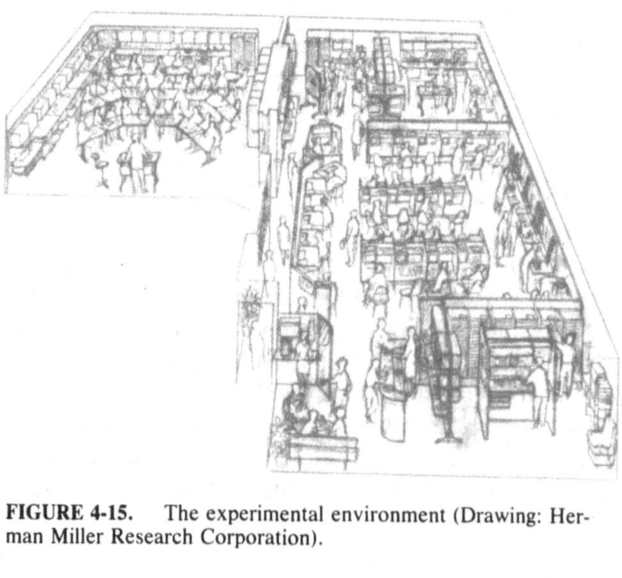

FIGURE 4-15. The experimental environment (Drawing: Herman Miller Research Corporation).

FIGURE 4-16. The learning center features auto-tutorial carrels (Photo: Herman Miller Research Corporation).

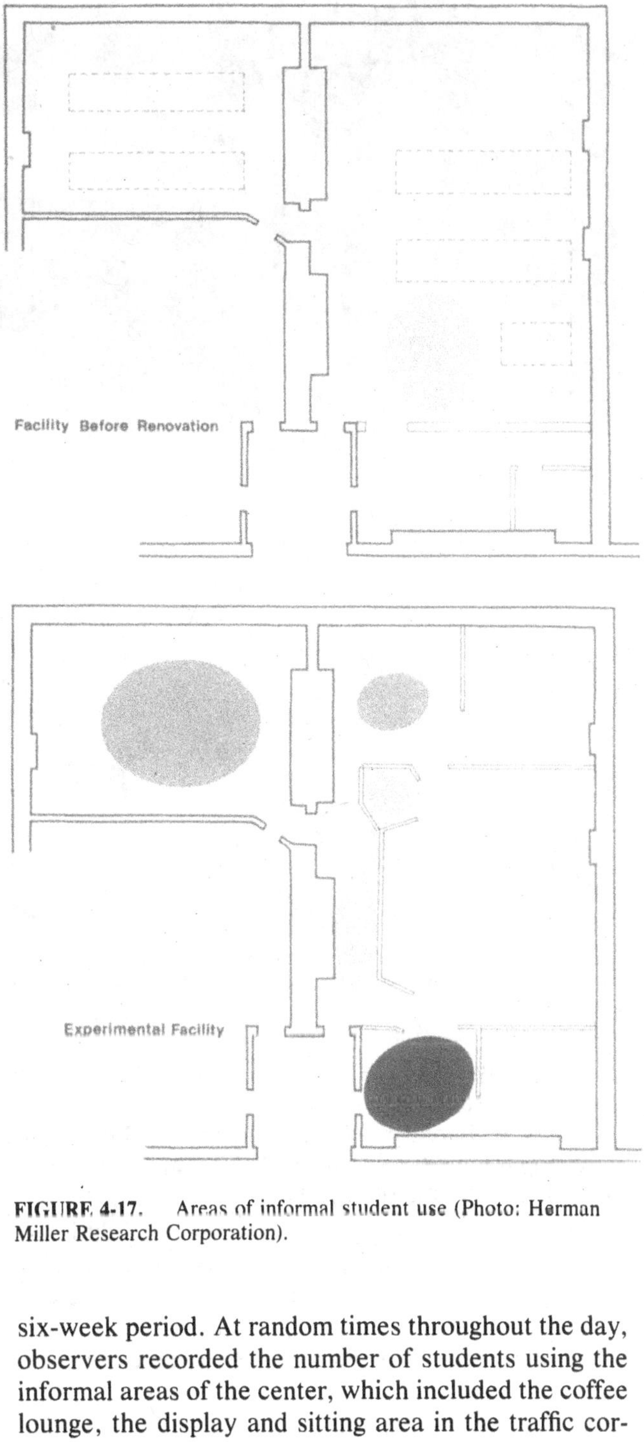

FIGURE 4-17. Areas of informal student use (Photo: Herman Miller Research Corporation).

The Facility Response Index was a measure based on the number and variety of activities the facility accommodated; user adjustment of the environment; and amount of time required for organization, storage, and retrieval of lab supplies and course materials. Comparisons of utilization patterns of the facility before and after renovation revealed a significant change in both scheduled and informal use of the space. The number of regularly scheduled classes held in the experimental environment increased 3.4 times over the use of the same space in the control year. The flexibility of the experimental environment allowed for the use of a variety of instructional formats in the new center (Figure 4-16). Providing auto-tutorial facilities in the new center was the major factor in expanding the use of space.

The Negotiation Index was a measure of the number and variety of services offered to students and faculty as well as the number of interactions with the Resource Store for services and assistance. In the facility before renovation no mechanism existed for providing services directly to faculty or students. Services to students were the individual responsibility of every faculty member to his or her own classes. In contrast, the experiment provided a Resource Service Store that was continuously staffed by part-time students which handled an average of 165 student-initiated events per day. In interviews, faculty members were consistently enthusiastic about the introduction of these support services.

The informal use of the facility by students, and the amount of user originated display, was termed a Possession Index. Acts of possession were most evident in the uses of a facility that go beyond the formal programs and organized activities. Observers documented the pattern of informal student use of the facility through daily observations conducted over a six-week period. At random times throughout the day, observers recorded the number of students using the informal areas of the center, which included the coffee lounge, the display and sitting area in the traffic corridor, and the sitting area in the lab and lecture areas when not being used by scheduled classes (Figure 4-17). The data revealed that the informal areas of the center were being used 69 percent of the time. The major activities that students were involved in included reading magazines and catalogues from the Resource Store mini-library, interacting in the coffee lounge, studying or visiting in the lecture-lab space, and getting advice from the tutors. In contrast, direct observation of informal use of the facility before renovation showed very little student use or student-ori-

FIGURE 4-18. Examples of personalization (Photo: Herman Miller Research Corporation).

ented displays. The space was not personalized to any noticeable extent. After renovation, articles and news clippings appeared in addition to prints and oil paintings (Figure 4-18). Students also began to bring in special projects for the display area.

The efficient use of space measured by credit hours and student class hours per square foot was classified as the Utilization Density Index. The data on credit hour and student class hour generation shows a dramatic increase in utilization density in the experimental facility over the same space before renovation. Substantial portions of the increase resulted from the auto-tutorial programs brought into the new facility with their high utilization efficiency, along with an increase in the number of lecture, laboratory, and seminar classes being taught in the experimental environment. The results of the experiment substantiated the initial premise that the physical environment has the potential to enhance and improve productivity and satisfaction.

University of Oregon, Willamette Hall

Attitude Survey	
Charette Process	
Community Meetings	
Design-In	✓
Focused Interviews	
Fishbowl Planning	✓
Game Simulation	✓
Group Dynamics	
Public Forum	
Task Force	✓
Training	
Workshop	✓

SUMMARY

The rapid expansion of the University of Oregon in the 1970s and the tradition of faculty participation in university governance led to a new planning process. The university retained the Center for Environmental Structure, which resulted in the publication of *The Oregon Experiment* (Alexander et al. 1975), the principle basis for future campus planning. Integral to the University of Oregon's planning process is the premise that people who are affected by an environment should be involved in the process for its modification or change. The success of such a process, however, requires support at the institutional level.

The Oregon Experiment consists of major principles such as piecemeal growth, coordination, diagnosis, and patterns, all of which are implemented by means of user participation. Piecemeal growth suggests that environmental changes should be small in scale, representing the commonly held values of the community, since smaller projects are less likely to be disruptive to the environment than large projects. Consequently, the university agreed that the new science complex should consist of several smaller buildings, each designed to stand alone.

Coordination reflects the fact that more than 100 individuals were directly involved in planning the science complex. Many were involved in the diagnostic process to understand what was right and wrong about the campus environment. The diagnosis, developed in the early stages of planning for the science complex, resulted in a "Manual for Prospective Architectural Consultants" that became the charge to the design team. Pattern statements describe a design situation, analyze it in terms of available information, and suggest ways in which problems might be resolved. Many of the pattern statements organizers drew from *The Pattern Language* (Alexander 1977).

A planning team began work at the university in 1985. The team consisted of The Ratcliff Architects, who brought workshop experience and a knowledge of the pattern language through Christie Johnson Coffin's asssociation with Christopher Alexander. Moore Ruble Yudell brought considerable experience in participatory planning workshops, and McLellan and Copenhagen brought experience in detailed planning of laboratory space. A series of participatory design workshops produced sketches and collages that indicated priorities for allocating and reorganizing departmental space. The workshops exposed goals in a common forum so that all participants were aware of the necessity of accommodating diverse and conflicting needs. Yudell states (1991), "They unleashed the enormous creativity of individuals who were enfranchised as creative participants in the making of their workplace and community." Opening day ceremonies were four years after the first workshop.

CLIENT

The University of Oregon's long history of faculty involvement in its overall decision-making process carried over into the planning of new facilities as a result of *The Oregon Experiment,* a process for involving the university community in developing its environment. Overcrowded conditions in the science facilities led to the planning of a new science complex.

The science faculty of the University of Oregon are appointed within a department as well as affiliated with interdisciplinary research units. These institutes are tightly integrated with the departments. Faculty members wanted the new science complex to facilitate their interactions within both groups. John Moseley, the university's vice president for research and active participant in the process stated, "The ideal arrangement of space would allow a faculty member's office, laboratory, and research assistants to be located in a place that was physically connected to both the department and the institute with which the faculty member was affiliated" (1991). This integration required making connections between new and existing buildings. Thus, the two basic issues in planning the new science facility was the allocation and organization of space. In order to achieve "piecemeal growth" as suggested by *The Oregon Experiment,* the user group decided that the science complex should consist of small buildings in scale with the other buildings in this area of the campus. These concerns were resolved successfully because they were addressed by the people at the university who would be most affected by the results, as well as state and DOE officials, U.S. Senator Mark Hatfield and his staff, three architectural and seven engineering practices, artists, and contractors, many of whom were geographically scattered.

Architect Christie Coffin described several factors that contributed to the successful implementation of the new science complex, which was funded and constructed within a very short period of time. Most important was the commitment and decision responsibility taken by all participants, the continuity of most of the participants throughout the process, the effective delegation of tasks to people who were knowledgeable, and the mutual trust of all participants, which allowed discussions to be open and fair.

Initially three user groups were identified. The "direct" users of the science complex — the faculty and staff who would occupy the new buildings — were represented by the Science Facilities User Group. They established several "major task groups" to contribute in defining the spatial program. This group discussed the list of space requests and eliminated overlapping requests in order to seek more efficient use of spaces, and to compare the space requests with national norms for comparable programs. Before selecting an architect, this group published guidelines for the architect consisting of diagrammed connections among the various disciplines and anticipating cross-disciplinary work.

The Campus Planning Committee, an ongoing body consisting of the campus planner David Rowe and faculty representation, monitored the process according to the principles expressed in *The Oregon Experiment*. The Campus Planning Office focused its efforts where they would make a difference, and delegated the rest of the work to faculty, staff, and consultants. The university administration was represented throughout the planning and design process, and also supported the participatory process by compensating the faculty and staff for the considerable time devoted to this project.

PROJECT

The process for the design of the new science complex consisted of a series of participatory design workshops conducted on campus over a four-month period. These workshops brought together people representing a broad range of viewpoints, and encouraged their participation in decisions about a variety of campus, spatial, and laboratory planning issues.

Early in the process, the planning team attempted to develop a common visual vocabulary with faculty and staff by presenting slides representing a wide variety of historic and contemporary buildings. Participants were asked to respond to two questions about each slide: Do you like it? and Do you like it for the science complex? Generally, pictures depicting buildings in well-landscaped settings were favored to more austere settings lacking landscape features. The concerns that emerged from these discussions were green space, human scale, durable materials, and friendliness.

Workshop participants represented a broad cross-section of backgrounds and experiences. Participants, ranging from 50 to 80 individuals in each workshop, included faculty, planning staff, students, and administrators. A member of the planning team introduced each workshop to establish goals and expectations. Workgroups from five to eight people discussed ideas, developed plans, and worked collaboratively to reach decisions. Each group included a member of the planning team who acted as a facilitator, answered questions, took notes, stimulated discussion, and remained careful not to influence the discussion.

The initial workshop consisted of a review of specific outdoor places on campus that were successful as well as where patterns were ignored. This workshop was based on one of the most significant patterns, namely "Site Repair," which suggests that the location of new buildings should be used to repair places that do not work (Figure 4-19). The architects and workshop participants walked the campus, recording potential building sites and general campus conditions on maps that also indicated special views and paths (Figure 4-20). Small groups consisting of representatives from science departments, the campus planning office, students, staff, and administrators considered alternative schemes for the location and massing of buildings.

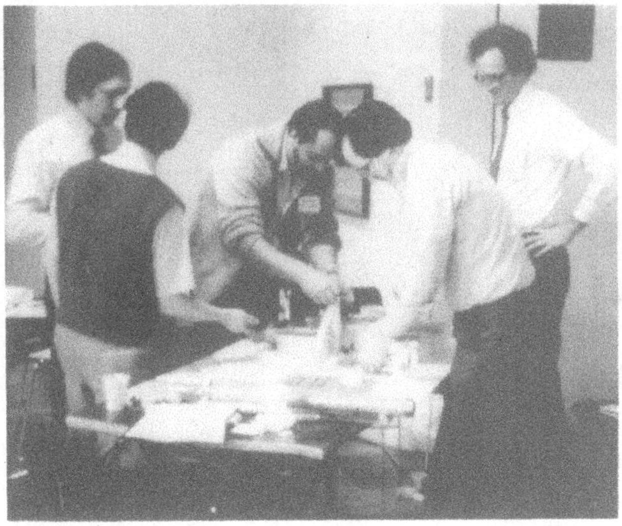

FIGURE 4-19. "Site-repair" workshop (Photo: Stephen Harby: Moore Ruble Yudell).

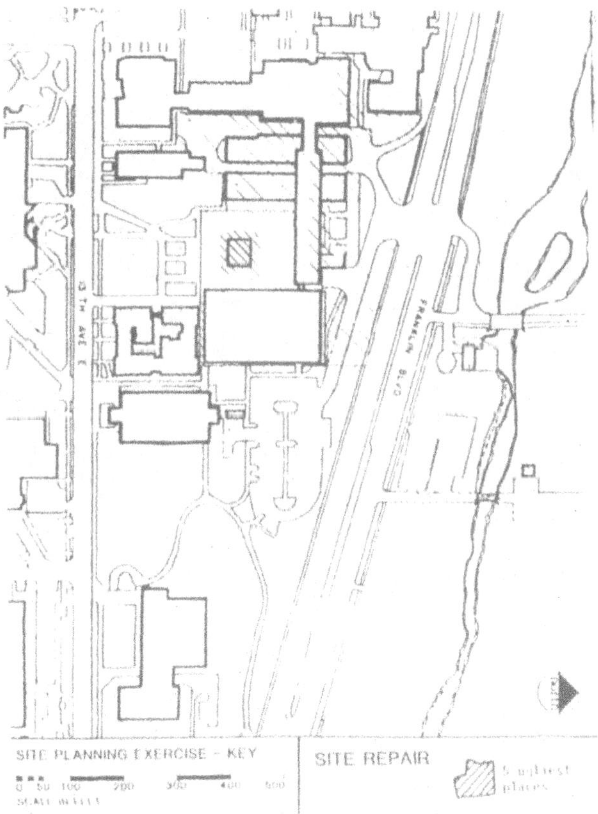

FIGURE 4-20. Site-planning exercise (Drawing: Courtesy Moore Ruble Yudell).

During this workshop, participants became sensitized to a variety of issues. Campus planners became aware of the needs and work patterns of scientists, while scientists became aware of campus planning issues. The maps were synthesized by the planning team and were discussed with all participants.

An important idea that emerged from this workshop was the possibility of creating south-facing courtyards (a pattern particularly suited to the Oregon campus) by the organization and location of new buildings. These new buildings could enhance important views and conceal unattractive views. This proposal led to the opportunity for the creation of a pedestrian path which was later to become Science Walk, for science students and faculty.

Workshops pertaining to departmental issues consisted of small groups organized according to discipline; these groups discussed spatial relationships between faculty, graduate research assistants, staff, and undergraduate students. Using colored paper to denote spatial categories such as laboratories, offices, and service areas, teams produced diagrams representing group consensus on the ideal organization of departments (Figure 4-21). All groups incorporated key patterns from *The Pattern Language* that were introduced by the planning team at various times.

"Department Hearth," for example, is a pattern that recommends a focal space that can become the social center of the department (Figure 4-22). The physicists presented a three-dimensional model that described horizontal and vertical connections to other departments, stood organized around an atrium that allowed for social interaction, and served as a focus for the entire science community.

Another pattern, "South Facing Outdoor Space," encourages a southern orientation for gathering spaces, and is particularly suited for a damp northern climate (Figure 4-23). The geologists, with an orientation towards the outdoors, opted for south-facing social spaces adjacent to south-facing porches and courtyards. The ideas generated in these workshops substantially influenced the design and planning of the science complex.

The Willamette Hall atrium became the heart of the science complex and one of the major meeting spaces on campus. Science Walk became an important social spine.

The laboratory workshop allowed for discussions about the research process and spatial requirements. An introductory talk presented examples that were related to necessary trade-offs between laboratory size and related services, which workshop participants would need to consider. Using a "kit of parts," participants were able to manipulate scale models in order to develop desired relationships between work spaces and offices (Figure 4-24).

Workshops occurred at intervals of four to six weeks apart, with the intervening time used for summarizing the results of previous sessions and planning future events. In addition to the workshops, the plan-

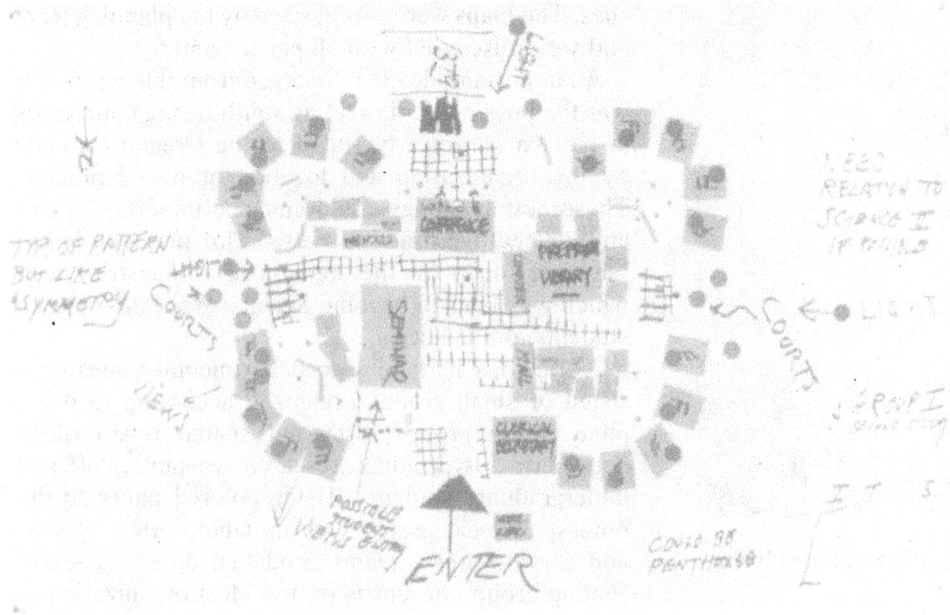

FIGURE 4-21. Departmental workshop (Drawing: Courtesy Moore Ruble Yudell).

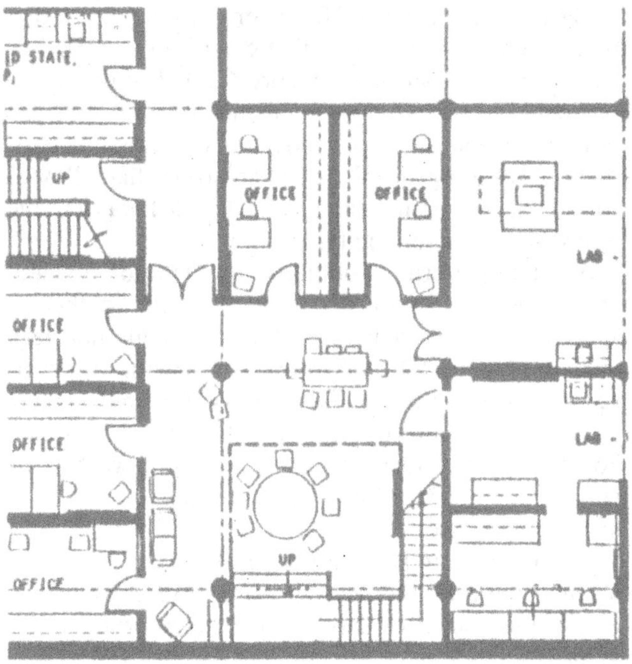

FIGURE 4-22. Plan of "department hearth" based on a pattern to create a social center for each department where seminars, discussions, and socializing over coffee would occur (Drawing: Courtesy of Ratcliff Architects).

FIGURE 4-23. South-facing outdoor space (Photo: Timothy Hursley).

ning team conducted numerous interviews and received information from user committees in order to develop a comprehensive program.

Dr. Moseley noted that involving the users so early and so substantively in the planning process allowed for substantial acceptance in the complex process of allocating space. Also, the users' success in developing an equitable model for spatial organization led to a high degree of "ownership" in the project. This sense of ownership made it easier for administrators to cope with problems that arose during the design and development stages of the project. While a large number of faculty and staff were involved in the process, it allowed for consensus decisions that would have otherwise been impossible.

AFTER-OCCUPANCY RESPONSES

In 1991, after the building was completed, The Ratcliff Architects were seeking user responses to the occu-

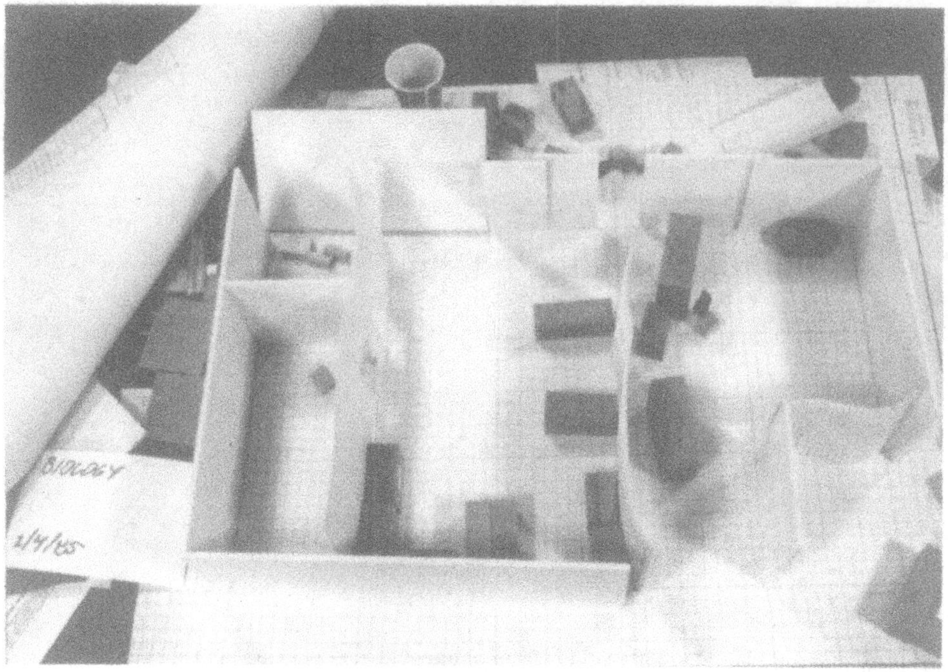

FIGURE 4-24. Departmental model (Photo: Stephen Harby: Moore Ruble Yudell).

pied building. They were interested in answers to questions related to the satisfaction of the architects' original intentions as stipulated in the program. When the architects learn of a problem, reports Christie Coffin, "we want to help fix it and devise strategies to avoid repeating the mistake." Reports from the Core Users Group indicated a satisfactory arrangement of rooms and friendly spaces that support collaboration in science. Scientists indicate success in recruiting excellent new scientists to use the new labs. Dr. Moseley comments, "Faculty who work in these buildings report that both planned and spontaneous interactions with other faculty in their department are enhanced by the easy connection between the buildings and by the attraction of the open space" (Figure 4-25(a)). Visits to the atrium coffee shop often result in meeting with colleagues and meaningful discussions.

Building users who responded to a more recent evaluation questionnaire conducted by this author reflected on the achievement of many of the original goals. The opportunity for random, unplanned meetings with people from different disciplines in the common area supported the goal of a sense of community. Similarly, the grouping of people with similar research interests was said to support collaboration. The atrium was seen as a good idea, but consumed an excess of space, especially since many of the perimeter offices were very small. Windowless offices, too, was cited as a dissatisfaction, particularly when laboratories with windows were shielded with foil.

The building appearance, the quality of light, and

FIGURE 4-25(a). Atrium space (Photo: Timothy Hursley).

FIGURE 4-25(b). Building exterior (Photo: Timothy Hursley).

the views to the mountains were all amenity features of Willamette Hall (Figure 4-25(b)). Several comments, however, pertained to the unattractive "hospital green" interior color scheme, and one irate respondent was outraged with the busts on the facade, which was described as "low art." Other building occupants commented on more specific malfunctions such as the lack of a freight elevator, making it difficult to elevate heavy equipment. Several problems identified by the users resulted from the inability of the architects, consultants, and user committees to accurately predict the way in which the building would be used. This is not an unusual occurrence as we have seen described in many other unique school buildings.

The design process was striking for its openness and high level of participation among a diverse group of consultants and university representatives, which was in keeping with the university's tradition of collaborative decision making.

ACKNOWLEDGMENT

This section was summarized with permission from the authors from the following articles contained in *Places:* 7:4 1991.

Coffin, C.J., "Making places for scientists."
Moseley, J., "From partnership to ownership: How users shaped the science complex."
Yudell, B., "Building community through participation."

In addition, valuable comments pertaining to the process were provided by Christie Johnson Coffin, project director of the new science complex for the Ratcliff Architects.

Pembroke State University, Native American Center

Attitude Survey	
Charette Process	
Community Meetings	✓
Design-In	
Focused Interviews	✓
Fishbowl Planning	
Game Simulation	
Group Dynamics	✓
Public Forum	✓
Task Force	
Training	
Workshop	

SUMMARY

A Native American community organization was formed to enable the preservation of a building that served as their cultural symbol. The principal goal of the Old Main Commission was to conduct a feasibility study for the renovation of a partially demolished building situated on the site of the nation's first Indian school. Located on the Pembroke State University campus in North Carolina, Old Main was devastated by fires that left only the outer walls standing. In an effort to restore the building, a commission was formed and a partnership was established between the citizens of Pembroke, representatives of Pembroke State University, and a design team from North Carolina State University. The university president's office, in conjunction with the governor's office, requested assistance from the design team.

As a result of numerous group meetings and surveys, a building program developed to reflect the needs of the Native American community and the local university. The design proposal, developed by North Carolina State University's Community Development Group, directed by Henry Sanoff, became the focus for legislative action which yielded 1.5 million dollars required for renovation. Public participation in the development of the building program was an effective strategy, since it made the process highly visible in the community and in the state.

The purpose of the project was to explore alternative uses for a university building that would additionally serve the community's educational interests. Working with Pembroke citizens, local public agencies, and representatives from Pembroke State University, the design team conducted a series of open workshops aimed at exploring options for a new Indian Educational and Cultural Center as a regional resource.

CLIENT

The citizens of the town of Pembroke initiated the Old Main Commission to act as advocates for the preservation of a campus building initially scheduled for demolition by state university officials. Pembroke, the center of the Lumbee people, is the largest of North Carolina's Indian population. Pembroke State University was also the site of the first Indian college in the United States, established in 1887. The Commission was concerned with the historic documentation of "Old Main," as well as with the investigation of the social and economic impact of the building's renovation on the attitudes of the Lumbee community.

PROJECT

The Old Main building on the Pembroke State campus was not only the site of the first Indian School in the country, but also it served as an important landmark and symbol of the Lumbee people. In the early 1970s, plans were announced by university officials that Old Main would be demolished to provide for a new federally financed auditorium to serve the university community. Various forms of protest arose until a "Save Old Main Movement" appeared with strong support from National Indian organizations. On the same day that the fate of Old Main was under review

FIGURE 4-26. Old Main after the fire (Photo: Ken Lambla).

by campus, community, and state education officials, two fires virtually gutted the interior of the building. The only visible remains were its outer brick walls and four white columns (Figure 4-26). Political pressure mounted at the local and state levels until leaders of the Lumbee community formed a commission to focus their concerns.

The Coastal Plains Regional Commission, a multistate organization, provided a grant to North Carolina State University's Community Development Group to conduct a building feasibility study that would be used by the Old Main Commission in securing renovation funds. The design team including Ken Lambla, John Meecham, and Carter Reese used the commission as as client and a catalyst for generating community interest. They began a series of open meetings to explore ways in which the emerging Indian Studies program at Pembroke State University, staffed by six faculty located in different departments, could become part of the new vision for the restored educational and cultural center.

To begin the process, the Old Main Commission considered Indian Studies and the display of cultural artifacts according to four areas of social impact. First, the renovation of Old Main could be perceived as a reinforcing influence for positive campus-community relations in the town of Pembroke. Second, the renovation process could restore faith in government within the Lumbee community, a faith that had been severely shaken in the past as a result of previous government action. Third, the renovation of Old Main could represent to the Lumbee people the restoration of their only remaining community symbol. And, fourth, the revitalized Old Main building would assume a new role as a gathering place and information center for Robeson County's Native American citizens, and as a major regional Indian center east of the Mississippi.

Initial discussions with community members and university officials helped to formulate the building's purpose as an Indian Studies and information center, a community assembly area, and a museum as a repositor of Indian artifacts. According to the Lumbee leaders, the principal requirements of any design solution were that the renovated facility would essentially provide a place for Indian activities, and that the building's appearance would remain substantially unaltered.

Although the process for reaching decisions is presented in seemingly linear and sequential stages, it was an iterative process, consisting of long and sometimes confused meetings between members of the design team and the commission. The results of these efforts were not only explicit desires for renovation, but also a better understanding on the part of commission members for the types of information necessary for making design decisions.

The Indian Studies program, staffed by six faculty members, and the commission's Indian Studies committee, which included students, educators, and administrators, developed the building program working together with the design team.

An activity analysis included space requirements and descriptions, or scenarios of the learning areas. The analysis was based on a systematic assessment of the adequacy of places and their corresponding areas currently used by faculty and students. This facility assessment revealed that most spaces were designed to accommodate traditional lectures, whereas to satisfy the curriculum requirements, a variety of spatial configurations were necessary to include opportunities for informal discussion, small-group work, independent research, and reading. Students and faculty voiced a major concern for a spatial layout that would encourage greater social interchange and subsequently increased cooperation. These discussions took into account students' feelings of isolation and needs for stronger out-of-class involvement between students and faculty.

The "suite" evolved as a spatial concept for describing the academic areas. The suite would include listening booths in the instructional materials center for recording oral history as told by members of the Pembroke community, and student work areas for individual projects (Figure 4-27). The public role of Old Main was developed by the museum committee, whose objectives included the collection of existing documents and artifacts related to the Lumbee origins, and cooperation with community and regional schools and civic organizations. The museum committee proposed to establish interest areas for displays and the continuation of geographical and archaeological research. The concept of "museum" is one which describes a range of institutions varying considerably in types of exhibit structure, organization, size, and location. The committee agreed that Old Main would serve as a resource center containing exhibits and film material, conducting workshops in dance and music, and serving as a clearing house for information pertaining to Lumbee and other Native American groups (Figure 4-28). The 80-person assembly area would act as a nucleus for the resource center's large-group activities that would be shared with the Indian Studies program.

Through close collaboration with university administrators and staff, additional space needs were identified that would enhance the management of the Indian Studies program, since a number of community functions occurred in different campus locations. The integration of functions such as Placement and Guidance, Public Information, Alumni Affairs, and Human Services, into a Support Services area was proposed to substantially enhance community–university relations.

FIGURE 4-27. Conceptual design of the educational component.

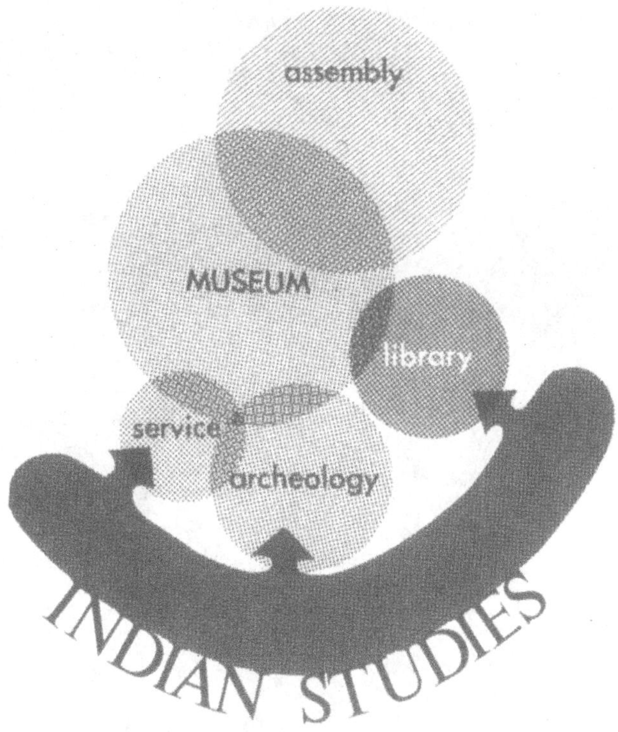

FIGURE 4-28. Conceptual diagram of the cultural center.

The objectives that evolved for the new facility included:

- To preserve the existing building facade
- To support and initiate programs directed at cooperation between university and community
- To integrate the Indian Studies program, the museum, and the community assembly area into a cultural center

The original Old Main building consisted of a central two-story auditorium with classrooms around the perimeter of each of the two levels. The requirement of supportive services increased the spatial needs beyond the limited area within the existing building, necessitating a departure from the original two-story building. Since the building goal was to contain the spatial requirements within the walls of the existing building, the proposed design solution consisted of a three-level core (A, B, and D) with two levels (A and C) around the perimeter (Figure 4-29). The assembly area and resource center were located on the first level (A) to provide direct access for community members using

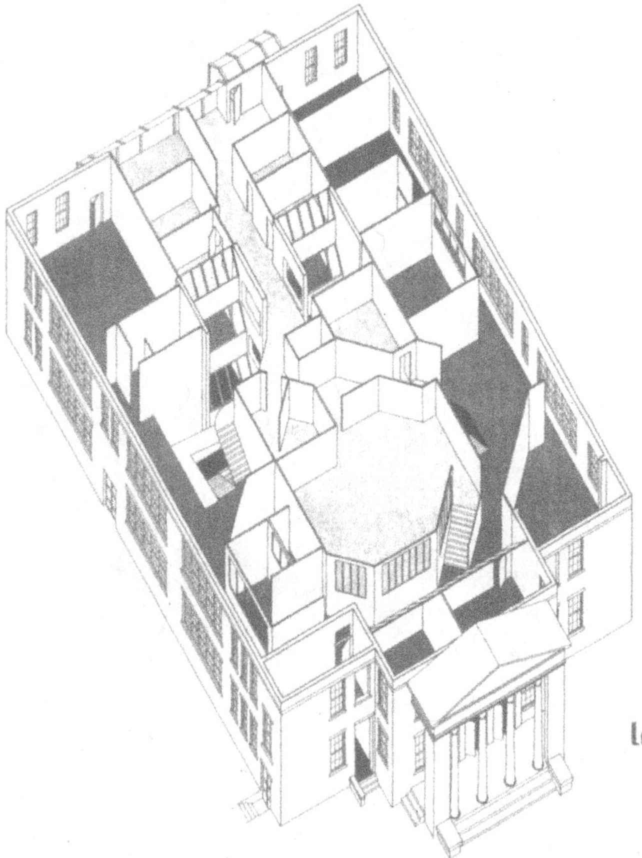

FIGURE 4-29. Axonometric floor plan (Drawing: Ken Lambla).

the building. University functions, such as the Indian Studies program, were located on level C.

IMPLEMENTATION

Although a proposed budget of 2.2 million dollars *was recommended* by the design team to the North Carolina State Legislature for the renovation of Old Main, only 1.5 million dollars *were appropriated,* and the architectural firm of Jordan, Snowdon, and McVicker *was selected* to implement the building program. During the six years between the completion of the feasibility study and the construction starting date, the spatial needs increased by 20 percent. The increased requirements necessitated some modification to the preliminary design proposal.

The basic concept of the cultural center *was incorporated* by the architects, Jordan, Snowdon, and McVicker into the final design scheme, though the media center expanded considerably from the original program (Figure 4-30). This change resulted from the increase in use of the campus radio station and television studio, which were important community functions. The central assembly area surrounded by exhibition space was the dominant theme of the Native American Cultural Center, located on the first floor. The increased area required for media support could not be accommodated within the volume of the existing building; consequentially, a one-story extension *was proposed* by the architects at the rear of the original building.

The Department of Indian Studies on the second floor also contained university Support Services, which corresponded to the intentions of the preliminary design proposal. Except for the small extension, the two-story part of the project was constructed within the limits of the exterior walls of the 1923 building, as recommended by the design programming team (Figure 4-31).

The architects Jordan, Snowdon, and McVicker maintain that the university-community involvement in the programming process permitted them to pursue effectively the necessary modifications to the building design because the working groups had already developed good communication links.

The Native American Resource Center at Pembroke State University has been in operation since 1982. The center includes a variety of authentic Indian artifacts, handicrafts, art, books, cassettes, and film strips about Native Americans, with special emphasis on the Lum-

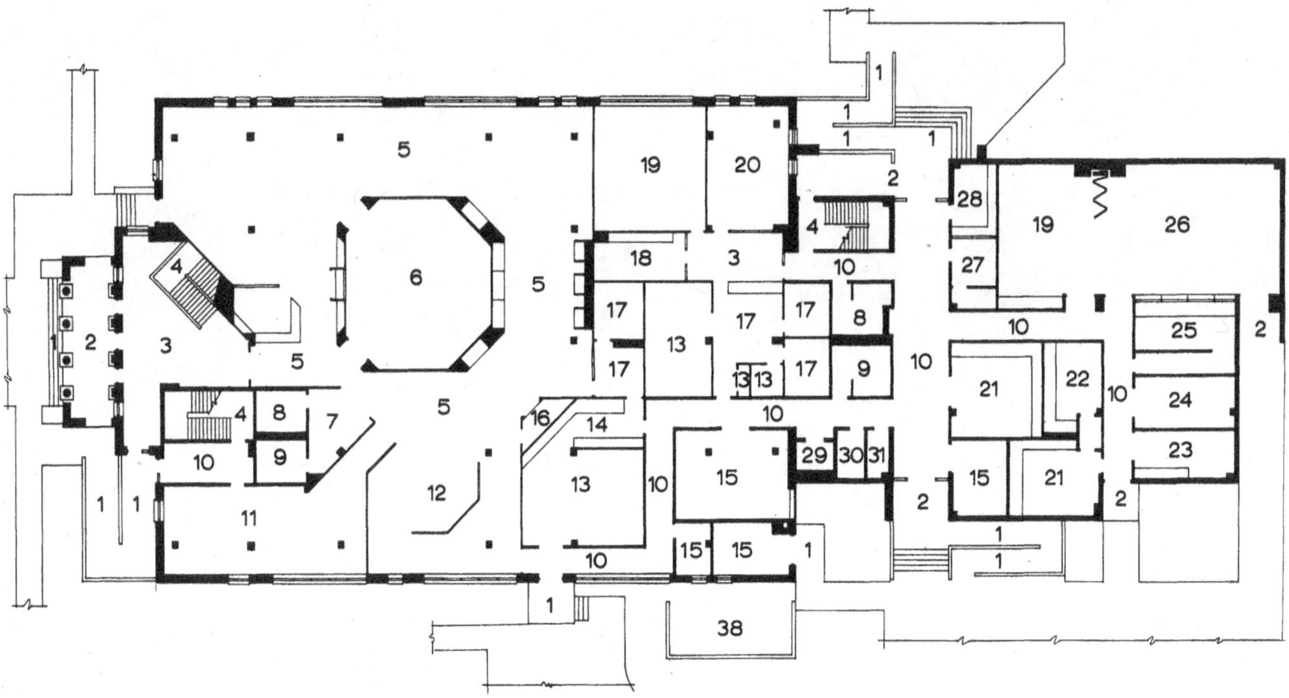

FIGURE 4-30. Floor plan of completed building (Drawing: Sam Snowden).

FIGURE 4-31. Restored building (Photo: Henry Sanoff).

bee Indians of Robeson County. The permanent exhibit includes prehistoric tools and weapons, 19th-century Lumbee household and farm equipment, and contemporary Indian art. Indian cultures from all sections of the United States are represented by characteristic artifacts.

The assembly room is well utilized for meetings of various campus and community organizations, workshops, and film viewing. The reading room contains books, records, and film strips on many Indian tribes. Tours are continuous throughout the year for school groups, senior citizens, and civic and community organizations.

5
Participatory Theories and Methods

Participatory Design Principles

An important point in the participatory process is individual learning through increased awareness of a problem. In order to maximize learning, the process should be clear, communicable, and open. It should encourage dialogue, debate, and collaboration. This learning process is valuable to all sides: school users, planners, and designers.

> A planner who previously used citizen participation only to educate the public as to his or her professional recommendations may also learn that he or she can equally well be educated from public involvement (*Williams 1976*).

The types and degrees of participation depend on several factors and vary in accord with the circumstances. For Alexander (1972),

> . . . the most modest kind of participation is the kind where the user helps to shape a building by acting as a client of an architect. The fullest kind of participation is the kind where users actually build their building for themselves.

Jim Burns (1979) classifies participation into four categories or "experiences" that can lead to ultimate agreement about what the future should bring:

Awareness. This experience involves discovering or rediscovering the realities of a given environment or situation so that everyone in the "Take Part" process is talking the same language based on their experiences in the field where change is proposed.

Perception. This experience entails going from awareness of the situation to understanding it and its physical, social, cultural, and economic ramifications. It means sharing with each other so that the understanding, objectives, and expectations of all participants become resources for planning and not hidden agendas that could disrupt the project later on.

Decision Making. This phase concentrates on working from awareness and perception to a program for the situation under consideration. In it, participants make actual physical designs based on their priorities, which professionals use as a resource to synthesize alternative and final plans.

Implementation. Many participatory processes stop with awareness, perception, and decision making, often with fatal results to a project because it ends people's responsibilities just when they could be of most value: when the how-to, where-to, when-to, and who-will-do-it must be added to what people want and how the building will look. People must stay involved throughout the processes; in other words, take responsibility with their professionals to see that there are results (Hurwitz 1975).

Purposes of Participation

Participation (from the Latin "pars," a part) means to be and to act as a part of a larger order of a higher totality or wholeness. Participation refers to the fact or conditions of sharing in common with others, and refers to making decisions with regards to the common good. Participation implies the presence of the users during the whole course of the architectural operation, which passes through three phases: the definition of the problem, the elaboration of the solution, and the evaluation of the results. Participation has a number of synonyms such as citizen involvement, citizen influence, cooperation, co-decision, and self-decision. This definition implies that participation is a general concept covering different forms of decision-making by a number of involved parties (Wulz 1985). Participation, however, is a concept laden with ideology and assumptions. Often the arguments made for participation are not based on a clear conceptual understanding or on an appropriate organizing framework. Important issues in any framework must include factors such as who is participating, how people are participating, and what are the effects of participation.

Participation means different things to different people and different things to the same people, depending on the issue, its timing, and the social and political setting in which it takes place. Participation can be addressed effectively if the task is conceptualized in terms of what is to be accomplished when the need is acknowledged to involve users. Conceptualizing the issue means asking simple questions of who, what, where, how, and when?

1. Who are the parties to be involved in the participation process?
2. What are the specifications we wish to have performed by the participation program?
3. Where do we wish the participation road to lead?
4. How should people be involved?
5. When in the design process is participation needed or desired?

These are simple questions, yet rarely are they asked prior to the development of a participation program.

What architects and public officials should realize is that participation is like a professional sport: it takes place in a public forum where there is competition between individuals and groups with conflicting goals; individuals and groups that participate play different roles at different times; the playing conditions change from time to time; the planning of strategies is a major activity; no one group wins every contest; and there is an ongoing need to evaluate performance in order to succeed. Like the manager of a professional sports club, the designer of a participation program needs to think about goals and objectives, about options and plays, resources and timing, strategy and performances. And, like sports, planning for a successful participation program involves a great deal of thought and analysis prior to the first public performance.

The planning that accompanies the design of any participation program should first include a determination of goals and objectives. For example:

- Is the participation intended to generate ideas?
- Is it to identify attitudes?
- Is it to disseminate information?
- Is it to resolve some identified conflict?
- Is it to measure opinion?
- It is to review a proposal?
- Or is it merely to serve as a safety valve for pent-up emotions?

The list of possible participation objectives will differ from time to time and from issue to issue. Once the goals and objectives of participation are stated, participation is perceived differently depending on the type of issue and the people involved. If differences in perception and expectations are not identified at the outset, and realistic objectives are not made clear, the expectations of those involved in the participation program will not have been met and they will become disenchanted.

One of the stumbling blocks to an effective participation program is the difficulty associated with the articulation of participation goals and objectives. Yet it is this articulation that forms the basis of any wise choice of participation methods. The difficulty in determining goals, objectives, and methods may be caused by confusion over what is meant by the planning of a participation program (Rosner 1978).

A *goal* is nothing more than a generalized statement of intended accomplishment. It is usually abstract and somewhat ambiguous. An *objective* is more specific. It is a statement of the changes on conditions that some activity is expected to produce; put another way, it is a function to be performed. A *method* is a vehicle by which an objective is to be achieved.

When participation goals and objectives are not clearly articulated, participants will have different expectations of what participation is to achieve.

Many architects and public officials find the involvement of users time consuming, inefficient, irrational, and not very productive. However, when the purposes are made clear, then it is possible to plan activities that are directly related to the objectives. Examples of objectives would be:

- To disseminate information
- To solicit and identify the attitudes and opinions of user groups
- To facilitate participation
- To generate new ideas and alternatives
- To establish priorities

These objectives would be the functions to be performed by some set of participation activities, and are the purposes to which some participation will be matched.

Planning for participation needs considerable time prior to the taking of any action. When sufficient time is allowed to analyze the issues, participants, resources, and participation goals and objectives prior to the choosing of participation methods, the chance of success is greatly enhanced. Poorly planned participation actions create a lack of confidence in public agencies and generate a stronger demand by people for the monitoring of agency activities.

The steps to successful participation planning are (Rosner 1978):

1. Identify the individuals or groups who will or should be involved in the participation activity being planned.
2. Decide where in the planning process the participants should be involved; that is, in development, implementation, evaluation, or some combination thereof.
3. Articulate the participation goals and objectives in relation to all participants who will be involved; that is, elected officials, public administrators, the affected people.
4. Identify participation methods to objectives in terms of the resources available.
5. Match alternative methods to objectives in terms of the resources available.
6. Select an appropriate method to be used in the achievement of specified objectives.
7. Implement chosen participation activities.
8. Evaluate the implemented methods to see to what extent they achieved the desired goals and objectives.

It is not suggested that taking the eight proposed steps will automatically ensure success, but it can be claimed that the process will minimize failure.

A collective review of the theories and practices of participation are synthesized into the following five statements:

1. *There is no "best solution" to design problems.* Each problem has a number of solutions. Solutions to design problems are traditionally based on two sets of criteria: (a) *facts* — the empirical data concerning material strengths, economics, building codes, and so forth; and (b) *attitudes* — interpretation of the facts, the state of the art in any particular area, traditional and customary approaches, and value judgments. Thus design and planning decisions are by nature biased and depend on the values of the decision maker(s).
2. *"Expert" decisions are not necessarily better than "lay" decisions.* Given the facts with which to make decisions, the users can examine the available alternatives and choose among them. The architect or planner involved in such an approach should be considered a participant who is expected to state his opinion, provide technical information, and discuss consequences of various alternatives, just as the users state their opinions and contribute their expertise.
3. *A design or planning task can be made "transparent."* Steps taken and alternatives considered by the architect-planners (traditionally in their own minds in the privacy of an office) can be brought to the surface for the users to discuss. By understanding the components of planning and design decisions and by "shopping" among the alternatives, the users in effect generate their own plan rather than react to one provided for them. The final product is more likely to succeed because it is better understood by the people who will use it.
4. *All individuals and interest groups should come together in an open forum.* In this way people can openly express their opinions, make necessary compromises, and arrive at decisions that are acceptable to all concerned. By involving as many interests as possible, not only is the product strengthened by the wealth of input, but the user group is strengthened as well by learning more about itself.
5. *The process is continuous and ever changing.* The product is not the end of the process. It must be managed, re-evaluated, and adapted to changing needs. Those most directly involved with the product — the users — are best able to assume those tasks.

As a summary, four essential purposes of participation can be identified:

1. Participation is inherently good.
2. It is a source of wisdom and information about local conditions, needs, and attitudes, and thus improves the effectiveness of decision making.
3. It is an inclusive and pluralistic approach by which fundamental human needs are fulfilled and user values reflected.
4. It is a means of defending the interests of groups of people and of individuals, and a tool for satisfying their needs, which are often ignored and dominated by large organizations, institutions, and their inflated bureaucracies.

Forms of Participation

Participation can be active or passive. A rough division of these two extremes results in opposing poles of expert-autonomous and user-autonomous architecture. The concept of expert-autonomous architecture denotes architecture stemming from the architect's own subjective ideas and values. Planning and design decisions are made by the architect himself alone, denying exposure to other opinions, i.e. the 'artistic' architect. At the other end of the scale, in user-autonomous architecture, the architect is more or less eliminated from the planning, design, and construction process. These two forms of architectural extremes may not appear very often today in their pure forms, but they do serve to illustrate the two opposing poles of the architectural design process: one where the architect reaches his own decisions and sets his personal stamp on his architecture, and the other, where the individual makes his own decisions and will not submit to anyone else's 'stamp' (Wulz 1986).

In the practical world of building, these two extremes are forced to reach a compromise with each other. The question is which one of the two is to make the decisive decisions in connection with the design of the architectural environment. The different forms and stages of participation are a result of the differences of influence by the architect and the user. The scale between those two poles provide the stages of influence by the architect and by the user. It is a reciprocal scale in which the decreasing influence of the architect is followed by increasing users' influence.

Levels of Participation

As a convenient organizing system, a review of the literature will examine participation as a function of the type of structure in which it occurs. There are important qualitative differences in participation within small groups, organizations, and communities; yet it is not always recognized that community participation involves all three structural levels.

Structural Factors. Certain factors appear to influence both participant behavior and participation outcomes. These important structural factors include:

- Group type: small face-to-face group, formal organizations, or larger community of multiple groups and organizations
- Purpose of participation: social control, partisan influence, or exchange
- Degree of autonomy: extent to which participants have an independent supply of resources
- Participant characteristics: race, socioeconomic status
- Structural conduciveness: legal and organization procedures, intra- and interorganizational relationships, and roles for participants
- Resources available: tangible and symbolic rewards controlled by participants

Behavior Factors. In addition to structural factors, certain behavioral factors are also relevant to our view of participation. These include:

- Exchange process: participation in planning, innovation, or conflict
- Participation outcome: whether the act succeeded or failed in terms of its goal
- Type and sequence of interaction: whether the interaction between participants was primarily coercive (conflict), utilitarian (competition), or normative (cooperation), and whether it changed over time
- Motivation: what goals participants sought
- Competence: capacity of participants to take effective roles in public decision making
- Internal cohesiveness: extent to which group members are united behind leaders

Analytical Assumptions. More interesting than the individual, structural, and behavioral factors are the potential relationships among them. Three primary types of analytical assumptions may be identified:

- Social control: in which the author views the relationship between citizens and government from the side of the authorities and their system-wide goals, as in Litwak and Meyer (1966)
- Exchange: in which citizen-government relationships are seen in terms of transactions in which each side calculates its costs and benefits, as in Mitchell (1967)
- Partisan influence: in which citizens attempt to influence government decisions, as in Lipsky (1968)

Units of Participation

As a background to this theoretical discussion, general participation studies have been categorized in terms of whether the size of the unit of analysis was the small group, the organization, or the community. All of these different groups depend on the number of participants involved, the topic, and the social relationship.

Small-Group Participation

Participation has been studied in small groups in which each participant has direct control over the innovation or strategy through intimate communication. In a review of the relevant literature, Godschalk (1972) notes that small-group participation occurs when members communicate on a face-to-face basis and are aware of each other as individuals. The small-group studies produced evidence for the "participation hypothesis," as Verba (1961) states that ". . . significant changes in human behavior can be brought about rapidly only if the persons who are expected to change participate in deciding what the change shall be and how it shall be made."

The basis for the participation hypothesis stems from the nature of the influence of the small group over its individual members, causing them to conform to group standards, once these have been set. Thus conformity in one form or another is the typical dependent variable in small-group studies. Conformity results from compliance with group norms, or rules, that describe expected behavior and prescribe punishments for noncompliance.

Small-group members tend to conform to group norms because of individual needs, internal pressures within the individual to be accepted by the group, and external pressures and sanctions imposed on the nonconformist by the group (Verba 1961). The character of the small group itself also affects the susceptibility of member opinions to group influence. Small groups tend to exert a great influence on member opinions because the member does not have the opportunity to be selective about the information he will expose himself to (unlike in the mass media); relations among members are diffuse and general, rather than specific to any particular type of behavior; and informal decision methods emphasize consensus, unlike voting which allows for opinion differences (Verba 1961).

In the small-group participation method, the group leader acts as the medium between external enforcement and internal demands. Democratic (participatory) or authoritarian (coercive) decision methods may be applied, but, in general, members have been found to prefer a democratic (normative) leadership style, and more readily accept decisions in which they have participated (Lewin, Lippitt, and White 1939). The "participation effect" in small groups has been described in terms of a type of social physics. Norms supposedly set up a "field of forces" acting on the group. Participation lowers the forces opposed to change, while external direction increases them and causes group tension and aggression. In this view the field of forces must appear to be influenced from within the group, so that group and individual goals can be fused. For effective participation, members must make a positive commitment by actively discussing the subject. The force for decisions must come from the group, and members must perceive other members as changing (Verba 1961). A major criticism of the early small-group participation studies was that the structure did not offer alternatives for group decisions, but merely sought member endorsement of the leader's goals. The underlying analytical assumption appears as one of social control: individual conformity as the desired outcome where leadership was a means of changing group attitudes. Participation has also been linked to conflict behavior in small-group studies based on game theory, in which the underlying analytical assumption is one of exchange. Game theory assumes that it is possible to assign values to the various choices in conflicting issues, so that there is an explicitly measurable basis for determining preferences. The game theory approach defines conflict as an exchange process based on competition or cooperation (Abt 1970).

Participation as an Organizational Strategy

Many of the social characteristics of society are integrally connected to the behavior of organizations and to the delivery of goods and services. In organizational development, participation refers to an approach that is rooted in trust, intimacy, and consensus. This relationship has been described by William Ouchi as Theory Z (1981), where Theory X is an assumption about human behavior stating that people are inherently lazy and need to be constantly watched; and Theory Y assumes that people are hard working and need only to be supported and encouraged. This distinction is significant since there is a growing number of type Z organizations where the decision-making process is typically a consensual, participative one.

Egalitarianism is a central feature of type Z organizations. Egalitarianism implies that each person can apply discretion and can work autonomously without close supervision because they are to be trusted. This feature accounts for high levels of loyalty and productivity in type Z organizations. Social scientists have described this as a democratic (as opposed to autocratic or apathetic) process in which many people are drawn into the shaping of important decisions. In type Z organizations, the decision making may be collective, but the ultimate responsibility for decisions still resides in one individual. The consensus process is one in which members of the group may be asked to accept responsibility for a decision that they do not prefer, but that the group, in an open and complete discussion, has settled upon. This combination of collective decision making with individual responsibility demands an atmosphere of trust. Through many years of research, Ouchi and others have demonstrated that type Z organizations were more profitable, and had emotionally more healthy employees than did autocratic organizations.

Theory Z emphasizes participatory management in an holistic atmosphere, in which the culture of an organization is considered. In order to implement changes, it is necessary to understand the organization's culture. Lindemer suggests type Z organizations function similar to an open system, where there is continual interaction with the environment and a state of balance or harmony is achieved. Interaction with the environment implies listening, but may also necessitate internal adjustments within the organization's structure. Corporate CEOs and school administrators are discovering that to implement changes they must first know the organization's culture before introducing such techniques as quality circles, a form of teaming and participatory management. The quality circle is a participative management tool designed to harness systematically the brain power of employees to solve an organization's problems of productivity and quality. While there are differences in the way industry and education operate, they do share one attribute: The public distrusts the quality of their products. Whether it is American cars or American high school graduates, both are perceived as not as good as they used to be. Quality circles are different than committees or task forces, since leaders and members are trained in specific techniques of the circle process, including brainstorming and consensus decision making. The circle itself determines what problems will be analyzed and solved.

This theory and approach opens the way for people to find and pursue points of communality involving their own interests and those of the organizations for which they work. This approach can also serve to enhance the performance and experience of everyone involved in an organization. People do indeed gain satisfaction from feeling competent, in control, and free to choose for themselves. Personal involvement in the shaping of the schoolroom will aid the development of responsibility, cooperation, and self-motivation.

Since schools are operating from a dynamic base, type Z management styles are a natural extension of their thrust. Theory Z emphasizes the environment beyond the local community and recognizes a new generation with diverse values.

Conclusion

Participation might be seen as direct human involvement in decision-making processes. In this type of participation, students, teachers, administrators, and public officials share in decisions that determine the quality and direction of their educational program. This approach requires the provision of effective communication media in order to provide suitable grounds for school user participation in designing. The experiences in design participation show that the main source of user satisfaction is not so much the degree to which particular needs have been met, but the feeling of having influenced the decisions. However, there are many benefits accruing from such an approach for community, users, and designers (Wrona 1981).

First, from the social point of view:

- It results in a greater meeting of social needs, and an increasingly effective utilization of resources at the disposal of a particular community.
- It enhances democracy in the whole investment system.
- It has a didactic effect leading to increased social awareness, and a generally higher intellectual level of school community.

Second, to the user group in design:

- An increased reconciliation of individual objectives
- An increased sense of having influenced the design decision-making process
- An increased awareness of the consequences of decisions made

Third, to the designer:

- Setting up a logical basis for interdisciplinary design ventures, operating through a mutual complement of professionals and nonprofessionals rather than through a domination of one group over the other
- Supplying the designer with more relevant and up-to-date information than was possible before
- Creating a methodological framework for an effective use of rational design methods and accurate design tools (such as the computer) without affecting the role and nature of creative processes now augmented by lay productions
- Enriching professional designers with nonprofessional aspects of social activity
- Expanding the role of professional designers to include the function of instructor and designer of the design process, which, admittedly, burdens them with new duties and responsibilities, but at the same time increases their social standing, esteem, and respect

The potential benefits offered by an organized approach to design participation constitutes logical, emotional, technological, and economic tenets for its use. A collective review of the theories and practices of participation can be summarized as follows:

1. The designer's job is no longer to produce finished and unalterable solutions, but to extract solutions from a continuous confrontation with those who will use his or her work. The designer's energy and imagination will be completely directed to raising the level of awareness of the school users in the discussion, and the solution will come out of the exchanges between the two; the designer states his or her opinions, provides technical information, and discusses the consequences of various alternatives, just as the users state their opinions and contribute their expertise.
2. Participation has a diversity of expression, and a design task resulting from this approach can be made "transparent" because the final decisions are understood by the people who made them.
3. Public forums should be convened and participation by all members of the community should be encouraged. In this way people can openly express their opinions, make necessary compromises, and arrive at acceptable decisions. This method not

only strengthens the product by the wealth of input, but also strengthens the user group by learning more about itself.

4. Although participation in the design process can create technological specialization by bringing numerous specialists in various fields to cooperate in the design process, a general effort should be made to educate the school community about various strategies that can be employed to achieve effective and efficient participation in designing.
5. Public comments and representation should be accepted into the design process continuously. The final decision is not the end of the process. It requires management, evaluation, and adaptability to changing needs.

Architecture in the future can be characterized by an increasing participation of the user in its organizational and formal definition. In order to respond to this situation, professionals will need to do everything possible to make design solutions less representative of its designers and more representative of its users. Even though many difficulties in applying design participation arise from the concept of democratic participation, the consideration for the interests of future users, and organizational and methodological problems reflect true participation.

Planning for Participation

Participation in design and planning has come to be construed by professionals and policymakers as an acceptable concept that can be applied to different community problems. However, in most instances, serious demands and responsibilities are placed upon participants. In addition to concern with technical complexity, sound design principles must also be incorporated into the development process. Without guidance, community groups may respond only to crisis situations and subsequently cannot achieve the broad goals that originally united the group. Often community participants cannot draw upon personal experiences for resolving building conflicts and may select courses of action that create unforeseen, deleterious consequences. Therefore, the management of participatory efforts directed at environmental change is important.

People will join together if it is clear that change can and will occur. Participation can function if it is active and directed, and a sense of achievement is experienced by those who get involved. At the same time, it requires a reexamination of traditional design procedures to ensure that participation becomes more than an affirmation of the designer's intentions. The guidance of user participation directed at environmental change requires new skills of the design professional, both design skills and skills for ensuring community participation in the design process.

Structuring group efforts can take many forms corresponding to the diverse array of environmental issues that confront communities daily. The basic ingredient in the participatory process is individual learning through increased awareness of a problem. Learning occurs best when the process is clear, communicable, open, and encourages dialogue, debate, and collaboration. As more participants learn about environmental issues and impacts, the decisions they make will have broad effects on the quality of the environment.

Thus, the designer's role is to facilitate the user group's ability to reach decisions pertinent to the environment through a communicable procedure. Most often this approach will take the form of creating awareness which permits citizens to be critical of environmental alternatives. Such design assistance is oriented toward sensitizing groups to environmental issues.

The facilitator's role is to help people develop their existing and/or potential resources in ways that will benefit themselves and others. Facilitation helps bring people together to determine what they wish to do and helps them find ways to work together in figuring out ways to do it. A facilitator's role is to make everyone know that they are included in what is going on and that what they have to say is being listened to by the group. Facilitation can also include systematic procedures by which people untrained in design can organize themselves to create a planned action. The basic ingredient in the participatory process is individual learning through increased awareness of a problem.

If people are to discover the principle of quality for themselves, they are more likely to do so in small groups. Above and beyond this, small-scale organization is needed to reduce alienation and to allow people to come to grips with rapid change. Significant changes in human behavior can be brought about rapidly only if the persons who are expected to change participate in deciding what the change shall be and how it shall be made. Participation, however, can take place through many modes of involvement including simulated experiences and structured group decision making.

Simulation methods are primarily educational since their purpose is to prepare people to act. Such methods are based on an abstraction of complex processes achieved by compressing time and capturing the interest of participants through "parlor game" strategies. Gaming simulations devised by architects ask participants to assume the decision roles normally included in "real life" situations. After participation in a game process, individuals may confront their own community problems with an increased awareness of the general issues, the process by which decisions are made, and appropriate decision strategies. This approach is utilized to make individuals more sensitive to issues and alternatives, and ultimately to influence individual behavior.

Another form of participation is the direct involvement of community residents in a systematically organized decision process. This process can be professionally designed for a specific community issue, or a general planning process can be utilized for typical classes of problems. Success in this approach is associated with the quality of guidance through the decision procedure. Leadership is necessary to insure that all the participants contribute to the fullest of their abilities. Similarly, the procedures are tailored to the willingness of people who are required to work together, yet are not intended to force involvement beyond a participant's competence. Overzealous attempts at total involvement of community residents in all stages of the design process may lead to their early withdrawal, particularly if progress toward implementation is slow.

An effective process for involving people must be carefully designed. The random involvement of people without a clear sequence of events and without clearly understood roles can result in chaos. There are a few essential ingredients for success in any type of participatory effort. Initially there needs to be a shared view of the goals of the project and what the participants want to achieve. As the process moves ahead the goals may change, yet the structure should be adhered to since open-ended processes that permit people to join and drop out usually end in frustration. To ensure continuity of the process, a steering committee, executive board, citizens council, or building committee should be formed at the outset. Their role should also include the need to maintain open communication between all participants at all times. Open dialogues often provide protection against hidden agendas that may emerge. The process must also have a clear beginning and end, through which participants understand their responsibilities and how they are interconnected with each other and with the designer. The role of the designer in this process is not only as the process facilitator, but as the technical specialist who makes recommendations and develops the necessary design documents. Since the process is open to lay people, communication systems that everyone can read clearly must be employed.

Organizing the Workshop

The term "workshop" is used to emphasize that participants engage in those experiences that provide the material for learning about human relations. The assumption is that learning is most functional when it grows out of personally involving experiences that require reflecting, developing, and testing of new insights and approaches to problem solving. These processes come into focus when participants are obliged to resolve their differences in pursuit of a common goal.

Workshops are an appropriate setting to achieve a high level of interaction between people sharing a common purpose. A workshop is a planned event whereby participants can learn from each other as they explore issues. An important component in the development of a workshop is building cohesion. Opportunities should be provided for groups to get so involved with each other that they begin to see each other as persons and, therefore, invest interest in each other. It is the intent of this experience to facilitate learning that might otherwise be haphazard and diffuse. In order to accomplish this, the experience must be structured to insure that there is a focus to the group process. It should also increase the probability that certain learning will occur for the participants. The structured experience, however, does not dictate what a participant should learn.

The structured experience is a function of the objectives of the experience, the content, and the techniques employed to focus learning. The learning goals of a structured experience may include cognitive, affective, and skill-building aspects. The cognitive aspect of the experience may include an awareness of the content or uses and how they can be effectively organized. The participant's self-awareness, insight, and empathy illustrate the effective aspects of learning goals. Development and implementation of characteristics such as listening and problem solving are skill-building aspects of the goals. The content areas refer to individual and group events, and include methods of interpersonal communication, group problem solving, sensory awareness, giving and receiving feedback, and team building. Techniques employed to direct learning include activities such as making or building something, discussions, summarizations, board games, interviews, inventories or check lists, role playing, and tasks.

An appropriate combination of objectives, content, and techniques will produce a structure that will generate an opportunity for learning. Workshops can vary widely in topics, time lengths, and goals, so all three elements must be carefully chosen. The content and quality of the experience is important enough to create the highest quality environment possible. Since the workshop participants will be using various awareness activities to heighten their sensitivity to the environment, the meeting space and graphic quality are important factors that may contribute towards a successful session. The quality of meeting space should reflect an awareness of the environment by insuring adequate ventilation and light, movable furniture, and a general setting that would make the participants feel comfortable. Arrangements setting the audience apart from the speaker are not desirable since it is important to establish a feeling of informality and encourage interaction.

Generally it is useful to promote an upcoming workshop, especially those open to the public, with mail flyers, press releases to the newspaper, and television and radio coverage. Participants attending workshops should receive an information packet including the program and workshop schedule. It is also useful to document the workshop by taking photographs, slides, video tapes, or audio cassettes as well as recording the decisions that were made.

Certain activities are basic to any environmental workshop. First, it is necessary to clearly state the workshop's goals, schedule, and events. Participants will become involved if they know what to expect. As an opening activity it is desirable to provide the participants with the opportunity to have a tangible personal experience that will relate to what they will encounter. This overview might take the form of a simple lecture, the presentation of environmental issues, or a slide show that introduces basic concepts of awareness, understanding, and action. The focus should be on active participation in activities that involve all the senses, allowing discovery and encouraging exploration. Each participant should carry away from the workshop new information and fresh insights.

When individuals come together to engage in group tasks, perceptions of why the group was formed will affect their performance. It is important that there be a leader who will clarify the members' roles and group objectives of the workshop. Appropriate role definitions will help reduce status barriers among members, encourage free communication, and decrease the tendency for high-status individuals to be unduly verbal. Workshop participants need to understand the context of their discussions and see the potential of their collective creativity before the process starts. Workshop participants should be divided into groups of five to nine people, since groups of fewer than five people may lack the knowledge or critical judgments available to analyze the problem and arrive at a decision. As groups enlarge beyond nine people, opportunities to participate decline, and dissatisfaction occurs. A group leader or facilitator is needed to help members share activities and learn to work together.

Antagonism and conflicts arise when groups create together just as they do in "real-life" situations. In both situations negative and destructive forces can emerge which can destroy personal relationships and group cohesiveness, or they can be used as positive forces for dynamic change and interchange. The core of the issue is to recognize conflict and to make it acceptable and visible, not attempt to squelch it or deny its validity. Conflict, when looked upon as an important resource, can become useful rather than destructive. One major source of conflict in community workshops occurs when participants feel that their viewpoints are not being heard and, for this reason, they become belligerent and antagonistic. It is the responsibility of the group facilitator to see that conflicts, when they arise, are settled amicably and constructively. One of the important ways of resolving conflicts is for the leader to listen to what is said and then to repeat it, making sure of what the person or the group has said. This is called the language of acceptance, which means that one person accepts the other person for what he or she is and how he or she feels, even though there may be disagreement.

A recorder working with each group is also an important contributor to the successful operation of the process. The recorder's function is to keep notes about what everyone in the group says so that in feedback sessions, each person has the assurance that he or she is being listened to and input is being valued. Summaries is one method of group feedback which helps to resolve conflicts. After each session, the group leader can summarize the important points that were made, insuring that everyone's point of view has been accurately stated. This approach insures that the process evolves on a basis of common agreements and people can identify and accept accomplishments before proceeding to the next activity.

Opinions, biases, and judgments have their place in participatory sessions, but their purpose is to allow choice and to encourage input rather than to prevent ideas from flowing. Summaries during the session allow the group to perceive what has been happening and to determine how to proceed. Agreements can be reached or disagreements can be made visible so they can be resolved constructively.

Concurrent with the exploration of people's perceptions of the issues, designers and planners need to develop a thorough data base in order to understand the technical aspects of the problem and synthesize them into issues, objectives, and activities. Finally, this information is diagrammed in a series of easily understood drawings and models. Based on the objectives that were agreed upon in the workshops, a series of program alternatives can be developed in diagrammatic design form. These findings are discussed in meetings with appropriate groups and may be presented to the larger community for approval. The intention is to arrive at a consensus about which of the design solutions best responds to the concerns of all participants. This final public forum, workshop, or design is a necessary step prior to implementation of the project.

Participatory Techniques

Gaming is a participatory approach to problem solving that engages a real-life situation compressed in time so that the essential characteristics of the problem are open to examination. This technique permits learning about the process of change in a dynamic environment and requires periodic decisions. Essentially, a complex problem is identified, its essence is abstracted, and the end result is a process referred to as simulation.

The basic format of this section is people working towards group consensus decisions. All the exercises are based on the premise that there should not be losers in design decision making. Every participant should be a winner. Therefore, the traditional process of voting is replaced by the consensus process.

In each exercise the individual makes choices, holds positions, and debates them, but the final goal of the exercise is a plan of action for an entire group of people; a goal which requires some compromising. Participants in these design groups learn about each others' value differences, and use the game props to clarify and reconcile them.

Each exercise provides props in the form of objectives and environmental settings. The range of possibilities has not been exhausted. It would be appropriate to add or eliminate items from any list of objectives, as well as maintain the opportunity for participants to include their own choices of objectives or settings.

The games included in this section have been developed to facilitate an understanding of strategies for solving school environment problems, and to impart information in a meaningful way. While games help to understand the complex interweaving of environmental and social forces, they can also be used to provide insights into situations so familiar that their characteristics are not perceived. Games help sharpen perceptions.

RELATING OBJECTIVES FOR LEARNING TO EDUCATION (ROLE)

This exercise encourages a dialogue among teachers, students, parents, administrators, and designers. Participants explore aspects of the school environment by considering a variety of approaches to teaching and learning. Educational objectives and learning methods were selected from the educational literature to allow participants the possibility of discussing numerous options (Figure 5-1). Introducing them stimulates a discussion about the purpose of learning, and the types of physical settings that would enhance student learning. In planning for efficient and effective achievement of educational *objectives,* it is necessary to consider the following:

- *Learning methods* to be used to accomplish the objectives
- *Role relationships* between student and teacher, whether student or teacher directed (The difference is primarily who makes the decision about the learning activity.)
- *Settings* or environments in which *learning methods* will be accomplished

This game is played by groups of three to five people. To begin, each player selects individually, from the list provided, no more than four *objectives* which seem to be the most important. Brief notes should be

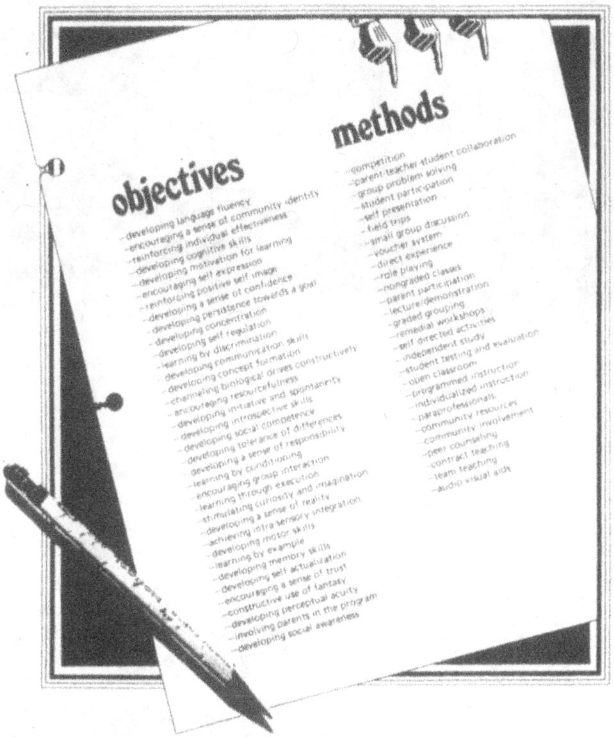

FIGURE 5-1. Educational objectives and learning methods.

FIGURE 5-2. Record sheet noting group decisions.

made justifying each choice. After each player has made choices, the individual lists are pooled. Through discussion, the group chooses from the aggregated list no more than four *objectives* that are agreeable to all participants. Group members are urged to support their individual choices forcefully, even if other members did not make the same choice, until they persuade or are persuaded by others that an *objective* should or should not be included in the final list. When consensus is reached, the group should record its choices.

The game *record sheet* (Figure 5-2) is used to report the final decisions. Next, participants should examine each objective to identify the appropriate *learning methods* (Figure 5-1) necessary to accomplish the *objective*. Three *learning methods* should be selected for each *objective*. Individual choices are then pooled for a group discussion, reaching a consensus about four *learning methods* for each *objective*. Each *learning method* should be qualified whether teacher directed (TD) or child directed (CD). (Note: This approach has also been used in many non-English speaking countries, as shown in the Japanese translation in Figure 5-3.)

Combining these two components — *objectives* and *learning methods* — the best *setting* (Figure 5-4) should be identified to fulfill the requirements established by the group. All decisions are to be noted on the game *record sheet*. A final discussion of all groups might consist of representatives from each group re-

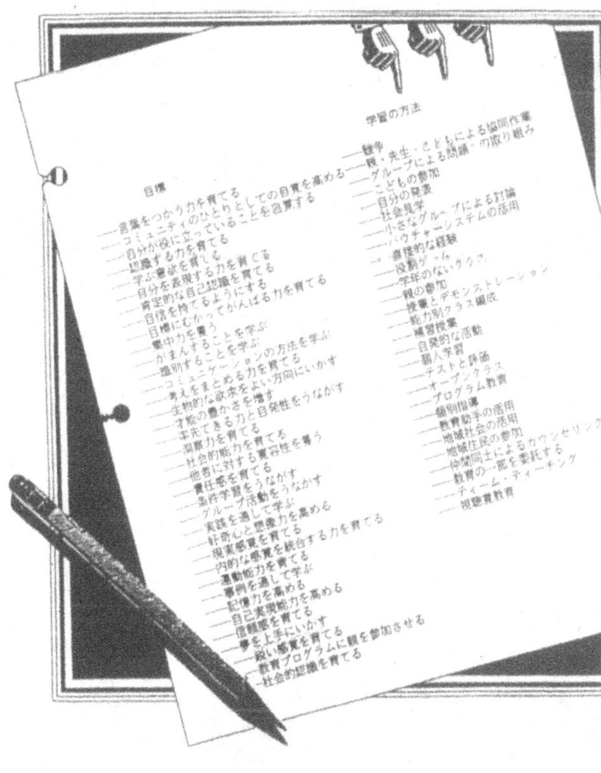

FIGURE 5-3. Japanese version of educational objectives and learning methods.

FIGURE 5-4. Photographs of a variety of educational settings that are matched to learning methods.

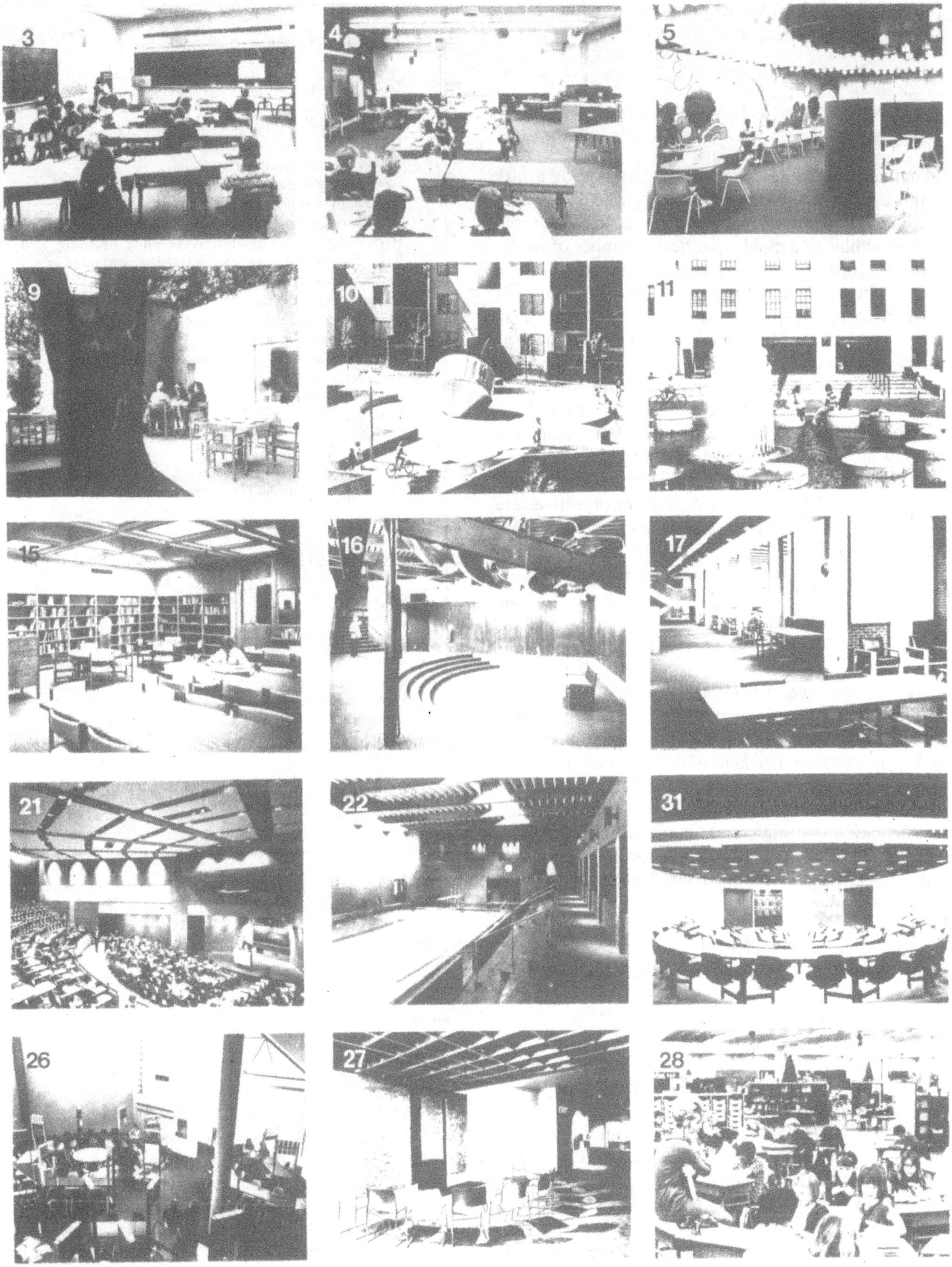

FIGURE 5-4. (continued)

porting their collective decisions, with a total group summation of all decisions.

LEARNING ENVIRONMENTS FOR CHILDREN

Planning the children's center or playroom is a task requiring the specialized knowledge of the architect as well as that of the early childhood teacher. The problem is similar to a child's puzzle. A number of pieces must fit together in some logical manner. Unlike a puzzle, however, there is not one correct solution or best fit of puzzle pieces. The differences may stem from a variety of values, goals, and needs of teachers, parents, and communities. Yet, the common aspect to all groups is the nature of activities children of all ages engage in, what they enjoy doing, and how they learn.

While goals are generalized statements about the overall purpose of an educational program such as *to advance and develop the child's functioning knowledge of his or her environment,* learning objectives are statements that describe the desired characteristics to be achieved by each child. From the goal statement, the following learning objectives might be generated:

- Positive self image
- Language development

An activity area or learning center is a place within the children's playroom described by materials and boundaries where particular learning experiences occur. The basic arrangement of the playroom is a function of the appropriate learning objectives and the organization of activity centers.

Planning appropriate environments for young children is a strategy for effectively accomplishing learning objectives. This interactional game process consists of three stages:

- Stating learning objectives
- Identifying and matching appropriate children's activity centers
- Planning the playroom or center

This structured experience can be used by groups of three to five people, although many groups can simultaneously participate. To begin, each person selects from the list provided no more than three objectives which seem to be most important to a particular age group, such as infants, toddlers, two-year-olds, etc. (Figure 5-5). The list of objectives have been culled from the early childhood literature. Through collaboration, the participants should agree to three statements that could be incorporated into a unified program for their age group. Then, two activity centers are identified where each objective can be accomplished. All decisions can be noted on the *record sheet* similar to the previous exercise.

Objectives

__ To develop self control
__ To involve parents in the educational experience
__ To reinforce a positive self image
__ To develop problem-solving skills
__ To develop communication skills
__ To encourage creativity and self-expression
__ To develop large and small muscles
__ To encourage cooperation
__ To develop sensory awareness (smelling, touching, etc.)
__ To be able to recognize symbols, letters, and numbers
__ To develop a sense of responsibility
__ To stimulate curiosity and imagination
__ To develop thinking and concentration
__ To encourage leadership
__ To develop a sense of confidence and self-reliance
__ To develop persistence towards a goal
__ To allow for privacy and introspection
__ To develop social skills
__ To develop respect for others
__ To encourge a sense of trust
__ To develop eye/hand coordination
__ To develop self-motivation

Activities

__Water play
__Art
__Dramatic play
__Manipulatives
__Eating or snacking
__Science and nature
__Sand play
__Math
__Protected outdoor
__Concept formation
__Cubby/locker
__Construction
__Reading
__Listening
__Block play
__Cooking
__Large group games
__Resting
__Indoor active
__Climbing
__Entry/reception
__Toilet
__Music

FIGURE 5-5. Developmental objectives and activity centers for young children.

To allow the effective participation of individuals not familiar with the purposes of activity centers, short scenarios are provided for each group. In addition to a description of the activity centers, there is a list of learning objectives that can be achieved in each center (Figure 5-6). It may be evident that the same objective may be achieved by different activity centers.

The game pieces represent what is common to all children's centers. How they go together, or what pieces are included, may vary between participating groups. This exercise, however, can provide the preliminary steps in planning for physical changes.

Art. The art work of children is a visual expression of their feelings. To express these feelings visually, children must think about themselves and their physical and social environment. For this reason art activities are valuable for: 1) intellectual development, 2) self-image, 3) self-expression, 4) communication, 5) problem solving, 6) exploration, 7) experimentation.

Block Play. Block play is another area where building structures from blocks allows children to express themselves. Children use their structures in both a realistic and imaginative manner. When children explore their ideas structurally, they observe physical principles and form concepts of size, weight, shape, and fit. Block play enables children to learn how to work and cooperate with their peers: 1) concept formation, 2) problem solving, 3) eye-hand coordination, 4) visual discrimination, 5) large-small muscle development, 6) cooperation, 7) self-expression, 8) positive self-concept.

Construction. Children delight in building activities in a construction area. They begin to develop skills in planning by defining the steps needed to reach a finished product. The hammering, sawing, and drilling develop: 1) large and small motor coordination, 2) eye-hand coordination, 3) visual discrimination, 4) problem solving, 5) self-confidence, 6) self-concept.

Dramatic Play. Fascinated by the experiences of everyday life, children enjoy interpreting these experiences and re-enacting them. They learn what it is like to be mother, father, police officer, storekeeper, and what their peers feel about people in such roles. They begin to learn: 1) socialization skills, 2) experimenting, 3) oral language, 4) pretending. They will begin to discover themselves as individual beings, similar to others, yet unique in their own way.

Indoor Activity. Children tend to become excessively active and excited. Under usual circumstances, they are able to exercise and reduce their excitement during active outdoor play. However, when weather conditions prevent normal outdoor activities, children must still have some means of releasing energy. An indoor active center can provide children with a variety of activities for energy release and large muscle development. Climbing and active games are two types of play that can be facilitated in this center. Objectives: 1) large-small muscle development, 2) eye-hand coordination, 3) positive self-image.

Manipulative Play. Manipulative skill is the ability to use one's hands and fingers with dexterity. It is important for young children to develop such skill so that they may later learn to read without difficulty. Puzzles, pegboards, and construction sets encourage children to learn both about their physical manipulations and about the relationships resulting from these actions. As a result, they develop: 1) eye-hand coordination, 2) perceptual skills, 3) concept formation, and 4) small motor skills.

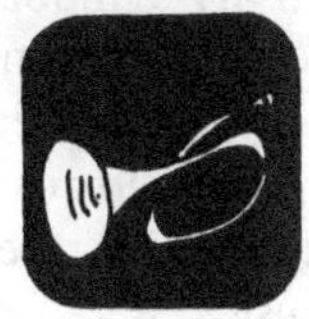

Music. The basic elements of music are sound and sound-making. This is quite evident when observing the activities of children. Making music and responding to it can enhance all areas of development. Singing, playing an instrument, and dancing are important to: 1) oral language development, 2) concept reinforcement, 3) cooperation in the social environment, 4) self-concept, 5) motor development.

Reading. If a pre-school child is to meet with later success in learning and enjoying reading, then he or she needs to become acquainted with books as early as possible. At this age, children are involved with learning a language and are fascinated with words and sounds. Provide opportunities, support, and encouragement for reading experiences whenever possible. Objectives: 1) recognition of symbols, 2) oral language, 3) concept formation, 4) visual-auditory discrimination.

Science. Pre-school children are born scientists. They are equipped with an imaginative curiosity to touch, see, hear, smell, taste. A science area integrates natural and man-made objects into the world of children and nurtures their curiosity and understanding of the environment and the interrelationships within it. Objectives: 1) concept formation, 2) experimentation, 3) sensory development, 4) problem solving.

Sand-Water Play. Flexibility, in form and function, is a primary characteristic of water and sand, and because of this flexibility, it offers children many opportunities for experimentation. Playing with varying objects in the water-sand and measuring introduce to children concepts of floating, sinking, and quantity. Objectives: 1) concept formation, 2) sensory development, 3) eye-hand coordination, 4) small muscle development, 5) experimentation, 6) exploration.

FIGURE 5.6. Learning objectives for activity centers.

Each of the symbol diagrams represents an activity center in the playroom, as well as activity areas in the children's center (Figure 5-7). Through comparisons between the activity symbols, it is possible to decide which centers should be adjacent to one another and which require some separation. To facilitate the planning process, a grid should be prepared to correspond with the size of the activity symbols. The size of the activity symbols corresponds to the area necessary for the activity center, which usually accommodates two to four children. Therefore the spaces between the symbols correspond to area for movement and circulation. The rules for locating the symbols are as follows:

- Each activity symbol should be placed on a vacant grid.
- Symbols should not overlap or occupy more than one grid cell.
- Blank space between activity symbols should be provided for circulation.
- Activity centers should be located on the basis of their requirements for privacy, quiet, or accessibility to each other.

While many of the activity centers appear to be related, their placement will require a decision about which are the most important relationships.

FIGURE 5-7. Symbol diagrams corresponding to activity centers (from Sanoff, H. & J., *Learning Environments for Children*. Humanics Ltd. 1988).

A final stage in the process explores the physical features of activity centers. Several drawings of different and unidentified centers are used to promote a discussion among participants about the appropriate character of the center and the image it evokes (Figure 5-8). While the drawings are not intended to offer design solutions, they can be instrumental in increasing participants' awareness to the "silent messages" conveyed by the physical environment.

FIGURE 5-8. Drawings of activity centers (from Sanoff, H. & J., *Learning Environments for Children*).

PLANNING OUTDOOR PLAY

Planning for outdoor play is an integral part of the design process and is a vital component of the child care center. Typically perceived as a staging area for large muscle development, the outdoor play area is not only important for the child's health but contributes to the child's learning experiences (Threlfall 1986). Outdoor play space offers opportunities for adventure, challenge, and wonder in the natural environment (Frost and Klein 1983). The only substantial difference between indoor and outdoor activity is that one has a roof over it. Both, however, need architectural and landscape definition, and both need to provide for the multiplicity of children's developmental needs. For example, a play yard with 12 tricycles, a rocking boat, a tumble tub, a jungle gym, a dirt area, and a sand table with water, has 17 separate play units but only four different kinds of things to do (Kritchevsky, Prescott, and Walling 1974). Variety can be an important measure of interest. Complexity, or the number of subparts of a piece of equipment, such as a sandbox with play materials, water, climbing boards, and crates, can also add to a child's interest.

The process of creating outdoor play spaces is age-group oriented and begins with developmental objectives that help to generate the activities in which children engage (Sanoff 1982). The teaching staff and design team work together to establish linkages between objectives for outdoor play, the related children's activities, and the play settings required.

To complement the indoor environment, the outdoors provides play settings that stress muscle development as well as natural settings that provide experience in the life cycle of plants and animals. The props used to enable the teachers to make spatial decisions included drawings of different play settings as well as statements of objectives and lists of activities. The planning group moves through a series of collaborative stages in which all members should reach consensus. Finally, the activities and play settings are organized into play zones which range from passive to active play, and from private to group activities (Sanoff 1982). This part of the planning process helps generate discussions about the purpose of outdoor play, usually dispelling many of the myths surrounding large muscle development as the primary purpose of children's outdoor activities.

Learning objectives for outdoor play are discussed in a similar way to those in the planning of the playrooms. Objectives such as problem solving, concept development, and social development are key concerns of the teachers. Supporting activities like role playing, climbing, feeling and handling, balancing, sliding, and construction compose the array of choices most frequently made. As a result of making these linkages, the subsequent choice of play equipment and play areas is based on a clear understanding of the developmental needs that the outdoor play area should serve. Other types of individual or quiet activities, group games, and opportunities for exercising imagination are also appropriate for outdoor use, but may not necessarily require the construction of special equipment.

An analysis of the building site and its topography would influence the location and options for various play settings. A site map should be used as the basis for planning areas where play settings can be clustered according to similarity of requirements. Play zones include areas for drama, nature, adventure, and large muscle development. Equipment and zone choices are then related to specific site requirements, such as solar orientation.

Process

Planning outdoor play is a method of facilitating the design of children's outdoor play areas. Participants involved in the playroom exercise can continue planning for their age group in an outdoor area contiguous to their playroom. Using the same list of educational objectives found in playroom planning, participants can select three activities, using the same consensus decision making process. Each objective would then be matched to three outdoor activities from the expanded list (Figure 5-9). The numbered activity settings (Figure 5-10) can then be matched to the appropriate activity as shown in the drawings. The setting drawings are provided to aid in visualizing how the activities can be spatially organized. When all activities are selected, they can be grouped into play zones (Figure 5-11) which range from active to passive

Activities

__Mixing	__Painting
__Feeling & handling	__Cooking
__Hitting	__Pouring
__Crawling	__Stretching
__Splashing	__Sliding
__Role playing	__Constructing
__Dressing up	__Planting
__Molding	__Swinging
__Contact with animals	__Throwing & catching
__Digging	__Balancing
__Climbing	__Vehicular motion

FIGURE 5-9. List of outdoor play-activity settings.

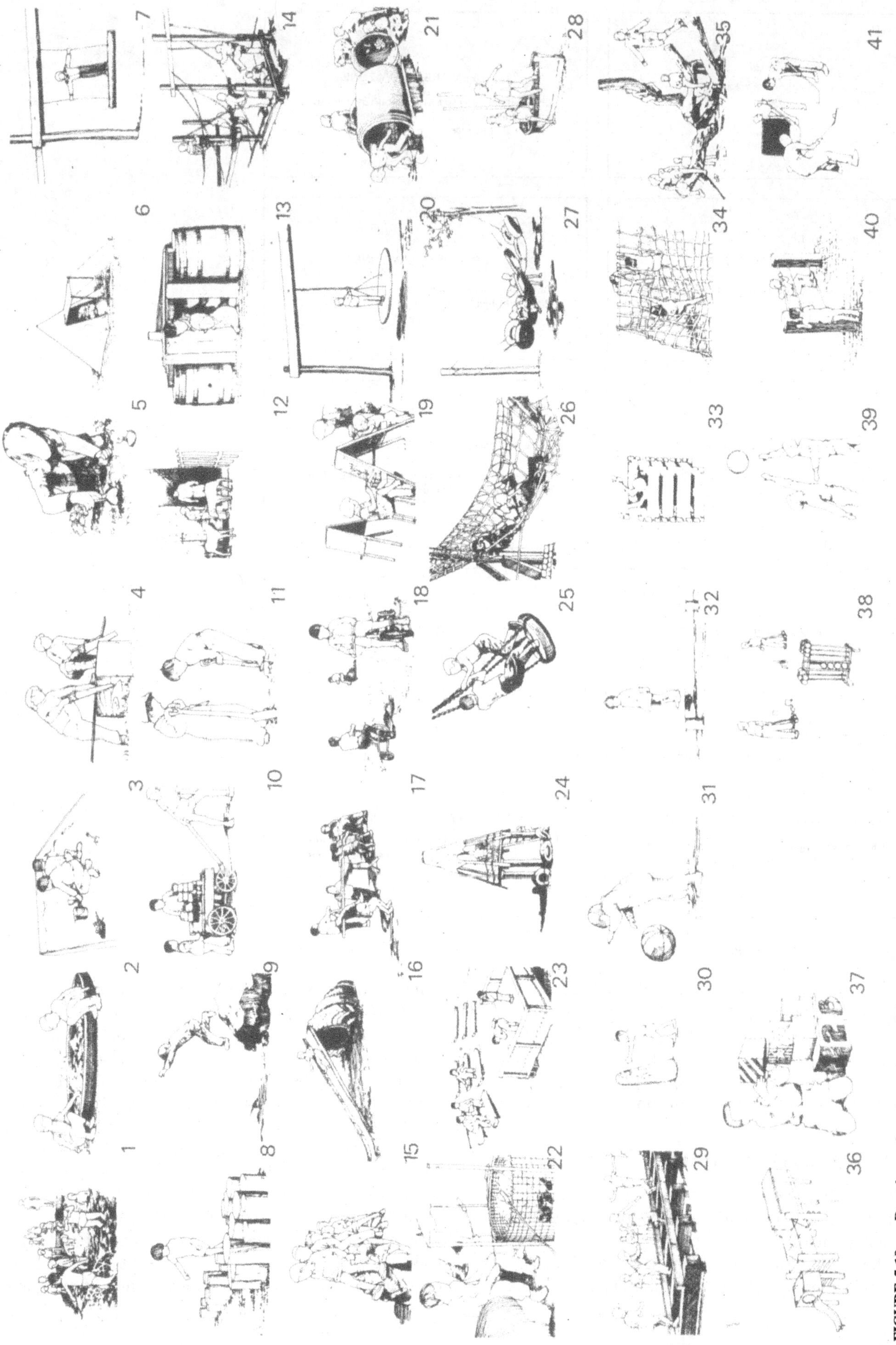

FIGURE 5-10. Drawings of outdoor play-activity settings (from Sanoff, H., *Planning Outdoor Play.* Humanics, 1982).

ZONES

OPEN AREA PLAY ZONE

Children use large spaces for group games and some individual activities, (which may require hard or soft surfaces).

PRIVATE PLAY ZONE

Children use small protected areas for individual or quiet activities.

CREATIVE PLAY ZONE

Children combine materials to make a different object.

DRAMATIC PLAY ZONE

Children exercise their imaginations to create roles.

LARGE MUSCLE DEVELOPMENT ZONE

Children overcome physical and mental obstacles, exercising all possible muscles.

ADVENTURE PLAY ZONE

Children spontaneously build and rebuild their environment.

NATURE ZONE

Children interact with natural objects.

MANIPULATIVE COORDINATION ZONE

Children develop coordination skills frequently with repetitive motion.

IMAGINATIVE PLAY ZONE

Children exercise imagination and limited muscular effort, but no object is necessarily produced.

FIGURE 5-11. Outdoor play zones.

play, and private to group activities (Figure 5-12). Zones are a planning strategy for enabling activities with similar requirements to be clustered together.

The diagrams of outdoor play equipment (Figure 5-13) are drawn to scale and allow participants to organize and locate the equipment on an actual site.

PHOTO QUESTIONNAIRES

Buildings and spaces convey messages reflecting the inner life, activities, and social values of the users. Characteristics like shape, color, or arrangement enable the making of vividly identified mental images of the environment. These environmental cues have something to say about the people who occupy buildings as well as the people who created these buildings. Similarly, people read these cues, make judgments, and act accordingly. These messages play an important role in people's comprehension of the environment. Specific environments can be evaluated about the appropriateness of the messages conveyed. An effective method for eliciting responses to the environment are through the use of visual techniques, such as drawings, photographs, and video.

Photo questionnaires and interviews are an effective means used to elicit evaluative comments about physical settings. People interpret the identity and meaning of their environment from the interaction of and their

Zones	Activities	Settings
Creative Play Zone		
Imaginative Play Zone		
Dramatic Play Zone		
Nature Zone		
Adventure Play Zone		
Private Play Zone		
Manipulative Coordination Zone		
Large Muscle Development Zone		
Open Area Play Zone		

FIGURE 5-12. Zones, activities, settings record sheet.

interaction with a wide variety of physical features. In the school environment, there are entrances, pathways, and a variety of inside places that evoke either good or bad feelings (Figure 5-14).

Becoming aware of perceived environmental effects is a necessary first step in striking the delicate balance between familiarity and monotony and boredom, and between variety and confusion and disorientation. With an understanding of how physical surroundings affect us psychologically, we can become more aware of our effects on them, and on ourselves, when we allow them to be changed. We will then start to realize the importance of our concern for our surroundings, and eventually work toward the improvement of their quality.

CLASSROOM ENVIRONMENT RATINGS

The physical assessment of classrooms can be accomplished by comparing user ratings of different settings using the same descriptive statements, as well as between the *actual* and *ideal* classroom. The technique, described as a Q-sort, consists of descriptive statements (below) printed on separate cards. Students sort the cards into piles according to the issue under consideration, such as "most like my classroom" or "most not like my classroom" (David 1982). This technique which David (1982) describes as a Classroom Environment Q-sort is most effective when it supplements other information-gathering approaches.

Classroom environment descriptive statements follow:

1. I have enough space to work without others crowding me.
2. My room has places where you can be by yourself if you want to.
3. I have a place of my own where I can keep my things.
4. In my room it's easy to concentrate on what you're doing.
5. I get to choose where I sit.
6. I can see everything that goes on in our room from where I sit.
7. I spend most of the day at my desk.
8. The furniture in my room is arranged to help us work together easily.
9. I feel like I have a place here that belongs to me.
10. I can fix up my place the way I want it.
11. There are lots of good places to work in my room.
12. It's quiet enough for me in my room.
13. We often change the way my room is arranged.
14. My room is neatly arranged.
15. My room is clearly organized.
16. My room is just the right size for me — not too big and not too small.
17. My room is pleasant to look at.
18. My room is a special place for me.
19. There are lots of comfortable places in my room.
20. I get to help decide how our room will be arranged.
21. There are lots of interesting things to do in my room.
22. I get to help add things to my room to make it even better.
23. There are places for me to display my work.

ROLE PLAYING

Direct human involvement in decision making integrates thought and action. With increased participation comes the inevitability of conflict resulting from value differences among participants. An effective approach to solve a problem within a controlled set of circumstances can be achieved through role playing,

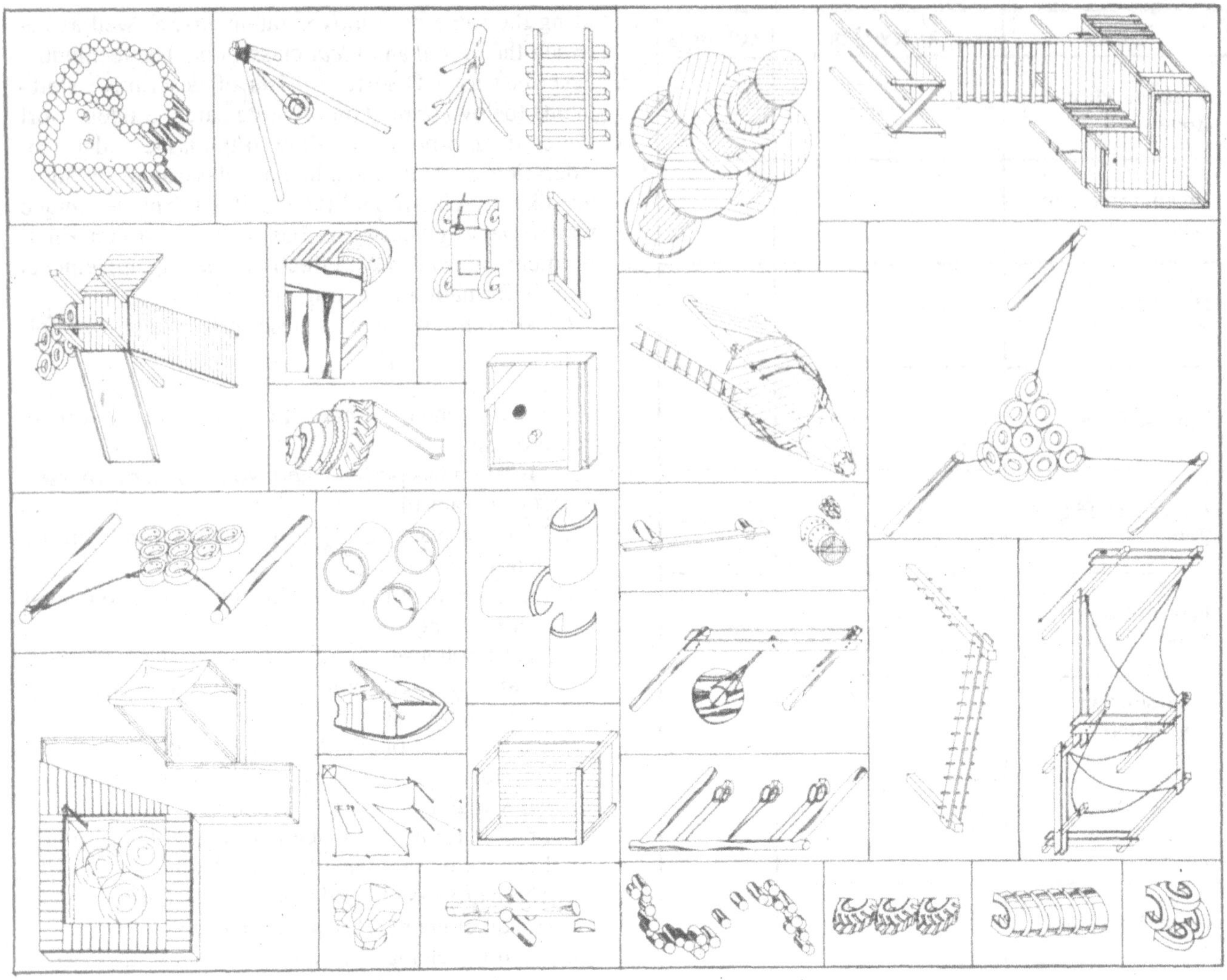

FIGURE 5-13. Outdoor play equipment (from Sanoff, H., *Planning Outdoor Play*).

in which a plot or basic conflict situation is designed. Information is given to each participant in the form of a profile which describes the character and the factors influencing the players' behavior. A scenario describes the setting in which the role playing activity will occur. In a free role play, compared to a structured event with rules, participants begin interacting immediately after receiving the profiles and scenario.

For example, a school building committee with broad-based representation from the administration, the teaching staff, the parents and students, and the architects has the potential for conflict during many stages in the design process, particularly in the earliest stages of establishing educational goals. From the architect's point of view, one of the main objectives of a role playing simulation is to prepare the design team for the unexpected conflicts that might occur during community meetings.

Typical profiles or scenarios for the composition of such a committee can be constructed (see box on page 204). The scenario can identify the purpose of the meeting with a playing time limited to between one and two hours. An observer can lead a follow-up discussion with the participants to ask several questions. What kinds of decisions were made? What influenced the decisions made? What did the participants learn? What did they feel they had done wrong? Were conflict situations successfully resolved? How closely did the role-playing situation approximate a real one?

In addition to the analytic component of a role-play simulation, there is an emotional, dramatic element as well. Participants openly express their beliefs and opinions, all of which are a reflection of their attitudes and values. The recognition of value differences that generate conflict early in the planning process enables designers to identify means for reconciliation of those

1. **Please select in order of preference where you would like to ATTEND CLASS.**

A__ B__ C__ D__

2. Your 1st choice is selected because :

3. Your last choice is due to :

FIGURE 5-14. Photo questionnaires (Photo: Henry Sanoff & Tun Sing Chen).

1. **Please select in order of preference where you would like to CONVERSE WITH OTHER PEOPLE.**

   A__ B__ C__ D__

2. Your 1st choice is selected because :

3. Your last choice is due to :

FIGURE 5-14. (continued)

1. Please select in order of preference where you would like to HAVE LUNCH.

A__ B__ C__ D__

2. Your 1st choice is selected because :

3. Your last choice is due to :

FIGURE 5-14. (continued)

differences. Conflicts can be resolved when dissenting participants are asked to restate ideas they oppose by identifying and stating the positive features of those ideas. This procedure attempts to maintain a positive discussion while enhancing individual listening skills.

Role-playing games can enable participants to analyze and practice solving specific problems that arise during the school design process. They simulate the communication of information and decisions in the actual situation in which they may be employed (Abt 1970).

Profiles of Committee Members for a Private Alternative School

Parent No. 1. You are sending your child to this school so he can be with children of his social level. The public schools expose your child to children you would not want him to become involved with — "children not of his own kind."

Parent No. 2. You feel that this school can offer your child better academic opportunities. You are interested in your child learning the three R's and getting good grades so that she can succeed in life.

Parent No. 3. You feel that the public schools don't understand your child. He does not get along with the teachers. They pick on him for things he does not do and accuse him wrongly. You feel that in this school with small classes and better teachers, he will be better understood and do well.

Headmaster. You, the headmaster, feel that education is self-directed. Each child pursues his/her own interests at his/her own rate of development. Each child receives individual instruction as required.

The Architect. You are designing a school for this community. To successfully achieve this end, you must find out from the building committee, parents, teachers, and headmaster what the educational objectives are. Each of the participants' contributing ideas may create conflict. Your role is to direct the group to reach some agreement about goals and objectives.

Building Committee Member — Builder. You, the builder, are concerned with the cost of construction. To you, a good school means sound brick construction at a low cost. You will support most ideas about education as long as they do not interfere with a sound building.

Building Committee Member — Minister. You, the minister, are concerned with religious education. You desire that more time be committed to the teaching of the Bible as an important part of the educational objectives.

Building Committee Member — Doctor. You, the doctor, feel that academic achievement is of utmost importance. There should be an emphasis on learning facts and information and do away with all this freedom nonsense of the child pursuing his or her own interests. Learn and get good grades so your child can get into a good college.

Teacher No. 1. You believe in a strict schedule: All children do all activities together. They are assigned tasks and must fulfill their assignments. One afternoon a week is set aside for "free time."

Teacher No. 2. You believe that with appropriate materials and guidance in their use, children can proceed at their own rate and interest. They are free to question the teacher and ask for help when needed. Children can move about freely with the teacher's permission.

GLOSSARY OF PARTICIPATION TECHNIQUES

The projects in this book employ a wide range of participatory techniques. They all require different resources and respond to different objectives identified by the architect or by the client. Each technique is briefly defined below, and their deployment is noted at the beginning of each project.

Attitude survey a technique statistically representative of all people that does not allow direct contact between architect and client(s)

Charette a process which convenes interest groups in intensive interactive meetings lasting several days

Community meetings planned by organizations to focus on a particular project or issue

Design-in a technique in which people work with plans and models to provide a clear idea of the impact of design solutions

Fishbowl planning refers to an open decision-making process that involves the use of several participatory techniques.

Focused group interview structured interview consisting of several individuals permitting discussion of ideas

Game simulations a technique of abstracting the essential elements of a problem without the normal constraints

Group interaction interpersonal techniques used to facilitate group interaction and problem solving

Public forum an open meeting held by an organization or agency to present information about a project at any time during the process

Task force a special purpose committee sponsored by an organization to be involved with a clearly defined task

Workshop working sessions to discuss issues in order to reach an understanding of their importance

The table shown in Figure 5-15 identifies the unique features associated with each technique. Usually several techniques are combined in the development of a plan for participation.

	Clarifies problem	Elicits community support	Uncovers hidden problems	Fosters creative solutions	Identifies constraints	Informs people	Generates objective information	Develops awareness of diverse interests	Promotes human resource development
Charette process	●			●	●			●	
Community meetings			●	●		●			
Design in	●		●	●	●				
Focus interviews	●		●		●				
Fishbowl planning		●	●		●	●	●		
Game simulation	●		●						●
Group dynamics	●							●	●
Public forum		●						●	
Task force	●			●			●		
Training						●		●	●
Workshop	●			●			●	●	●

FIGURE 5-15. Comparison of participatory techniques and their advantages.

References

Abt, Clark C. (1970). *Serious Games*. New York: Viking.

Adams, Raymond S., and Bruce J. Biddle (1970). *Realities of Teaching: Explorations with Video Tape*. New York: Holt, Rinehart & Winston.

Ahrentzen, Sherry (1982). Students' responses to openness, softness, and seclusion in elementary school classrooms. *Journal of Man-Environment Relations*, 1.3:42–53.

Alexander, Christopher, Murray Silverstein, Shlomo Angel, Sara Ishikawa, and Denny Abrams (1975). *The Oregon Experiment*. New York: Oxford University Press.

Alexander, Christopher, Sara Ishikawa, and Murray Silverstein (1977). *The Pattern Language*. New York: Oxford University Press.

Astin, A.W. (1968). *The College Environment*. Washington, DC: American Council on Education.

Banning, J.H. (1978). *Campus Ecology: A Perspective for Student Affairs*. Portland, OR: National Association of Student Personnel Administrators.

Banning, J.H. (1980). The campus ecology manager role. In U. Delworth and G.R. Hanson (eds.), *Student Services: A Handbook for the Profession*. San Francisco: Jossey-Bass.

Barker, Roger G., and Paul V. Gump (1964). *Big School, Small School*. Stanford, CA: Stanford University Press.

Beggs, David W. III (1964). *A Practical Application of the Trump Plan*. Englewood Cliffs, NJ: Prentice-Hall.

Bennett, Neville, J. Andreae, P. Hegarty, and B. Wade (1980). *Open Plan Schools*. Atlantic Highlands, NJ: Humanities.

Bennett, Guy (1985). When form follows function . . . success is all but assured. *Middle School Journal*, 16:2–24.

Bremer, John, and Michael von Moschzisker (1971). *The School Without Walls: Philadelphia's Parkway Program*. New York: Holt, Rinehart & Winston.

Burns, Jim (1979). *Connections: Ways to Discover and Realize Human Potentials*. New York: McGraw-Hill.

Burns, Jim (1983). Designing for (and with) the Christian Brothers. *A/A Journal*, 72,2:60–63.

Casper, Dale E. (1987). *Grade School Architecture: Projects and Trends in the 1980's*. Monticello, IL: Vance Bibliographies.

Castaldi, Basil (1977). *Educational Facilities: Planning, Remodeling and Management*. Boston: Allyn & Bacon.

Chase, Larry (1983). Quality circles in education. *Educational Leadership*, 40,5:18–330.

Cohen, Harold L., and James Filipczak (1971). *A New Learning Environment*. San Francisco: Jossey-Bass.

Cohen, Uriel, Ann B. Hill, Carol G. Lane, Tim McGinty, and Gary T. Moore (1989). *Recommendations for Child Play Areas*. Milwaukee: University of Wisconsin-Milwaukee, Center for Architecture and Urban Planning Research.

Cohen, Uriel, Gary T. Moore, and Tim McGinty (1978). *Case Studies of Child Play Areas and Support Facilities*. Milwaukee: University of Wisconsin-Milwaukee, Center for Architecture and Urban Planning Research, Report R78–2.

Coleman, James S. (1961). *The Adolescent Society*. New York: Free Press.

Conyne, R.K. (1975). Environmental assessment: Mapping for counselor action. *Personnel and Guidance Journal*, 54:150–155.

Cooper, Bruce S. (1971). *Free and Freedom Schools: A National Survey of Alternative Programs*. Washington, DC: President's Commission on School Finance.

Cremin, Lawrence (1970). *American Education: The Colonial Experience*. New York: Harper & Row.

Crookston, B.B. (1975). Milieu management. *National Association of Student Personnel Administrators Journal*, 13:45–55.

Curtis, Paul, and Roger Smith (1974). A child's exploration of space. *School Review,* 82,4:671–679.

Daher, D.M., J.G. Corazzini, and R.D. McKinnon (1977). An environmental redesign program for residence halls. *Journal of College Student Personnel,* 18:11–15.

David, Thomas (1982). Functional dimensions of classroom environments. In John C. Baird and Anthony D. Lutkus (eds.), *Mind Child Architecture*. Hanover, NH: University Press of New England.

de Carlo, Gian Carlo (1974). Why/how to build school buildings. In Gary J. Coates (ed.), *Alternative Learning Environments*. Stroudsburg, PA: Dowden, Hutchinson & Ross.

Delle, Robert, Arlene Gaubertm, and William Picard (1989). *Middle grades assessment program for evaluating J. Landry Senior Middle School,* Hahnville, LA.

Dober, Richard P. (1963). *Campus Planning*. New York: John Wiley.

Dober, Richard P. (1992). *Campus Design*. New York: John Wiley.

Dorman, Gayle (1981). *Middle Grades Assessment Program: Users Manual.* Chapel Hill, NC: Center for Early Adolescence, University of North Carolina.

Dorman, Gayle (1987). *Improving Middle-Grade Schools: A Framework for Action*. Chapel Hill, NC: Center for Early Adolescence, University of North Carolina.

Doyle, Michael, and David Straus (1977). *How to Make Meetings Work: The New Interaction Method.* Chicago: Playboy Press.

Drucker, Peter (1969). *The Age of Discontent: Guidelines to Our Changing Society.* New York: Harper & Row.

Duke, Daniel L. (1978). *The Retransformation of the School: The Emergence of Contemporary Alternative Schools in the United States*. Chicago: Nelson-Hall.

Educational Change and Architectural Consequences: A Report on Facilities for Individualized Instruction (1971). New York: Educational Facilities Laboratory.

Elmore, Richard F. (1988). Choice in public education. In W.L. Boyd and C.T. Kerchner (eds.), *The Politics of Excellence and Choice in Education*. New York: Falmer Press.

Eisner, Elliot W. The ecology of school improvement. *Educational Leadership,* 40,5:24–29.

Elkin, David (1981). *The Hurried Child.* Reading, MA: Addison-Wesley.

Evans, G., and B. Lovell (1979). Design modification in an open-plan school. *Journal of Environmental Psychology,* 71:41–49.

Evans, Nancy J. (1983). Environmental assessment: Current practices and future directions, *Journal of College Student Personnel,* 24,4:283–299.

Facility Management Institute (1983). *The Story of the Lyle C. Roll Building*. Ann Arbor, MI: Herman Miller Research Corp.

Field, T.M. (1980). Preschool play: Effects of teacher/child ratios and organization of classroom space. *Child Study Journal,* 10,3:191–205.

Frabboni, Franco (1990). School-territory integration: Towards an educating city. In *The Educating City*. Proceedings of the First International Congress of Educating Cities, Barcelona.

Fritz, John (1975). *My Encounter with Alternatives*. Toronto: Canadian Education Association.

Gandini, Lella (1991). Not just anywhere: Making child care centers into "particular" places. *Child Care Information Exchange,* 78:5–9.

Gandini, Lella (1992). Education and caring spaces. In Carolyn Edwards, Lella Gandini, and George Forman (eds.), *The Hundred Languages of Children: The Reggio Emilia Approach to Early Childhood Education*. Norwood, NJ: Ablex.

Garbino, J. (1980). Some thoughts about school size and its effects on adolescent development. *Journal of Youth and Adolescence,* 9,1:19–31.

Getzels, Jacob W. (1974). Images of the classroom and visions of the learner. *School Review,* 82,4:527–540.

Glass, Gene V., L.S. Cahen, M.L. Smith, and N.N. Filby (1982). *School Class Size: Research and Policy.* Beverly Hills, CA: Sage.

Godschalk, David (1972). *Participation, Planning, and Exchange in Old and New Communities: A Collaborative Paradigm*. Chapel Hill, NC: North Carolina University Press.

Gold, A. (1975). The resurgence of the small school in the city. *Phi Delta Kappa,* 56.5:313–315.

Goldberg, Bruce (1991). Redesigning schools: Architecture and restructuring. *Radius,* 3,1:1–7.

Gordon, William J.J. (1961). *Synectics*. New York: Collier Books.

Greenman, Jim (1988). *Caring Spaces, Learning Places: Children's Environments That Work.* Redmond, WA: Exchange Press.

Gump, Paul V. (1980). School environments. In Irwin Altman and Joachim F. Wolwhill (eds.), *Children and the Environment*. New York: Plenum.

Gump, Paul V. (1987). School and classroom environments. In Daniel Stokols and Irwin Altman (eds.), *Handbook of Environmental Psychology,* Vol. 1. New York: John Wiley.

Gump, Paul V., and R. Ross (1979). What's happening in schools of open design? and *JSAS Catalog Selected Documents in Psychology,* 9.12:11816.

Guthrie, J.W., and M.W. Kirst (1988). *Conditions of Education in California 1988*. Berkeley: Policy Analysis for California Education. (Policy Paper No. 88-3-2).

Halprin, Lawrence, and Jim Burns (1974). *Taking Part: A Workshop Approach to Collective Creativity.* Cambridge, MA: MIT Press.

Harms, Thelma, and Richard M. Clifford (1980). *Early Childhood Environmental Rating Scales*. New York: Teachers College Press, Columbia University.

Hawkins, Donald E., and Dennis A. Vinton (1973). *The Environmental Classroom*. Englewood Cliffs, NJ: Prentice Hall.

Holland, J.L. (1973). *Making Vocational Choices: A Theory of Careers*. Englewood Cliffs, NJ: Prentice Hall.

Holt, James (1974). Involving the users in school planning. *School Review*, 82,4:667–670.

Huebner, L.A., J.A. Royer, J. Moore, D.L. Cordes, and S.C. Paul (1979). Stress management through an ecosystem model in a school of medicine. In L.A. Huebner (ed.), *Redesigning Campus Environments: New Directions for Student Services* (No. 8). San Francisco: Jossey-Bass.

Hunt, Michael E. (1985). Enhancing a building's imageability. *Journal of Architectural and Planning Research*, 2:151–168.

Hurwitz, Janet G. (1975). Participatory planning in an urban neighborhood. Soulard, St. Louis, Missouri: A case study. *DMG Journal*,9,4:348–357.

Joyce, Bruce R., Richard H. Hersh, and Michael McKibbin (1983). *The Structure of School Improvement*. New York: Longman, Inc.

Kantrowitz, Min (1986). POE. *Progressive Architecture*, 67,4:118–123.

Katz, Lillian (1990). Impressions of Reggio Emilia. *Young Children*, 45,6:11–12.

King, Stanley, and Merinda Conley, Bill Latimer, Drew Ferrari (1989). *Co-design: A Process of Design Participation*. New York: Van Nostrand Reinhold.

Knirk, Frederick G. (1979). *Designing Productive Learning Environments*. Englewood Cliffs, NJ: Educational Technology.

Kritchevsky, Sybil, Elizabeth Prescott, and Lee Walling (1974). Planning environments for young children: Physical space. In Gary Coates (ed.), *Alternative Learning Environments*. Stroudsburg, PA: Hutchinson and Ross.

Kurtz, John M. (1977). Habitable schools: Programming for a changing environment. In Wolfgang F.E. Preiser (ed.), *Facility Programming*. Stroudsburg, PA: Dowden, Hutchinson and Ross.

Lindemer, George C. (1984). Open system Theory Z: A natural for middle school management. *American Middle School Education*, 7,1:9–12.

Lipsitz, Joan (1977). *Growing Up Forgotten: A Review of Research and Programs Concerning Early Adolescence*. Lexington, MA: D.C. Heath.

Lipsky, Michael (1968). Protest as a political resource. *The American Political Science Review*, 62:1144–1158.

Litwak, Eugene, and Henry J. Meyer (1966). A balance theory of coordination between bureaucratic organizations and community primary groups. *Administrative Science Quarterly*, 7:31–58.

MacDonald, Donald (1989). Deinstitutionalizing architecture for children: The Stanford arboretum center. *Children's Environments Quarterly*, 6,4:40–47.

Mack, D. (1976). Privacy: A child's need to be alone in the classroom. *Teacher*, 93,6:52–53.

Malaguzzi, Loris (1984). If the eye jumps over the wall. Catalog of exhibition. Department of Education, City of Reggio Emilia-cited by Gandini, L., Educational and caring spaces. In Carolyn Edwards, Lella Gandini, and George Forman (eds.), *The Hundred Languages of Children: The Reggio Emilia Approach to Early Childhood Education*. Norwood, NJ: Ablex.

Malaguzzi, Loris (1992). History, ideas, and basic philosophy. In Carolyn Edwards, Lella Gandini, and George Forman (eds.), *The Hundred Languages of Children: The Reggio Emilia Approach to Early Childhood Education*. Norwood, NJ: Ablex.

McGuffey, C.W. (1982). Facilities. In Herbert J. Walberg (ed.), *Improving Educational Standards and Productivity*. Berkeley, CA: McCutchan.

McPartland, James M., and Edward L. Dill (1977). *Violence in Schools*. Lexington, MA: Lexington.

Milgram, Stanley (1970). The experience of living in cities. *Ekistics*, August,145–150.

Miller, J.A. (1988, October 4). Educational summit's promise: "Social compact" for reforms. *Education Week*, 9(5) 1:10.

Mitchell, William C. (1967). The shape of political theory to come: From political sociology to political economy. *American Behavioral Scientist* 2:8–37.

Moore, Gary T., Carol G. Lane, Ann B. Hill, Uriel Cohen, and Tim McGinty (1989). *Recommendations for Child Care Centers*. Milwaukee: University of Wisconsin-Milwaukee, Center for Architecture and Urban Planning Research.

Moore, Gary T. (1986). Effects of the spatial definition behavior settings on children's behavior: A quasi-experimental field study. *Journal of Environmental Psychology*, 6:205–231.

Moore, Gary T. (1987). The physical environment and cognitive development in child care centers. In Carol S. Weinstein and Thomas G. David (eds.), *Spaces for Children: The Built Environment and Child Development*. New York: Plenum.

Moos, Rudolph H. (1979). *Evaluating Educational Environments: Procedures, Measures, Findings, and Policy Implications*. San Francisco: Jossey-Bass.

Morton, Roger (1992). Albuquerque is offering a successful alternative. *School and College*, 31,1:6–8.

Murphy, Jim (1972). By the people. *Progressive Architecture*, 53,2:88–95.

Murphy, Jim (1975). A second look. *Progressive Architecture*, 57,12:56–59.

Murphy, Joseph (1991). *Restructuring Schools: Capturing and Assessing the Phenomena*. New York: Teachers College Press.

Natale, Jo Anna (1992). Great expectations. *The Executive Educator*, 3:32–35.

A Nation Prepared: Teachers for the 21st Century. (1986). New York: Carnegie Forum on Education and the Economy.

Neill, Alexander S. (1960). *Summerhill: A Radical Approach to Child Rearing*. New York: Hart.

New, Rebecca (1990). Excellent early education: A city in Italy has it. *Young Children*, 45,6:4–10.

O'Hanton, James (1983). Theory Z in school administration. *Educational Leadership,* 40,5:17.

Osmon, Fred L. (1971). *Patterns for Designing Children's Centers.* New York: Educational Facilities Laboratory.

Ouchi, William (1981). *Theory Z: How American Business Can Meet the Japanese Challenge.* Reading, MA: Addison-Wesley.

Palmer, Mickey (1981). *The Architect's Guide to Facility Programming.* Washington, DC: The American Institute of Architects and Architectural Record Books.

Phillips, D., S. Scarr, and K. McCartney (1989). Child care quality and children's social development. *Developmental Psychology,* 23:537–543.

Places and Things for Experimental Schools. (1972). New York: Educational Facilities Laboratory and U.S. Office of Education.

Plath, Karl (1965). *Schools Within Schools: A Study of High School Organization.* New York: Teachers College, Columbia University.

Postman, Neil, and Charles Weingarten (1971). *The Soft Revolution.* New York: Delacorte.

Preiser, Wolfgang F.E., Harvey Z. Rabinowitz, and Edward T. White (1988). *Post Occupancy Evaluation.* New York: Van Nostrand Reinhold.

Prescott, Elizabeth, Elizabeth Jones, Sybil Kritchevsky, Cynthia Milich, and Ede Haselhoef (1976). *Assessments of Child Rearing Environments: An Ecological Approach.* Pasadena, CA: Pacific Oaks College.

Prescott, Elizabeth, and Thomas G. David (1976). *The Effects of the Physical Environment in Child Care Systems.* Concept paper. Pasadena, CA: Pacific Oaks College.

Preskill, Hallie (1990). *Saturn School of Tomorrow: Formative Evaluation Report.* St. Paul, MN: The College of St. Thomas.

Proshansky, Etta, and Maxine Wolf (1974). The physical setting and open education. *School Review,* 82,4:557–574.

Rabinowitz, Harvey Z. (1975). *Buildings in Use Study.* Milwaukee: Center for Architecture and Urban Planning Research, University of Wisconsin, Milwaukee.

Rohe, William, and E. Nuffer (1977). *The Effects of Density and Partitioning on Children's Behavior.* Paper presented at the 85th annual meeting, American Psychological Association, San Francisco, Mimeo.

Rorty, Richard (1990). Education without dogma. *Dialogue,* 88:44–47.

Rosner, Judith (1978). Matching method to purpose: The challenge of planning citizen participation acitivities. In Stuart Langton (ed.) *Citizen Participation in America.* New York: Lexington Books.

Rutter, Michael, Barbara Maughan, Peter Mortimore, Janet Ouston, and Alan Smith (1979). *Fifteen Thousand Hours: Secondary Schools and Their Effects on Children.* Cambridge, MA: Harvard University Press.

Rust, Val D. (1977). *Alternatives in Education: Theoretical and Historical Perspective.* Beverly Hills, CA: Sage.

Saint, Andrew (1987). *Towards a Social Architecture: The Role of School-Building in Post-War England.* New Haven: Yale University Press.

Sanoff, Henry, and Joan Sanoff (1981). *Learning Environments for Children.* Atlanta: Humanics.

Sanoff, Henry, (1983). *Planning Outdoor Play.* Atlanta: Humanics.

Sanoff, Henry (1984). *Design Games.* Los Altos, CA: William Kaufman.

Sanoff, Henry (1989). Participatory strategies for the design of child care facilities. *Children's Environment Quarterly,* 6,4:32–39.

Schein, Edgar (1985). *Organizational Culture.* San Francisco: Jossey-Bass.

Schlechty, Philip C., and Ann W. Joslin (1988). Images of schools. In Ann Lieberman (ed.), *Rethinking School Improvement.* New York: Teachers College.

Schools (1992). In Clay Miller (ed.), *Progressive Architecture Plans.*

Schools as a resource (1984). *Architects Journal,* 180, November 14:79–83.

Schools as a resource (1984). *Architects Journal,* 180, November 21:67–68.

Schools as a resource (1984). *Architects Journal,* 180, November 28:63–66.

Schuh, J.H. (1979). Assessment and redesign in residence halls. In L.A. Huebner (ed.), *Redesigning Campus Environments: New Directions for Student Services* (No. 8). San Francisco: Jossey-Bass.

Schwartz, Steven (1978). User participation in environmental change. In Roger Brauer (ed.), *Priorities in Environmental Design Research.* Washington, DC: Environmental Design Research Association.

Smith, P.K., and K.J. Connolly (1980). *The Ecology of Preschool Behavior.* Cambridge, England: Cambridge University Press.

Smith, Vernon, Robert Barr, and Daniel Burke (1976). *Alternatives in Education: Freedom to Choose.* Bloomington, IN: Phi Delta Kappa.

Sommer, Robert (1974). *Tight Spaces: Hard Architecture and How to Humanize It.* Englewood Cliffs, NJ: Prentice Hall.

Spaulding, A., and E. Crittenden (1983). Design of a school for non-handicapped and handicapped children in a remote area. *Exceptional Education Quarterly,* 4:16–23.

Taylor, Ann (1983). Effects of the physical environment on learning. *Exceptional Education Quarterly,* 4:1–115.

Threllfall, M. (1986). Inside/outside: The school environment. *Children's Environment Quarterly,* 3,3:30–39.

Treadway, D.M. (1979). Use of campus-wide ecosystem surveys to monitor a changing institution. In L.A. Huebner (ed.), *Redesigning Campus Environments: New Directions for Student Services* (No. 8). San Francisco: Jossey-Bass.

Trump, J. Lloyd (1959). *Images of the Future: A New Approach to the Secondary School.* Washington, DC: National Association of Secondary-School Principals.

Tucker, Marc S. (1988). Peter Drucker, knowledge work, and the structure of schools. *Educational Leadership,* 45,5:44–47.

Turner, Paul V. (1985). *Campus: An American Planning Tradition.* New York: The Architectural History Foundation, and Cambridge, MA: MIT Press.

Vance, Mary (1987). *School Buildings: Monographs Published 1976–1987.* Monticello, IL: Vance Bibliographies.

Verba, Sydney (1961). *Small Groups and Political Behavior: A Study of Leadership.* Princeton, NJ: Princeton University Press.

Weinstein, Carol S. (1979). The physical environment of the school: A review of the research. *Review of Educational Research,* 49,4:577–610.

Weinstein, Carol S. (1982). Privacy-seeking behavior in an elementary classroom. *Journal of Environmental Psychology,* 2:23–35.

Weinstein, Carol S. (1987). Designing preschool classrooms to support development. In Carol S. Weinstein and Thomas G. David (eds.), *Spaces for Children: The Built Environment and Child Development.* New York: Plenum.

Whitebrook, M., C. Howes, and D. Phillips (1989). *Who Cares? Child Care Teachers and the Quality of Care in America.* Oakland, CA: Child Care Employee Project.

WICHE (Western Interstate Commission for Higher Education) (1973). *The System Model: Designing Campus Environments.* Boulder, CO: WICHE.

Williams, Sydney A. (1976). City participation in city and regional planning: An effective methodology. *Town Planning Review,* 47:349–358.

Wineman, Jean, and Craig Zimring (1986). POE. *Progressive Architecture,* 67,4:115–117.

Woodbridge, Sally B. (1980). School designed both with and for a Navaho community: An unusual programming process responds to a desire for self-determination. *AIA Journal,* 69:40–49.

Wrona, Stephen (1981). *Participation in Architectural Design and Urban Planning.* Poland: Warsaw Polytechnic.

Yudell, Buzz (1991). Building community through participation. *Places,* 7,4:22–29.

Zimring, Craig, and Jan Reizenstein (1981). A primer on post-occupancy evaluation, *AIA Journal,* 70,13:52–58.

Index